INCLUSION, EXCLUSION
AND RELIGIOUS FREEDOM IN
CONTEMPORARY AUSTRALIA

EDITORS MICHAEL QUINLAN AND A. KEITH THOMPSON

SHEPHERD
STREET PRESS

Published in 2021 by Connor Court Publishing Pty Ltd under the imprint Shepherd Street Press.

Shepherd Street Press is an imprint of Connor Court Publishing and The School of Law, The University of Notre Dame Australia, Broadway.

Shepherd Street Press Editorial Executive:

Michael Quinlan
A. Keith Thompson
Iain T. Benson

Connor Court Publishing Pty Ltd
PO Box 7257
Redland Bay QLD 4165
sales@connorcourt.com
www.connorcourtpublishing.com.au
Phone 0497-900-685

Printed in Australia

ISBN: 9781922449559

Front Cover Image: Abanoned Church, South Australia, Wikipedia Commons.

Peer Review Policy
This book has been prepared in compliance with the Peer Review Policy of the Shepherd Street Press which provides for double blind peer review by at least two expert reviewers.

The editors also wish to acknowledge the assistance they have received from Alex Du Maurier, a final year Honours student. Among other tasks, Alex has assisted in ensuring compliance with the fourth edition of the Australian Guide to Legal Citation.

TABLE OF CONTENTS

INTRODUCTION

As the world battles a global pandemic it might have been hoped that people would – at least during the pandemic – be a bit nicer to each other, a bit more tolerant and a bit more accepting of difference. Alas that seems not to be so. The Western World – particularly the United States and Europe - has been riven by conflict with riots, rising crime rates, a rising lack of civility and the continued spread of cancel culture and division. While violent rioting has been rare in Australia that tide of conflict, cancel culture and antipathy towards religious faith has been washing this way too. This book hopes to bring some measure of calm to that maelstrom by arguing that we need to seek real tolerance which means a real acceptance of difference.

The chapters of this book had their birth at The University of Notre Dame Australia Religious Liberty Conference held in Sydney in 2019. Since then those papers have been developed and refined and been subject to the academic peer review process. In these pages you will find chapters written by authors across Australia and abroad. In this brief introduction I want to give readers a teaser of the contents and encourage them to delve into these pages with a sense of expectation and a willingness to embrace difference.

In his chapter "Is Religious Liberty Loving in Principle?" Dr Alex Deagon considers the historical roots of the idea of religious tolerance. He finds this idea of tolerance ultimately sourced in Genesis 1:26-27 in which man and woman are described as being created in the image of God. For Dr Deagon religious liberty is loving in principle and hence inclusive because it starts from the proposition that every person possesses innate human dignity and worth because they are a human being. Dr Deagon discusses contemporary Australian issues in which religion might be perceived as exclusionary such as the Israel Folau affair and the selection and regulation policies of religious schools. Speaking of Christian schools with policies of this kind, he argues that they provide "choice for parents who wish to educate their children in accordance with such an ethos, a loving community for those parents and children, and the capacity for that community to contribute to the public good in a distinctive way."

Dr Deagon argues that Christianity fosters the virtues of humility, sacrifice, forgiveness and trust which are inclusive because these virtues can be practised by all. He also argues that coercion is incompatible with Christianity which requires religious liberty for all. As he explains:

> For coerced belief is not true belief, and is antithetical to love which must be voluntary. The law of love indicates that just as we would not want to be coerced into belief so the beliefs of others should not be coerced. Similarly, just as we would not want to coerce others to violate their beliefs, so others should not coerce us to violate our beliefs. Fundamentally then, Christianity requires religious liberty because love does not compel belief.

In his chapter "Law, Judges and the Exclusionary Nature of Inclusion" Shaun de Freitas critiques judicial characterisations of religious belief – and religious belief alone - as being irrational, illogical, strange, bizarre or supernatural. De Freitas argues that the moral worth of religious belief is dependent on one's perspective on morality but that much which is generally accepted by society as good has come from religious modes of thought:

> Why is it that religion is viewed as contributory when it comes to certain moral matters such as, for example, efforts at curbing slavery and racism, but when it comes to views on, for example, when hu-

man life begins and ends; the teaching in public schools of the source
and development of the earth and humans; and views on marriage
and acceptable forms of sexual conduct; it (religion) is marginalised
or relegated to the private sphere?

De Freitas argues that other modes of thought which are not subject to
such dismissive approaches by the Courts may be – but are rarely characterised by judges as – irrational, illogical, strange, bizarre or supernatural. As
he argues:

> Surely there is much irrationality and strangeness in the eyes of many
> religious believers (and even from certain non-religious believers)
> when observing a certain non-religious believer's views that, for ex-
> ample, Intelligent Design theory should be excluded from public
> school education, or that abortion does not constitute the killing of
> human life or that an adult person who is experiencing pain and suf-
> fering should have the right to have his/her life terminated according
> to regulated medical procedures.

De Freitas argues that it is unjust and unfair to single out the religious and
religious beliefs for alleged irrationality, bizarreness and lack of reason.
This approach trivialises the beliefs and attitudes of one section of the
community resulting in their exclusion and a lack of inclusion and diversity.
He concludes that:

> The labelling of liberal democracies as being inclusive and the law's
> expressed commitment towards inclusivity remain questionable
> when taking into cognisance the substantive marginalisation of reli-
> gion that takes place in such societies.

Mark Fowler moves the book from the broad to the particular in his chapter "Judicial Apprehension of Religious Belief under the Commonwealth
Religious Discrimination Bill." If passed this Bill would be Commonwealth
recognition of the importance of providing legislative protection for religious believers from discrimination. It might, to use Charles Taylor's words,
"establish norms of conduct that operate as sign-posts indicating the direction in which society is heading." At the moment, in the absence of legis-

lation of this kind, those signposts are not indicating that society is heading in a direction favourable to respect for religion. Fowler focusses on what he argues is a serious flaw in the Bill: the threshold for an applicant or respondent to access the Bill's protections. The relevant threshold is that the putative religionist's conduct must be such that "a person of the same religion as the first person could reasonably consider [the conduct] to be in accordance with the doctrines, tenets, beliefs or teachings of that religion." As Fowler persuasively argues the impact of this test is that a Court is required to make an assessment not of the sincerity or genuineness of the religious believer but their belief measured against the "doctrines, tenets, beliefs or teachings of that religion" as understood by a "co-religionist."   As Fowler observes this approach is contrary to much jurisprudence and would shut out from the protection of the Bill (if passed into law) protection for the genuinely or sincerely held beliefs of a religious person with an "unorthodox" position on the relevant doctrine, tenet, belief or teaching. Fowler argues that:

> Where a religious believer is subjected to detrimental treatment as a consequence of their sincere religious expression, whether that expression is doctrinally correct according to the view of fellow believers should be irrelevant to the determination of whether the believer has been discriminated against. Similarly, the reliance of a body on an 'exemption' should not turn on a court's assessment of doctrinal correctness, whether by regard to fellow adherents or otherwise. Use of such means contemplate the possibility that a sincerely and genuinely held belief will be defeated as a belief that is not religious simply because of a dispute as to doctrinal interpretation. That is not necessary, when the ultimate question is whether the manifestation accompanying the belief is to be accommodated in a plural society.

Fowler argues that the approach taken by the Bill undermines what the Bill should be seeking to achieve – respect for the dignity of the individual. The dignity of the religious believer whose convictions do not squarely align with their co-religionists – perhaps a believer who has thought long and hard about a particular doctrine – is treated by the Bill as less worthy of respect and protection than the dignity of others.

My chapter of the book, "The exclusivity demands of religion meet the exclusivity demands of inclusion: the case for a new approach to inclusion in Australia", considers the current meaning and usage of the term 'inclusion' in the Western world and particularly in Australia. It has a particular focus on inclusion in the business and workforce context. The chapter argues that successful religions tend to have clear moral codes and to make significant demands on their followers. It is of the essence of such religions that they are in a sense 'exclusive': they expect their adherents to comply with their moral tenets in their lives. These moral tenets are increasingly at odds with the perspectives of many other people in society. I argue that a failure to extend inclusion to those who share different religious perspectives on moral matters and demanding or expecting conformity on contentious moral matters is not properly to be understood as inclusion. I conclude that there is a need for a new approach to inclusion which is far more respecting of difference:

> Forcing people to act in ways which they cannot and punishing them
> if they do not is not inclusive. Preventing people from doing what
> they must is not inclusive. Inclusiveness which operates in these ways
> – contemporary inclusion – is not the way to build a harmonious and
> productive workplace or by extension a harmonious and productive
> society. To do so requires real respect for the many differences which
> exist between individuals. It requires true inclusion. When applied to
> a society, true inclusion means recognising that everyone is different
> and not seeking to enforce conformity.

Like Mark Fowler, Michael Stokes focusses his discussion on one piece of contemporary law: in his case, s17 of the *Anti-Discrimination Act 1998* (Tas). This provision proscribes conduct which offends, humiliates, intimidates, insults or ridicules a person on the basis of a protected characteristic such as sexual orientation. This provision has led to complaints to the Anti-Discrimination Commissioner against a Catholic Archbishop, a religious Minister and a street preacher. Stokes argues that the provision is not, when properly construed, available in relation to conduct about a class of people but that it is limited to proscribing conduct aimed at an individual. He argues that:

> [i]f s17 of *the Anti-Discrimination Act* (Tas) extends beyond targeting individuals to prohibit general comment which some people find offensive, it imposes unacceptable constraints on public comment and criticism and should be amended to limit it to conduct causing real harm or repealed.

If the provision does extend to prevent preaching on moral matters it could be considered to be a legislative embodiment of 'inclusion' where, as Stokes explains, "the behaviour of those who voice strong moral views about the behaviour of others is [viewed as] intolerant, disrespectful and unjustifiable." On this understanding of inclusiveness "[i]nclusion tends to exclude those with strong views of right and wrong because they are seen as wrong and as in the wrong in that they fail to understand that their moral views are [according to those with a relativist perspective] merely preferences. Hence if they are critical of the behaviour of others, they are acting on the basis of personal dislike." If this approach to 'inclusiveness' is the approach taken towards religious believers, it is not in fact inclusive of their moral and religious perspective or of their conscience.

Michael Stokes' chapter is followed very appropriately by Dr Paul Taylor's chapter which asks the question a religious reader of Michael Stokes' chapter may leave that chapter with: "What on earth does Australia think of religious freedom? Not very inclusive." Dr Taylor examines the framework of Australian anti-discrimination legislation against the international human rights standards contained in the *International Covenant on Civil and Political Rights* (*ICCPR*). He finds the approach to protection of religious freedom sadly wanting. While noting that there is no hierarchy of internationally recognised human rights and that Article 18 of the *ICCPR* identifies the need for states to protect the dignity of religious believers, he notes that advocates of religious freedom as contemplated by Article 18 – rather than those opposed to such protections – are viewed as being non-inclusive. As he correctly observes:

> In the debate which has attended successive inquiries and legislative proposals on freedom of religion, those who urge greater protection are represented as non-inclusive.

> Yet some forms of contemporary opposition to freedom of religion reflect a view that is not inclusive, and fail to give recognition to the co-existence of rights that is intended under the ICCPR and related UN instruments.

Taylor identifies the framing of Australia's anti-discrimination laws – in which religious freedom protections are generally couched in terms of exception or exemption from otherwise applicable anti-discrimination protections - as part of the perception problem. This structure readily leads to the perspective: If discrimination is wrong then surely it is wrong for religious believers or their religions to be able to lawfully do what others cannot. In the Western world, as generally accepted moral positons move increasingly away from those traditionally held by organised religions, conflicts between those who adopt contemporary moral positions and those who retain the moral traditions of their religious faith are bound to occur and with greater frequency. As Taylor observes this disparity between religious convictions and the prevailing point of view is precisely why and when the protections envisaged by Article 18 are most needed. As he argues:

> [Freedom of religion] is surely most needed precisely when there is a tendency of undue restriction to occur because minority belief systems do not fit with the doctrine of the State or popular standards. It is inimical to human rights protections, in particular under Article 18, that belief systems should be sanitised of incompatibility with prevailing social standards. The obligation of the State under the *ICCPR* is to ensure that the *ICCPR* standards of protection on the part of the State to determine whether religious beliefs or the means used to

express them are legitimate.

Taylor does not make this point but to be recognised as a religion in Australia, applying the standards of the High Court, involves belief in a supernatural Being, Thing or Principle and the acceptance of canons of conduct to give effect to that belief. [1] On this test, a religion requires canons of conduct and this really presupposes differences in the expectations and demands on the conduct expected by religious believers to comply with their religion to the expectations and demands placed in general by society on the conduct of citizens.   In other words, difference comes with the territory of religious belief and religious believers have obligations which others do not. Treating them as if they were not subject to "canons of conduct" would not be treating them equally. Respecting their religious freedom is not elevating their human rights above others but treating them consistently with their inherent dignity. In respecting these human rights – along with others - the *ICCPR* is inclusive. As Taylor concludes:

> The *ICCPR* provides an integrated scheme for protection for fundamental rights, enjoyed in parallel with each other, in an interface which gives explicit recognition to the coexistence of other rights in terms of limitation, by definitional thresholds, and interpretative provisions, among other things. It is decidedly focussed on the individual, not only to guard against threats to liberty and personal security, but also in support of personal and collective autonomy without undue interference. In practice these are enjoyed in variety and plurality by everyone, or should be.

Professor Keith Thompson's chapter provides an historical consideration of the painful and the (literally) hard fought origins of tolerance in the acceptance of religious difference.   Professor Thompson argues against forgetting the wisdom learnt through those struggles which is that societies need to find a way to live with difference and that way is not enforced con-

---

[1]   *Church of the New Faith v Commissioner of Pay-Roll Tax (Vic)* (1983) 154 CLR 120, 136.

formity. As he puts it:

> If all minorities are to enjoy peaceful lives in any society, none of
> them can be straitjacketed into an identity with which they are not
> comfortable.

Professor Thompson also argues that there are limits to the extent to which
the law can be employed to protect people and that the law cannot protect
people from thoughts and ideas. He sees more harm than good coming
from legislative overreach. As a consequence he concludes that:

> While we can and should pastorally empathise with all of those who
> are victims of abuse including those who have inherited dignitary
> harm, our discrimination laws should not direct punishment of in-
> tangible harm.

In the book's final chapter "Religious freedoms and inclusivity" Charles
Wilson recognises the limits of the protections of religious freedom currently afforded in Australia by the *Constitution*'s s 116, by the common law
and by existing anti-discrimination law. He identifies the increasing divisiveness of debate about inclusivity. Having first recognised the limits of
the law to restore civility, while noting that "legislation and the decisional
law do establish norms of conduct that operate as sign-posts indicating the
direction in which society is heading," Wilson argues that the solution for
the divisiveness he identifies is to be found not so much in legislation but in
a change of heart of private individuals and groups. Wilson calls for "a renewed appreciation of our innate capacity for inclusivity and collaboration
as a change of heart." He concludes that:

> We must build respect and friendship with those of different out-
> looks because of an attitude of inclusivity and open-heartedness, and
> connection to our shared humanity. Individuals and groups commit-
> ted to real inclusivity will draw their inspiration from their faith tradi-
> tions, shared openly. Their humble sharing, without any intention to
> justify or convert, will see all advance beyond where we find ourselves
> today. As we explore our differences and seek willingly to understand
> each other, we can move beyond the tension between 'inclusivity' and

'religious freedoms.' In place of that tension, we can arrive at love of the innate equality of all people and a deep sense of our shared humanity.

Amen. Amen. Amen.

Professor Michael Quinlan

National Head of School, Law and Business

The University of Notre Dame Australia

February 12, 2021

ABOUT OUR CONTRIBUTORS

Alex Deagon is a Senior Lecturer in the Faculty of Law at the Queensland University of Technology. He specialises in legal philosophy, law and theology, freedom of religion, and constitutional protections for freedom of speech and religion. He teaches Theories of Law, Constitutional Law, and Evidence.

Shaun de Freitas is a Professor at the Faculty of Law of the University of the Free State where he serves as Academic Head of the Department of Public Law. He specialises in freedom of religion and teaches Constitutional Law. He is also Adjunct Professor at the School of Law, University of Notre Dame Australia (Sydney).

Mark Fowler is an Adjunct Associate Professor at the University of Notre Dame, Law School, Sydney and an Adjunct Associate Professor at the School of Law, University of New England. He is an Appeals Panel member for the Australian Council for International Development, a member of the Australian Charities and Not-for-Profits Commission's Adviser Forum and has served as a member of the Queensland Law Society's Human Rights Working Group. He is Principal of Fowler Charity Law.

Michael Quinlan is a Professor and Dean at the Sydney School of Law of The University of Notre Dame Australia. Before that Michael specialised in insolvency and insurance litigation for 23 years at Allens including 14 years as a partner. He also serves as the Junior Vice President of the St Thomas More Society and as a Director of Freedom for Faith.

Paul Taylor is a Senior Research Fellow at The University of Queensland and Adjunct Professor at the Sydney School of Law of The University of Notre Dame Australia. He has held Visiting Fellowships at Wolfson College,

Cambridge and at the Centre for International and Public Law, College of Law, Australian National University. His principal academic interests are international human rights law and conflict of laws.

Keith Thompson is a Professor and Associate Dean at the Sydney School of Law of The University of Notre Dame Australia. He previously worked as International Legal Counsel for The Church of Jesus Christ of Latter-day Saints through the Pacific and African continent and as a partner in a commercial law firm in Auckland, New Zealand.

Charles Wilson is a Barrister, living in Brisbane, Australia, practising in the area of Private Client Law. He was a convener of interfaith dialogue and a moving voice for a Human Rights Act in Queensland. Charles' work is built on a deep commitment to religious freedom of all.

1

IS RELIGIOUS LIBERTY LOVING IN PRINCIPLE?

Alex Deagon

Abstract

Religious liberty is often viewed as fundamentally unloving; an excuse to discriminate against and exclude those who are different to the accepted norm of the religion. In Australia, this has been patently exposed through the public debates about Israel Folau's social media statements and the selection policies of religious schools. This chapter argues from an evangelical Christian perspective that religious liberty is loving and the progeny of a Christian framework based on the law of love. Free religious speech contributes to social good by providing an alternative paradigm of the good and seeks to bring all people into relationship with the ultimate Good. Yet the method of persuasion must also be loving. This requires individual cultivation and application of the fundamental Christian virtues modelled and exemplified through the Crucifixion and Resurrection of Christ. This framework upholds inclusivity because all people are viewed to have equal dignity, worth and capacity to practice the Christian virtues. Thus, while we could say that Folau's evangelism is loving in principle because he is aiming to proclaim the good news of salvation to people, we could question the mode of his delivery with regard to the Christian virtues and the way it is perceived as hate speech which harms inclusivity. Similarly, we could use the Christian virtues as a standard to interrogate the selection and regulation policies of religious schools. Despite the appearance of exclusion, such policies may actually express love and inclusion through creating a religious community able to incubate and contribute diverse views which uphold the dignity and worth of humans, contributing to the common good.

I Introduction

Religious liberty is often viewed as fundamentally unloving in principle, an excuse to engage in actions which discriminate against and exclude those who are different to the accepted norm of a religion. In Australia, this has been patently exposed through the public debates about Israel Folau and religious schools. Folau's social media statements have been characterised as hate speech which conflicts with Rugby Australia's values of inclusivity and diversity, excluding members of the LGBTIQ+ community by undermining their intrinsic worth and dignity, and negatively distinguishing them from the general community.[1] Similarly, many have argued that religious exemptions in s 38 of the *Sex Discrimination Act 1984* (Cth) which allow religious schools to discriminate against students and staff on the basis of sexual orientation or gender identity are unduly exclusionary, damaging, and should be removed.[2]

---

1   See, eg, Jack Anderson, 'Explainer: does Rugby Australia have legal grounds to sack Israel Folau for anti-gay social media posts?', *The Conversation* (online, 30 April 2019) <https://theconversation.com/explainer-does-rugby-australia-have-legal-grounds-to-sack-israel-folau-for-anti-gay-social-media-posts-116170>.

2   See, eg, Mary Lou Rasmussen et al, 'There's no argument or support for allowing schools to discriminate against LGBTIQ teachers', *The Conversation* (online, 16 October 2018) <https://theconversation.com/ theres-no-argument-or-support-for-allowing-schools-to-discriminateagainst-lgbtiq-teachers-104765>.

Conversely, Folau and his Christian supporters see his comments as an expression of his religious freedom to proclaim and teach his faith to all people, which is ultimately a loving and inclusive action because it seeks to bring all people into the community of Christ despite differences between them.[3] Those who support the *Sex Discrimination Act* exemptions for religious schools suggest that freedom for schools to select and regulate staff may be necessary for those schools to cultivate a distinctive ethos for the school community. This provides choice for parents who wish to educate their children in accordance with such an ethos, a loving community for those parents and children, and the capacity for that community to contribute to the public good in a distinctive way.[4]

This chapter takes the latter view from an evangelical Christian perspective, arguing that religious liberty is loving and the progeny of a Christian framework based on the law of love; to love your neighbour as yourself.[5] It is not an argument that love in the Christian framework is the only foundation for religious liberty, or even the most persuasive foundation. This chapter is more modest; it proposes that the principle of religious liberty can be conceived through a purely Christian framework grounded in the law of love. Consequently, the idea of religious liberty, and associated actions (within limits), are loving and inclusive. For example, free religious speech, from the Christian perspective, contributes to social good by providing an alternative paradigm of the good and seeks to bring all people into relation-

---

3   See eg, David Mark, 'Israel Folau's legal battle against Rugby Australia begins', *ABC News* (online, 28 June 2019) <https://www.abc.net.au/news/2019-06-28/israel-folau-rugby-australia-legal-battle/11257778>.

4   See Alex Deagon, 'Equal Voice Liberalism and Free Public Religion: Some Legal Implications' in Iain T Benson, Michael Quinlan and A Keith Thompson (eds), *Religious Freedom in Australia: A New Terra Nullius?* (Connor Court, 2019) 292, 320-7 ('Equal Voice Liberalism').

5   Romans 13:8-10 (English Standard Version). Biblical references throughout this chapter are to the English Standard Version unless otherwise indicated. See also Alex Deagon, *From Violence to Peace: Theology, Law and Community* (Hart Publishing, 2017).

ship with the ultimate Good: God Himself. The term 'religious liberty' was coined by the early Christian (albeit heretical) writer Tertullian and reflects a fundamental belief in the dignity and worth of all human beings as specially created in the image of God, with wills, rationality and desires.[6] The law of love indicates that true and genuine belief can never be coerced, but must always be freely chosen as the mind is persuaded by faith.

Yet the actions associated with religious liberty, such as the method of persuasion, must also be loving. This requires individual cultivation and application of the fundamental Christian virtues modelled and exemplified through the Crucifixion and Resurrection of Christ, including love as selfless sacrifice, forgiveness, humility, grace, patience, and kindness, as will be explained in Part III.[7] When these virtues are not adhered to and religious speech is hateful, it harms social good by undermining the dignity and worth of those subject to the speech. This provides substantive limits to the claim that the range of permitted actions associated with religious liberty is not absolute, a claim which is in principle universally accepted but in practice universally contested. Examples of this contestation are the very broad limits in s 17 of the *Anti-Discrimination Act 1998* (Tas), contrasted with the narrowing of these limits in s 41 of the first exposure draft of the *Religious Discrimination Bill 2019* (Cth).[8] Any legal limit must not be based on the content of the religious expression as such, but on the capacity of that action to be 'hateful' by undermining the virtues which underpin the principle of religious liberty and consequently remove the dignity of the individual as a creation of God. This framework also upholds inclusivity

---

6   See especially Timothy Shah and Allen Hertzke (eds), *Christianity and Freedom: Volume. 1, Historical Perspectives* (Cambridge University Press, 2016).

7   See generally John Milbank and Adrian Pabst, *The Politics of Virtue: Post-Liberalism and the Human Future* (Rowman and Littlefield, 2016).

8   A second exposure draft was released on 10 December 2019. Though no change was made to the substance of s 41, the addition of a section early in the draft means s 41 is now s 42. Hence in the remainder of this chapter the section will be referred to as s 42 (of the second exposure draft) of the *Religious Discrimination Bill 2019* (Cth).

because all people are viewed to have equal dignity, worth, and capacity to practice the Christian virtues.

Thus, while we can say that Folau's evangelism as an expression of religious liberty is loving in principle because he is aiming to proclaim the good news of salvation to people, we could question his specific actions, the mode of his delivery with regard to the Christian virtues and the way it is perceived as hate speech which harms inclusivity (and may well breach some anti-discrimination law) – as many Christian leaders did.[9] Similarly, we could use the Christian virtues as a standard to interrogate the selection and regulation policies of religious schools, and the form and content of the religious exemptions which allow them, ensuring they uphold a distinctive religious ethos rather than simply exclude others due to prejudice. Though other religious schools and the state generally may not accept the validity of the Christian virtues as a standard, it is a helpful measure to determine whether religious schools are in fact acting in an inclusive and loving way. Despite the appearance of exclusion, such policies may actually express love and inclusion through creating a religious community able to incubate and contribute diverse views which uphold the dignity and worth of humans, contributing to the common good. Where the reality of unloving exclusion exists, the standard of Christian virtues can be applied to inform and motivate religious schools to more diligently pursue that standard.[10]

II What is Religious Liberty?

The principle of religious liberty is not merely limited to private individual belief and action. It extends beyond our private belief and acts of worship to public and associational contexts such as proselytization, social and business

---

9   See, eg, 'What would you say to Israel Folau?', *Eternity* (online, 11 April 2019) <https://www.eternitynews.com.au/australia/what-would-you-say-to-israel-folau/>.

10   Cf Marion Maddox, *Taking God to School: The end of Australia's egalitarian education?* (Allen & Unwin, 2014).

interactions, employment, cultural and charitable activities, education, and so on. For many religious people, these external manifestations of religion are just as central and important to them as private belief, prayer and worship.[11] Article 18 of the *International Covenant on Civil and Political Rights*[12] (*ICCPR*) reflects this:

1. Everyone shall have the right to freedom of thought, conscience and religion. This right shall include freedom to have or to adopt a religion or belief of his choice, and freedom, either individually or in community with others and in public or private, to manifest his religion or belief in worship, observance, practice and teaching.

2. No one shall be subject to coercion which would impair his freedom to have or to adopt a religion or belief of his choice.

3. Freedom to manifest one's religion or beliefs may be subject only to such limitations as are prescribed by law and are necessary to protect public safety, order, health or morals or the fundamental rights and freedoms of others.

4. The States Parties to the present Covenant undertake to have respect for the liberty of parents and, when applicable, legal guardians to ensure the religious and moral education of their children in conformity with their own convictions.[13]

This indicates the actions associated with the principle of religious liberty are rights exercised by individuals and groups, individually and in community with others, and publicly or privately. It includes freedom of belief and to change beliefs, but also extends to manifestation. Note, in particular, art

---

11   Nicholas Aroney, 'Freedom of Religion as an Associational Right' (2014) 33(1) *University of Queensland Law Journal* 153, 161 nn 46 ('Freedom of Religion').

12   *International Covenant on Civil and Political Rights*, G.A. Res 2200A (XXI), U.N. GAOR, 21st Sess., Supp. No. 16 U.N. Doc.A/6316 (16 December 1966, entered into force on 23 March 1976) ('*ICCPR*').

13   Ibid art 18.

18(4) of the *ICCPR*, which obliges states to have respect for the liberty of parents to educate their children in conformity with religious convictions. One effective method of achieving this obligation is facilitating the ability of faith-based schools to educate in accordance with their faith-based ethos as parents may wish to choose this. Religious liberty in principle, and with particular regard to associated actions, is subject only to legal limitation which is *necessary* (not merely reasonable) to protect public safety, order, health, morals or fundamental rights and freedoms of others. This is a high threshold which requires substantive proof before any legal limitation is appropriate.[14]

Section 116 of the Australian Constitution also states that 'the Commonwealth shall not make any law for establishing any religion, or for imposing any religious observance, or for prohibiting the free exercise of any religion, and no religious test shall be required as a qualification for any office or public trust under the Commonwealth'. Chief Justice Latham in *Adelaide Company of Jehovah's Witnesses Inc v Commonwealth* (*'Jehovah's Witnesses'*)[15] argued that since the 'free exercise of religion' is protected, this includes but extends beyond protecting religious belief or the mere holding of religious opinion; the protection 'from the operation of any Commonwealth laws' covers 'acts which are done in the exercise of religion' or 'acts done in pursuance of religious belief as part of religion'.[16] Subsequent cases noted these acts must

---

14   See Alex Deagon, 'Maintaining religious freedom for religious schools: options for legal protection after the Ruddock Review' (2019) 247(1) *St Mark's Review: A Journal of Christian Thought and Opinion* 40, 49-50 ('Maintaining religious freedom').

15   (1943) 67 CLR 116.

16   Ibid 124–5 (Latham CJ). This follows Griffith CJ in the 1912 case of *Krygger v Williams* (1912) 15 CLR 366, 369 (Griffith CJ), indicating that s 116 not only protects religious belief/opinion or the private holding of faith, but also protects 'the practice of religion – the doing of acts which are done in the practice of religion'. For further discussion and questions regarding the current applicability of this 'action-belief dichotomy', see Gabriel Moens, 'Action-Belief Dichotomy and Freedom of Religion' (1989) 12 *Sydney Law Review* 195.

be religious conduct, or 'conduct in which a person engages in giving effect to his [sic] faith in the supernatural'.[17] Religious conduct protected by s 116 extends to 'faith and worship, to the teaching and propagation of religion, and to the practices and observances of religion'.[18]

From these principles at least seven actions associated with the principle of religious liberty can be deduced:

1. Freedom of belief, including freedom to choose or change belief.

2. Freedom of worship.

3. Freedom to establish places of worship.

4. Freedom to interpret Scripture without government interference.

5. Freedom to read Scripture in public.

6. Freedom to preach and proselytise (engage in teaching and propagation of the religion with intent to produce more followers).

7. Freedom from being required to affirm particular beliefs as a condition for holding a job in the public sector, stand for elections, study in university, or work in professions such as teaching or law (note s 116 also protects any person seeking to hold a public office under the Commonwealth from being subject to a religious test).

The principle of religious liberty is therefore broad and refers to all these actions. It stems from a historical (western) context where Christianity was the dominant religion of the society and different denominations of Christianity would vie for political power over the centuries from the fall of Rome to the rise of the modern secular state. As different denominations came in and out of power, and oppressed other denominations (and other

---

17   *Church of the New Faith v Commissioner of Pay-Roll Tax (Vic)* (1983) 154 CLR 120, 136 (Mason ACJ and Brennan J).

18   Ibid 135–6 (Mason ACJ and Brennan J).

minority religions such as Judaism) to varying extents, diverse thinkers and communities started to construct more robust frameworks for the principle of religious liberty as a bulwark against compelled religion.[19]

III Christian Conceptions of Religious Liberty

The principle of religious liberty has a distinctly Christian pedigree, on the basis of key theological doctrines such as intrinsic human dignity through God's creation of humans in his image, and Christ's assumption of human nature through the Incarnation.[20] Arguments for universal religious liberty are in some writings of the church fathers, including Justin Martyr, Athenagoras, Tertullian and Lactantius.[21] Tertullian in particular advocated for religious freedom (and first coined the term 'religious liberty') in an unprecedented, universal and inclusive way, claiming 'it is only just and a privilege inherent in human nature that every person should be able to worship according to his own convictions... It is not part of religion to coerce religious practice, for it is by choice not coercion that we should be led to religion'.[22] An important source for Tertullian was the Bible. Tertullian's approach reflects the biblical view of the dignity and worth of a human being as the *Imago Dei*, clearly articulated in Genesis 1:26-27.[23]

---

19   For the historical overview of this process see Robert Wilken, *Liberty in the Things of God: The Christian Origins of Religious Freedom* (Yale University Press, 2019). In the following section this chapter adopts a conceptual approach.

20   For the full account of this argument with further references see Alex Deagon, 'Reconciling John Milbank and Religious Freedom: "Liberalism" through Love' (2019) 34(2) *Journal of Law and Religion* 183 ('Reconciling John Milbank and Religious Freedom').

21   See Timothy Shah, 'The Roots of Religious Freedom in Early Christian Thought', in Timothy Shah and Allen Hertzke (eds), *Christianity and Freedom Volume I: Historical Perspectives* (Cambridge University Press, 2016); Robert Wilken, 'The Christian Roots of Religious Freedom', in Timothy Shah and Allen Hertzke (eds), *Christianity and Freedom Volume I: Historical Perspectives* (Cambridge University Press, 2016).

22   Tertullian, 'Apology', in *Corpus Christianorum*, Series Latina 1 (Turnholt, 1954) 1127.

23   See Wilken, *Liberty in the Things of God* (n 19) 13-6.

Historically, Christians have always understood that the beliefs grounding their ethics are matters of faith or persuasion. In particular, as the glory of Christ is revealed to the mind, the mind is persuaded. As the mind is transformed by faith, it participates in the glory of Christ by imitating Christ and then loves one's neighbour as a reflection of Christ, which is the law of love articulated by the Apostle Paul in the New Testament.[24] This fulfils the codified law since 'love does no wrong to a neighbour'. Law can be understood as a principle or set of principles which govern relationships within a community. Love, as modelled by Christ, involves the voluntary sacrifice of oneself for another. So the law of love, to 'love your neighbour as yourself', is the voluntary giving of oneself for another as the principle which governs individual relationships within a community.[25] This law of love, modelled on and enabled by the Incarnation and crucifixion of Christ, consequently encourages love for one's neighbour in terms of humility and sacrifice. Importantly, this is not forced or coerced, but rather freely volunteered as an imitation of Christ in trust that the action will be reciprocated.[26]

On the principle of religious liberty more specifically, the 'law of love' approach seeks to create a harmonious and inclusive space where a person can freely express, debate and choose faith perspectives without being subject to state, community or individual violence. There should not be arbitrary legal or political constraints on the expression of perspectives. Love, in fact, requires going beyond the boundaries of law or moral duty. In particular, we need to go beyond mere legal duty (for example, to just avoid hate speech, blasphemy or vilification) and selfish interest (the aggressive pursuit of our own agenda without due consideration to alternative views, or the prideful need to be seen as right), desiring to truly act with humility, love and sacrifice just like Christ did in humbling himself to death on a cross for our

---

24   Romans 13:8-10.
25   Deagon, *From Violence to Peace* (n 5) 7.
26   Colossians 3:8-17.

forgiveness:

> Do nothing from selfish ambition or conceit, but in humility count others more significant than yourselves. Let each of you look not only to his own interests, but also to the interests of others. Have this mind among yourselves, which is yours in Christ Jesus, who, though he was in the form of God, did not count equality with God a thing to be grasped, but emptied himself, by taking the form of a servant, being born in the likeness of men. And being found in human form, he humbled himself by becoming obedient to the point of death, even death on a cross.[27]

In this practical sense, love of neighbour in a religious liberty context means doing or refraining from particular associated actions through properly cultivating the Christian virtues: listening and engaging rather than pre-judging, interpreting expressed views charitably and asking questions to clarify and learn rather than assuming or misrepresenting the views of others, and not engaging in malicious or contemptuous conduct. Love of neighbour avoids 'anger, wrath, malice, slander' and lying,[28] and pursues 'kindness, humility, meekness and patience' with honesty, forbearance, compassion and forgiveness.[29] Most importantly, perspectives should be adopted by means of peaceful persuasion rather than coercion.

As British theologian John Milbank has said, 'virtue is democratic because its practice is open to all, especially the supreme virtues of love, trust, hope, mercy, kindness, forgiveness and reconciliation, which we have all in the West, whether avowedly Christians or not, inherited from the teachings of the Bible'.[30] These Christian virtues of humility, sacrifice, forgiveness and trust characterise the acknowledgement and expression of different faith perspectives, producing peaceful persuasion to the good and true which is inclusive because it can be practiced by all. The Christian perspective pro-

---

28   Philippians 2:3-8.
28   Colossians 3:8-9.
29   Colossians 3:12-3.
30   Milbank and Pabst (n 7) 7.

duces a space for religious liberty and discourse which is characterised by the 'fruit of the Spirit': 'love, joy, peace, patience, kindness, goodness, faithfulness, gentleness, self-control'; for 'against such things there is no law'.[31] The Christian virtues are beyond law and yet fulfil the law by their nature, and therefore allow us to persuade without coercing, which produces true religious liberty.

For coerced belief is not true belief, and is antithetical to love which must be voluntary. The law of love indicates that just as we would not want to be coerced into belief, so the beliefs of others should not be coerced. Similarly, just as we would not want to coerce others to violate their beliefs, so others should not coerce us to violate our beliefs. Fundamentally then, Christianity requires religious liberty because love does not compel belief. Even if one assumes Christianity is true with both temporal and eternal implications, it does not follow that Christianity must be compelled, because coerced religion is not true religion and so is impotent. It is mere externality or legalism, or hypocrisy, and from the Christian perspective this is far worse than a genuine, consistent and considered non-belief.

IV   The Limits of Religious Liberty

One question is how this framework might regulate the expression of particular perspectives, especially odious or violent ones. This is the 'limits' question. Is there complete liberty to express all kinds of perspectives? What about perspectives which incite violence? An initial point is though religious liberty as a principle is inviolable, the permitted actions associated with religious liberty are not absolute. When one considers the wide array of religious and non-religious perspectives, and the implications for public conduct and public policy, it is clear there must be some limit. The point of dispute is not the fact there must be a limit, but where exactly that limit lies.

---

31   Galatians 5:22-3.

A second point is determination of whether a particular perspective is 'odious' or unworthy of expression is largely a moral question which is evaluated on the basis of one's own perspective. Genuine application of religious liberty in principle must allow the possibility for conduct or articulation of perspectives potentially viewed as offensive. These can then be freely evaluated by people and rejected on their merits rather than by state *fiat*.[32]

Though it is almost universally accepted that there is a limit to the range of permissible actions associated with religious liberty, the pragmatics of that principle are contested. Different parties draw different lines in relation to what the appropriate limits are. For example, s 17(1) of the *Anti-Discrimination Act 1998* (Tas) states that 'a person must not engage in any conduct which offends, humiliates, intimidates, insults or ridicules another person on the basis of an attribute… in circumstances in which a reasonable person, having regard to all the circumstances, would have anticipated that the other person would be offended, humiliated, intimidated, insulted or ridiculed'. From s 16 such attributes include race, sexual orientation, gender identity, and political or religious activity. This is a very broad limit, for one person's religious speech or religious activity may well 'offend' another. For example, this was the provision that caught Archbishop Porteous when he distributed a Catholic pamphlet to Catholic parishioners which said 'Don't Mess with Marriage'. Transgender activist and federal Greens candidate, Martine Delaney, impugned this document on the basis that it breached the provision by insulting, offending or humiliating an individual or group because of a listed attribute (homosexuality), and brought a case to the Tasmanian Anti-Discrimination Commission.[33] The case was eventually dropped, though not before considerable time and expense spent by the

---

32   See Deagon, 'Reconciling John Milbank and Religious Freedom' (n 20) 208.

33   Delaney had already pursued similar actions with the Exclusive Brethren a decade earlier. See Bernard Doherty, 'The "Brethren Cult Controversy": Dissecting a Contemporary Australian "Social Problem"' (2013) 4(1) *Alternative Spiritualities and Religion Review* 33, nn 33.

Archbishop.[34] More significantly, the Commissioner had decided that there was a case to answer.[35]

Conversely, s 42 of the Government's proposed *Religious Discrimination Bill 2019* (Cth) overrules the 'offend or insult' threshold in the Tasmanian Anti-Discrimination Act, and explicitly states that a statement of religious belief 'does not constitute discrimination for the purposes of any anti-discrimination law'. This is a narrower limit which implies that any limits on religious speech as an action associated with religious liberty cannot be based on the content of the speech as such. Rather, any limit on action must be based on the capacity of the action to undermine the virtues which underpin the principle of religious liberty, particularly the ability to freely and inclusively express, debate and choose particular perspectives in a way which upholds the dignity of an individual created by God.[36] Actions such as the forced marriage and conversion of minors would infringe that limit. Similarly, if particular speech involves coercion to that or other perspectives through incitement to violence, or affronts to dignity through malicious insults or incitement to hatred, such a perspective is incompatible with the principle of religious liberty in the Christian framework. That is, such speech is fundamentally 'unloving' and exclusive, for it does not seek the good of our neighbour, and therefore it is not a legitimate exercise of the principle of religious liberty.

Some religious speech, such as proselytization which states that particular individuals will go to 'hell' unless they believe in the religion, can be viewed

---

34   See, eg, 'Anti-discrimination proceedings dropped but Archbishop Porteous disappointed', *The Catholic Weekly* (online, 7 May 2016) <https://www.catholicweekly.com.au/anti-discrimination-proceedings-dropped-but-archbishop-porteous-disappointed/>.

35   See Fiona Blackwood, 'Catholic Church has discrimination case to answer over anti same-sex marriage booklet', *ABC News* (online, 13 November 2015) <https://www.abc.net.au/news/2015-11-13/catholic-church-has-discrimination-case-to-answer/6939942>.

36   Deagon, 'Reconciling John Milbank and Religious Freedom' (n 20) 208.

as offensive or exclusive. But that does not mean it is necessarily 'unloving' or really exclusive in the sense described above. For example, from the perspective of orthodox Christianity, if one believes that hell is a reality for those who reject Christ and stay in their sin, then it is extremely loving to proclaim the good news of Christ to them in an inclusive attempt to persuade them to come to Christ and be saved through Him. There is a story concerning Penn Jillette, one half of the famed magicians Penn and Teller, and an atheist. Once after a show Penn was approached by a man who proselytized to him, sharing the gospel with him and giving him a Bible. Penn said the following after that conversation:

> The man was really kind and nice and sane and looked me in the eyes and talked to me and then gave me this Bible. And I've always said that I don't respect people who don't proselytize. I don't respect that at all. If you believe that there's a heaven and hell and people could be going to hell or not getting eternal life or whatever, and you think that it's not really worth telling them this because it would make it socially awkward. How much do you have to hate somebody to believe that everlasting life is possible and not tell them that? This man cared enough about me to proselytize and give me a Bible. I'll tell you, he was a very, very, very good man, and that's really important…that was a really good man who gave me that book.[37]

So from this perspective, the principle of religious liberty expressed through the action – attempted propagation of the religion – was fundamentally loving and inclusive because it seeks the good of the neighbour by providing (according to the religion) the means of salvation, and it affirms the dignity of the person spoken to by acknowledging their will to freely choose without coercion. As Penn implied, how this is communicated is as important as the content communicated – for Penn, 'the man was nice and kind' and actually talked to him as a person, affirming his dignity. Of course, this is

---

37   See Art Moore, 'Mystery Man Who Gave Bible to Famous Atheist Revealed', *Living Waters* (Web Page, 9 May 2018) <https://www.livingwaters.com/mystery-man-who-gave-bible-to-famous-atheist-revealed/≥.

just an anecdotal example, and Penn remains an atheist. But it effectively illustrates the practice of the Christian virtues mentioned earlier which undergird the principle that religious liberty is loving and inclusive.

Thus, broadly and conceptually, the principle of religious liberty in a Christian framework is loving because it is informed by and aims to proclaim the sacrificial love of Christ, seeks the good of the neighbour, and affirms the dignity of the neighbour through cultivation of the Christian virtues, the highest of which is love:

> Love is patient and kind; love does not envy or boast; it is not arrogant or rude. It does not insist on its own way; it is not irritable or resentful; it does not rejoice at wrongdoing, but rejoices with the truth. Love bears all things, believes all things, hopes all things, endures all things. Love never fails.[38]

The more practical implication of this is that the principle of religious liberty, and associated actions, should be legally protected (and appropriately limited) because it is loving for all people. That returns us to the current issues concerning religious liberty in Australian law and politics: religious schools and Folau. These will be considered in turn.

V Is Religious Liberty Loving? Discrimination and Religious Schools

Though controversy regarding religious schools may have deeper historical roots going back to the state aid debates, the contemporary discourse about religious freedom and discrimination in the schools context only makes sense if we take into account the 2017 same-sex marriage debate.[39] During that debate religious freedom was raised as an issue. Marriage has traditionally been understood as a religious institution with particular immutable characteristics, including that it is by definition only between a man and

---

38   1 Corinthians 13:4-8.
39   See generally Stephen Chavura, John Gascoigne and Ian Tregenza, *Reason, Religion and the Australian Polity: A Secular State?* (Routledge, 2019).

a woman.[40] Religious freedom advocates were concerned about the freedom of religious ministers and religious associations (including schools) to continue teaching this traditional understanding of marriage if the legal definition were to be altered to recognise same-sex marriage.[41] When the law recognising same-sex marriage was being considered in Parliament, many amendments to strengthen religious freedom protections in the wake of the change were voted down. To placate those concerned, then Prime Minister Malcolm Turnbull ordered a review into whether the human right to freedom of religion is adequately protected in Australian law. The panel conducting the review was chaired by Philip Ruddock, a senior minister in the economically and socially conservative government led by John Howard from 1996-2007. The review consequently became known as the 'Ruddock Review'.

The Ruddock Review found that there was no systemic, imminent danger to religious freedom in Australia, but there is inadequate legal protection for religious freedom and there are isolated occasions where religious freedom is violated or curtailed, as well as a rising social hostility to and ignorance of religion in general.[42] The Panel made a number of recommendations to address this, most of which will not be considered here. One of the most contentious recommendations was that religious schools should retain the freedom to discriminate against staff and students through religious exemptions to anti-discrimination law as long as they do so in accordance with a publicly accessible policy document. As mentioned in the Introduction, there was significant public objection to this recommendation – with many

---

40   See John Witte Jr., *From Sacrament to Contract: Marriage, Religion, and Law in the Western Tradition* (Westminster John Knox Press, 2012).

41   See, eg, Neville Rochow, 'Speak Now or Forever Hold Your Peace – The Influence of Constitutional Argument on Same-Sex Marriage Legislation Debates in Australia' [2013] (3) *Brigham Young University Law Review* 521, 526–7.

42   See Philip Ruddock, *Religious Freedom Review: Expert Panel Report* (Report, 18 May 2018) < https://www.ag.gov.au/sites/default/files/2020-03/religious-freedom-review-expert-panel-report-2018.pdf>.

apparently unaware that these exemptions for religious schools have existed for decades and were actually reaffirmed and extended in 2013 by the Rudd-Gillard Labor government.[43]

Sections 14 and 16 of the *Sex Discrimination Act 1984* (Cth) provide that it is not lawful to discriminate against employers or contract workers on the basis of protected attributes (such as sex, sexual orientation, gender identity, pregnancy, and so on) in the context of employment. Section 21 of that Act provides that it is not lawful to discriminate in the provision of education on the basis of these attributes. The contentious 'religious exemptions' are contained in s 38 of that Act, which reads:

> (1) Nothing in paragraph 14(1)(a) or (b) or 14(2)(c) renders it unlawful for a person to discriminate against another person on the ground of the other person's sex, sexual orientation, gender identity, marital or relationship status or pregnancy in connection with employment as a member of the staff of an educational institution that is conducted in accordance with the doctrines, tenets, beliefs or teachings of a particular religion or creed, if the first-mentioned person so discriminates in good faith in order to avoid injury to the religious susceptibilities of adherents of that religion or creed.

> (2) Nothing in paragraph 16(b) renders it unlawful for a person to discriminate against another person on the ground of the other person's sex, sexual orientation, gender identity, marital or relationship status or pregnancy in connection with a position as a contract worker that involves the doing of work in an educational institution that is conducted in accordance with the doctrines, tenets, beliefs or teachings of a particular religion or creed, if the first-mentioned person so discriminates in good faith in order to avoid injury to the religious susceptibilities of adherents of that religion or creed.

> (3) Nothing in section 21 renders it unlawful for a person to dis-

---

43　See *Sex Discrimination Amendment (Sexual Orientation, Gender Identity and Intersex Status) Act 2013* (Cth). Section 50 extended the exemptions in s 38 of the *Sex Discrimination Act 1984* (Cth) to cover the new protected attributes of sexual orientation, gender identity and intersex status.

criminate against another person on the ground of the other person's sexual orientation, gender identity, marital or relationship status or pregnancy in connection with the provision of education or training by an educational institution that is conducted in accordance with the doctrines, tenets, beliefs or teachings of a particular religion or creed, if the first-mentioned person so discriminates in good faith in order to avoid injury to the religious susceptibilities of adherents of that religion or creed.[44]

Essentially, this means religious schools can 'discriminate' on the basis of any sex-related attribute (or put positively, select and regulate) for their communities in order to uphold the religious ethos of that school. There is currently no requirement for a publicly available policy on the matter, so the public document requirement actually, in effect, narrows the exemptions. The public outcry was due to the perception that discrimination because of religion is exclusive and immoral, an affront to the dignity of members of the LGBT community, and therefore unloving. This question ought to be considered in accordance with the religious liberty framework articulated above.

The fundamental question is why religious schools should be permitted to discriminate against staff and students. Or, to rephrase the question in a less pejorative way, why should religious schools have a positive right to select and regulate the school community, including staff and students? The answer is because it allows the school to maintain a distinctive religious ethos. As mentioned earlier, art 18(4) of the *ICCPR* obliges nations to have respect for the liberty of parents to educate their children in conformity with religious convictions. One of the most effective methods of achieving this obligation is facilitating the ability of faith-based schools to educate in accordance with their faith-based ethos as parents may wish to choose this. Whether framed as exemptions to discrimination or as a legal right to select, allowing faith-based schools to select staff designed to consistently uphold

---

44   *Sex Discrimination Act 1984* (Cth) s 38.

this ethos is an essential aspect of maintaining the ability to educate in accordance with an ethos. Australia may be failing to comply with its international obligations if it removes religious exemptions for faith-based schools to choose staff in accordance with their religious convictions.[45]

Since religious groups in particular provide the associational structures (including visionary and didactic resources) for training in discourse concerning advancement of human development and the common good, it is essential for moral engagement and civic virtue (and democracy itself) that these groups be protected by and from the state.[46] As legal scholar Hans-Martien Ten Napel argues, 'it is precisely within such faith and other communities that mature visions of the good life can develop, which simultaneously contribute to the notion of the common good'.[47] Thus, at least from the Christian perspective, it is loving and beneficial for all people if religious associations, including schools, are free to run according to their own rules, because this enables the development of more diverse and inclusive visions of how to achieve the public good.

The broad definition of religious liberty explained earlier means the actions associated with the principle of religious liberty extend not just to belief and worship, but also to teaching, propagation, identifying conditions of membership and standards of conduct, and appointing officers, leaders and employees.[48] Such practices are all protected, even if the organisations are formed for broader social, commercial or educational purposes.[49] These insights provide a persuasive basis for allowing religious schools the autonomy to choose employees and students who uphold their doctrines in belief and conduct. A religious school may want to preserve their dis-

---

45   See Deagon, 'Maintaining religious freedom' (n 14) 49-50.

46   Deagon, 'Equal Voice Liberalism' (n 4) 323-4.

47   Hans-Martien Ten Napel, *Constitutionalism, Democracy and Religious Freedom* (Routledge, 2017) 97.

48   Carolyn Evans, *Legal Protection of Religious Freedom in Australia* (Federation Press, 2012) 35.

49   Aroney, 'Freedom of Religion' (n 11) 161 nn 46.

tinctive identity as religious in order to be a community which approaches questions of education from that particular religious perspective. Indeed, they may see the practice of education itself as a religious injunction which is to be performed in accordance with their religious convictions. So it is not enough for only the headmaster and religious studies teacher to uphold Christianity, for example. The entire community is designed to cultivate a consistent ethos. Maintaining this religious identity allows the school to present a unique perspective in a democracy, and legally compelling them to accept employees or students with views or conduct inconsistent with that perspective undermines their religious identity and, consequently, their democratic position as equal and valued citizens.[50] Facilitating this action as part of the principle of religious liberty is therefore loving and inclusive in the sense of loving neighbour as self, because it affirms the unique, equal and valued position of religious people and communities as citizens.

Facilitating the action of schools to select and regulate their community as a function of the principle of religious liberty is loving in another sense. It is important to note the ability to 'discriminate' in this context actually preserves equality between religious and non-religious institutions. Generally applicable laws, such as different kinds of anti-discrimination legislation, can fall disproportionately or unequally on those whose religious practices conflict with them. Those who do not engage in religious belief or practice are sometimes not subject to the same practical restrictions resulting from the law. The exemptions are necessary in order to preserve equality or neutrality, and specific exemptions are required to address this specific situation where there is an unequal or disproportionate application of law.[51] So, in other words, since loving your neighbour as yourself entails affirming their dignity by treating them equally, it is loving and inclusive for exemptions to

50 Deagon, 'Equal Voice Liberalism' (n 4) 325.
51 Alex Deagon, 'Defining the Interface of Freedom and Discrimination: Exercising Religion, Democracy and Same-Sex Marriage' (2017) 20 *International Trade and Business Law Review* 239, 276-8.

exist for religious organisations to remedy an unequal application of the law. An example to illustrate this principle is political parties. Political parties, by their nature, discriminate on the basis of political opinion. It would be absurd for the law to compel a particular party to hire someone who repudiates the ethos of the party in thought or conduct, and anti-discrimination law which rejects discrimination on the basis of political opinion has long recognised exemptions for political parties.[52] The same notion applies to schools.

Another issue is religious freedom advocates are concerned that the 'exemptions' framework actually undermines religious freedom. Neil Foster has persuasively argued that framing religious freedom protection as 'exemptions' from anti-discrimination laws might give the impression that powerful religious lobby groups are simply bullying politicians into giving them a special privilege to engage in otherwise unlawful conduct (which is not an unfounded concern), and in general equality is more important than religious freedom. A better approach is to 'see the limits drawn around discrimination laws as an integral part of a structure designed to reflect the relevant human rights as a whole'.[53] In other words, since equality and religious freedom are both positive rights under international law, and there is no hierarchy of human rights, it is more accurate to provide positive protection for religious freedom which reflects its status as a human right alongside and not inferior to the right of equality. Since there seems to be a common reluctance to maintain the exemptions in their current form, one other option is to remove the exemptions completely and in their place pass positive religious freedom rights for religious educational institutions. These would enable schools to select staff consistent with their religious and institutional

---

52   See, eg, 'Political belief', *Queensland Human Rights Commission* (Web Page, 28 June 2019) <https://www.qhrc.qld.gov.au/your-rights/discrimination-law/political-belief>.

53   Neil Foster, 'Freedom of Religion and Balancing Clauses in Discrimination Legislation' (2016) 5 *Oxford Journal of Law and Religion* 385, 389 ('Freedom of Religion and Balancing Clauses').

ethos and to enforce generally applicable procedures and rules with regard to student advocacy, conduct, dress and so forth.[54] Though opponents of religious liberty may not feel differently about a right framed in positive terms if the effect is the same, it would at least have the cosmetic appeal explained by Foster. It would address the perception that schools are engaging in 'unloving' behaviour by seeking special privileges to discriminate based simply on prejudice. The 'positive rights' framework recognises that schools are creating a community with a distinct ethos which will contribute to public good, and that ultimately seeks the good of the neighbour.

This proposition might sit awkwardly with those who do not adhere to the doctrines of the particular religious institution. Nevertheless, if we desire a healthy and inclusive democracy which genuinely and equally tolerates freedom to differ, we must allow associations the freedom to publicly conduct themselves in such a way as to maintain their unique identity on their terms. Only this will facilitate a robust, collective political encounter of perspectives for consideration and critique by citizens so they are fully informed to love their neighbour by pursuing the common good.

VI Is Religious Liberty Loving? Folau and 'Hateful' Religious Speech

The final issue to consider is where Israel Folau's statements on social media fit in relation to this framework of the principle of religious liberty and associated actions. To briefly summarise the facts, on his personal Instagram/social media account, Folau posted a picture saying that atheists, liars, homosexuals, drunks and others would go to hell unless they repent, along with some associated passages from the Bible. Rugby Australia, Folau's employer, stated that Folau had breached the code of conduct which is part of his employment contract, and sacked him. Rugby Australia's position is that Folau's posts were offensive and did not adhere to ARU's values of

---

54   See Deagon, 'Maintaining religious freedom' (n 14) 53-4.

diversity and inclusivity. Folau pursued Rugby Australia in the Federal Court for unlawful dismissal under the *Fair Work Act 2009* (Cth), claiming that he was dismissed because of his religion.[55] He maintained the position that his Instagram account is a mechanism for him to propagate and teach his Christian faith, and he is actually being loving because he wants people to repent and come to know Jesus.

Though the case will ultimately remain unresolved, the following points are pertinent. Folau's statement was not technically hate speech or discrimination because he didn't target a particular group in exclusion of other groups (in effect every person was a target), substantially attack any of the groups he specified or incite hatred or violence against them, or treat any person detrimentally on the basis of a protected attribute. Saying someone is going to hell unless they repent is not hate speech or discrimination from a legal standpoint.[56] However, under the broad s 17 of the *Anti-Discrimination Act 1998* (Tas), it is possible that Folau's speech could 'offend or insult' a person on the basis of sexual orientation so that his conduct breaches that law. This would not be the case under other narrower anti-discrimination laws in Australia and would be prevented by the operation of s 42 of the *Religious Discrimination Bill* if that were to come into force. The contested nature of limiting actions associated with the principle of religious liberty is again exposed.

As discussed above, teaching and expression of biblical principles, and prop-

---

55   Israel Folau and Rugby Australia ultimately settled the case on 4 December 2019, leaving the legal position unresolved. Both parties issued an apology and Rugby Australia paid an undisclosed amount of money to Folau. See 'Rugby Australia and Israel Folau settle legal dispute over sacking' *ABC News* (online, 5 December 2019) <https://www.abc.net.au/news/2019-12-04/rugby-australia-israel-folau-mediation-settlement/11765866>.

56   Cf *ICCPR* art 20(2), which states: '[a]ny advocacy of national, racial or religious hatred that constitutes incitement to discrimination, hostility or violence shall be prohibited by law.' Folau's speech clearly did not incite to discrimination, hostility or violence.

agation of the faith, are well-accepted actions associated with the principle of religious liberty.[57] Employers cannot contract out of statutory obligations so it ultimately is not relevant if Folau in fact agreed not to make such posts (and this issue remains unresolved) – he cannot be dismissed on the basis of his religion. Section 772(1) of the *Fair Work Act 2009* (Cth) states: '[a]n employer must not terminate an employee's employment for one or more of the following reasons, or for reasons including one or more of the following reasons:

> (f) race, colour, sex, sexual preference, age, physical or mental disability, marital status, family or carer's responsibilities, pregnancy, religion, political opinion, national extraction or social origin.

Under this provision, if Folau was able to prove that 'religion' was one of the reasons he was dismissed, he would have been successful. It seems clear that he was dismissed for posting this religious speech (which allegedly breached a code of conduct rule that was part of his contract), and the posting of religious speech as part of an attempt to teach or propagate a religion is an action associated with religious liberty and plausibly part of a person's 'religion'. Thus it appears that 'religion' was at least one of the reasons for his dismissal and consequently Folau may have won his case.

However, these considerations do not resolve the broader question of whether Folau's conduct was a legitimate action associated with the principle of religious liberty in the sense articulated in this chapter. In a fundamental sense, his post was loving because it sought the good of his neighbour. It was loving in the inclusive Penn Jillette sense – he is warning people about the consequences of sin and telling them about the solution for sin, which is a legitimate expression of religious liberty. However, as many Christian commentators have noted, his method of delivery could

---

57   It is also something explicitly supported under other legislation. See, eg the *Charities Act 2013* (Cth) which presumes the advancement of religion as a public benefit.

have been more loving in the sense of practicing the Christian virtues.[58] His post lacked nuance and sensitivity, the seasoning of grace to go with the natural offensiveness of truth. There was little demonstration of listening, kindness, compassion, humility, patience, and in particular, emphasis on the forgiveness and mercy that Christ offers to all those who genuinely come to him. The importance of practicing the Christian virtues as we engage in debates about faith, and the nature and limits of actions associated with the principle of religious liberty, may be the most significant lesson from the Folau saga.

VII　　Conclusion

Religious liberty is loving in principle. The range of associated actions which are permitted as a function of this principle is not absolute or limitless, and the principle itself can be damaged by failing to exhibit love through cultivating the Christian virtues while engaging in the expression or manifestation of religion. Nevertheless, religious liberty is fundamentally loving according to the principle of 'love your neighbour as yourself' because the principle of religious liberty seeks the good of the neighbour. It seeks the good of the neighbour by enabling the associational frameworks which can develop unique and diverse individual and group perspectives on what is required for the public good, and through individual and group efforts to bring people into right relationship with God – the ultimate Good. These pursuits are grounded in the Christian perspective and affirm the dignity and worth of all human beings; therefore, religious liberty is inclusive and should be robustly protected by the law.

58　　See, eg, 'What would you say to Israel Folau?', *Eternity* (Web Page, 11 April 2019) <https://www.eternitynews.com.au/australia/what-would-you-say-to-israel-fo-lau/>.

Bibliography

Adelaide Company of Jehovah's Witnesses Inc v Commonwealth (1943) 67 CLR 116.

Anderson, Jack, 'Explainer: does Rugby Australia have legal grounds to sack Israel Folau for anti-gay social media posts?', *The Conversation* (online, 30 April 2019) <https://theconversation.com/explainer-does-rugby-australia-have-legal-grounds-to-sack-israel-folau-for-anti-gay-social-media-posts-116170>.

Anti-Discrimination Act 1998 (Tas).

'Anti-discrimination proceedings dropped but Archbishop Porteous disappointed', *The Catholic Weekly* (online, 7 May 2016) <https://www.catholicweekly.com.au/anti-discrimination-proceedings-dropped-but-archbishop-porteous-disappointed/>.

Aroney, Nicholas, 'Freedom of Religion as an Associational Right' (2014) 33(1) *University of Queensland Law Journal* 153.

Blackwood, Fiona, 'Catholic Church has discrimination case to answer over anti same-sex marriage booklet', *ABC News* (online, 13 November 2015) <https://www.abc.net.au/news/2015-11-13/catholic-church-has-discrimination-case-to-answer/6939942>.

Charities Act 2013 (Cth).

Chavura, Stephen, John Gascoigne and Ian Tregenza, *Reason, Religion and the Australian Polity: A Secular State?* (Routledge, 2019).

Church of the New Faith v Commissioner of Pay-Roll Tax (Vic) (1983) 154 CLR 120.

Deagon, Alex, 'Defining the Interface of Freedom and Discrimination: Exercising Religion, Democracy and Same-Sex Marriage' (2017) 20 *International Trade and Business Law Review* 239.

Deagon, Alex, 'Equal Voice Liberalism and Free Public Religion: Some Legal Implications' in Iain T Benson, Michael Quinlan and A Keith Thompson (eds), *Religious Freedom in Australia: A New Terra Nullius?* (Connor Court, 2019) 292.

Deagon, Alex, *From Violence to Peace: Theology, Law and Community* (Hart Publishing, 2017).

Deagon, Alex, 'Maintaining religious freedom for religious schools: options for legal protection after the Ruddock Review' (2019) 247(1) *St Mark's Review: A Journal of Christian Thought and Opinion* 40.

Deagon, Alex, 'Reconciling John Milbank and Religious Freedom: "Liberalism" through Love' (2019) 34(2) *Journal of Law and Religion* 183.

Doherty, Bernard, 'The "Brethren Cult Controversy": Dissecting a Contemporary Australian "Social Problem"' (2013) 4(1) *Alternative Spiritualities and Religion Review* 33.

English Standard Version.

Evans, Carolyn, *Legal Protection of Religious Freedom in Australia* (Federation Press, 2012).

Foster, Neil, 'Freedom of Religion and Balancing Clauses in Discrimination Legislation' (2016) 5 *Oxford Journal of Law and Religion* 385.

International Covenant on Civil and Political Rights, G.A. Res 2200A (XXI), U.N. GAOR, 21st Sess., Supp. No. 16 U.N. Doc.A/6316 (16 December 1966, entered into force on 23 March 1976).

Krygger v Williams (1912) 15 CLR 366.

Maddox, Marion, *Taking God to School: The end of Australia's egalitarian education?* (Allen & Unwin, 2014).

Mark, David, 'Israel Folau's legal battle against Rugby Australia begins', *ABC News* (online, 28 June 2019) <https://www.abc.net.au/news/2019-06-28/israel-folau-rugby-australia-legal-battle/11257778>.

Moens, Gabriel, 'Action-Belief Dichotomy and Freedom of Religion' (1989) 12 *Sydney Law Review* 195.

Moore, Art, 'Mystery Man Who Gave Bible to Famous Atheist Revealed', *Living Waters* (Web Page, 9 May 2018) <https://www.livingwaters.com/mystery-man-who-gave-bible-to-famous-atheist-revealed/>.

'Political belief', *Queensland Human Rights Commission* (Web Page, 28 June 2019) <https://www.qhrc.qld.gov.au/your-rights/discrimination-law/political-belief>.

Rasmussen, Mary Lou, Andrew Singleton, Anna Halafoff and Gary D Bouma, 'There's no argument or support for allowing schools to discriminate against LGBTIQ teachers', *The Conversation* (online, 16 October 2018) <https://theconversation.com/ theres-no-argument-or-support-for-allowing-schools-to-discriminateagainst-lgbtiq-teachers-104765>.

Religious Discrimination Bill 2019 (Cth).

Rochow, Neville, 'Speak Now or Forever Hold Your Peace – The Influence of Constitutional Argument on Same-Sex Marriage Legislation Debates in Australia' [2013] (3) *Brigham Young University Law Review* 521.

Ruddock, Philip, *Religious Freedom Review: Expert Panel Report* (Report, 18 May 2018) < https://www.ag.gov.au/sites/default/files/2020-03/religious-freedom-review-expert-panel-report-2018.pdf>.

'Rugby Australia and Israel Folau settle legal dispute over sacking' *ABC News* (online, 5 December 2019) <https://www.abc.net.au/news/2019-12-04/rugby-australia-israel-folau-mediation-settlement/11765866>.

Sex Discrimination Act 1984 (Cth).

Sex Discrimination Amendment (Sexual Orientation, Gender Identity and Intersex Status) Act 2013 (Cth).

Shah, Timothy and Allen Hertzke (eds), *Christianity and Freedom: Volume. 1, Historical Perspectives* (Cambridge University Press, 2016).

Shah, Timothy, 'The Roots of Religious Freedom in Early Christian Thought', in Timothy Shah and Allen Hertzke (eds), *Christianity and Freedom Volume I: Historical Perspectives* (Cambridge University Press, 2016).

Ten Napel, Hans-Martien, *Constitutionalism, Democracy and Religious Freedom* (Routledge, 2017).

Tertullian, 'Apology', in *Corpus Christianorum*, Series Latina 1 (Turnholt, 1954).

'What would you say to Israel Folau?', *Eternity* (online, 11 April 2019) <https://www.eternitynews.com.au/australia/what-would-you-say-to-israel-folau/>.

Wilken, Robert, *Liberty in the Things of God: The Christian Origins of Religious Freedom* (Yale University Press, 2019).

Wilken, Robert, 'The Christian Roots of Religious Freedom', in Timothy Shah and Allen Hertzke (eds), *Christianity and Freedom Volume I: Historical Perspectives* (Cambridge University Press, 2016).

Witte Jr., John, *From Sacrament to Contract: Marriage, Religion, and Law in the Western Tradition* (Westminster John Knox Press, 2012).

2

LAW, JUDGES AND THE EXCLUSIONARY NATURE OF INCLUSION

Shaun de Freitas

"I apologize to the rationalists even for calling them rationalists. There are no rationalists. We all believe fairy-tales, and live in them. Some, with a sumptuous literary turn, believe in the existence of the lady clothed with the sun. Some, with a more rustic, elvish instinct, like Mr. McCabe, believe merely in the impossible sun itself. Some hold the undemonstrable dogma of the existence of God; some the equally undemonstrable dogma of the existence of the man next door." (GK Chesterton, Ch. 20 in "Heretics")

"judges' publicly proclaimed interpretive commitments may be more akin to religious commitments than is generally believed; despite their best arguments, they are unable to convince one another of the most appropriate mode of interpretation." (Howard Kislowicz, "Judging Religion and Judges' Religions", *Journal of Law and Religion*, Vol. 33, 1(2018), 51)

ABSTRACT

This chapter brings to the fore a dominant favouring of certain meanings in liberal democratic societies. This also relates to views pertaining not only to harm, equality, human dignity, the public interest and freedom, but also to inclusivity itself; views that frequently clash with interpretations from religious believers. This comes as no surprise, bearing in mind that those in power determine the parameters of freedom to fit their own interests and that insights related to inclusivity will be driven accordingly. Consequently, views related to inclusivity emanating from the dominant favouring of certain types of meanings in liberal democracies may give rise to an incompatibility between the law's understanding of, and approach towards inclusivity and the protection of freedom of religion; an incompatibility that has surfaced on many fronts, including matters of substantive moral concern. Bearing this in mind, this chapter focuses on an exclusionary (marginalising) approach by the judiciary in its labelling of religion as irrational and bizarre, and this points to an understanding of inclusivity that contrasts with the judiciary's support of the promotion of diversity. It is argued that not only religion but also non-religion may be susceptible to that which may be irrational and bizarre 'in the eyes of the other', which give rise to an understanding of inclusivity as being compatible with religious freedoms and progressive towards the furtherance of diversity.

1. Introduction

There is a plethora of scholarship that criticise the marginalisation of religion in societies that pride themselves on being democratic and supportive towards the protection and furtherance of human rights. Running like a golden thread through much of this criticism is the view that there is substantive exclusion by the law of religious interests, irrespective of expressed or implied loyalties towards inclusivity. Steven Smith, in his *The Disenchant-ment of Secular Discourse*, reminds us of the current monopolisation of mean-ings related to concepts such as equality, human dignity and harm. Smith refers to the 'cage of secular discourse'[1] within which public conversation and especially judicial and academic discourse occurs today.[2] This 'cage of secular discourse' referred to by Smith has gained in power to an extent that has produced, in many instances, an intolerant and excluding approach towards religion by the civil authorities, the law, and public institutions of basic and tertiary education.[3] Stanley Fish comments, "there can be no jus-tification apart from the act of power performed by those who determine the boundaries and that any regime of tolerance will therefore be founded by an intolerant gesture of exclusion".[4] In other words, the delineation of the boundaries of freedom requires power and the powers that be will naturally introduce a delineation that excludes interests that are not aligned

---

1   A phrase, says Steven Smith, that was coined by Max Weber, Steven D Smith, *The Disenchantment of Secular Discourse*, (Cambridge, Massachusetts & London, En-gland: Harvard University Press, 2010), 23.

2   Smith (n 1) 23. Similarly, Larry Alexander observes that, "Fairness, neu-trality and impartiality are concepts, like equality, that are empty vessels for substantive norms", Larry Alexander, "Liberalism, Religion, and the Unity of Epistemology", *San Diego Law Review*, Vol. 30, (1993), 775-776.

3   As Susan Mendus explains, in secularist liberal societies a distinction is made between the 'right' and the 'good' where the former should en-joy priority over the latter. In other words, a person may practise her own beliefs pertaining to what is good, as long as this does not come into conflict with views on the 'right', the latter signifying those matters that should give government the authority to interfere, Susan Mendus, *Toleration and the Limits of Liberalism*, (Hampshire, London: Macmillan Education Ltd., 1989), 119. But here one needs to ask the question as to who gets to choose what should be included under the category of the 'good' and what should be categorised under the category of the 'right'? As Mendus points out, in the determination as to what the 'right' itself should be, a specific sense of what is good is required in the first place, which in turn involves the relevance of foundational beliefs, whether religious or non-religious, see Mendus, ibid 119-120.

4   Stanley Fish, "Mission Impossible: Settling the Just Bounds between Church and State", *Columbia Law Review*, Vol. 97, 8(1997), 2261.

with the interests of the controlling power. Therefore, there will always be some or other form of intolerance and exclusion. However, where such intolerance and exclusion treat sincerely held convictions that do not violate nor pose a risk to the public order or fundamental human rights in an ignorant, derogatory, marginalised or superfluous manner, then such intolerance and exclusion require attention and consequent remedying. Not to pay heed to this would run counter to the ideals of democracy and therefore to the furtherance of diversity.

Meaning attributed to 'inclusivity' (whether explicitly or by implication) by the powers that be in liberal[5] democracies surely overlaps with the monopolisation of meaning alluded to in the above. The law, with its domination aligned with a specified 'cage of secular discourse', views such discourse as rational, which consequently generates the potentiality that forms of meaning that may challenge such secular discourse may be viewed as nonsensical.[6] This, in turn, poses substantive risks for the inclusion of religious interests and consequently for the furtherance of diversity. Paul Horwitz speaks of the general inclination of the judiciary to smuggle in a set of assumptions that give unfair advantage to non-religious interests,[7] and the judiciary's labelling of religion as potentially being irrational or bizarre serves as an example of this, which results in practices of exclusion regarding religious interests.

---

5   'Liberal' in this regard denotes an approach that views the public sphere as neutral towards religion and that the private sphere should rather be the domain of the religious. This liberalism also places the emphasis on individualism and its inextricable relationship to voluntariness; the faith in the possibility of public reason and an understanding of equality as denoting that there should be no privileged religious class, see Paul Horwitz, *The Agnostic Age. Law, Religion, and the Constitution*, (Oxford: Oxford University Press, 2011), 10-17.

6   Steven Smith comments that, "reason does not manufacture moral criteria *ex nihilo*. It needs something to work with", (n 1) 53. This 'something to work with' may emanate from belief, whether religious or non-religious.

7   Horwitz, (n 5) xxix.

The dominant approach in liberal democratic societies today represents the view (whether explicitly or by implication) that inclusivity is served by means of protections anchored in concepts such as equality and human dignity related to, for example, the removal of religious instruction from public schools; or in compelling a privately funded university to include students whose conduct pertaining to sexual orientation may be in opposition to the foundational policies (or doctrine) endorsed by such a university; or in prohibiting the awarding of exemptions to marriage officers who do not want to officiate before certain couples due to conscientious objection against certain types of sexual conduct; or to include the appointment of spiritual leaders in churches whose conduct related to sexual orientation is not in conformity to the essential doctrine of the church; or to have religious adoption agencies also include same-sex couples as prospective parents. Regarding these examples, there are those who find themselves restricted or excluded, such as the taxpayer, parents, students, marriage officers, members of churches and those running religious adoption agencies – all of these have a different or contrasting understanding of what 'inclusivity' means. Consequently, and similar to the 'neutrality of the public sphere' premise related to the civil authority's approach to religion (which is driven by a specific type of liberalism that marginalises religion), interpretations of 'inclusivity' by the powers that be as witnessed in the above examples, exclude other interpretations. This comes as no surprise, as meanings attributed to inclusivity are inextricably connected to ultimate concerns.

Bearing this in mind, this chapter focuses on what also comes forth as a practice of exclusion against the background of (and paradoxically so) liberal democracy's support of inclusivity, and this is approached by drawing attention to the explicit labelling of religion by the judiciary in liberal democracies today as that which may be irrational and bizarre.[8] In this regard,

---

8   'Bizarre' is defined as "strange in appearance or effect, eccentric or gro-

a dominant type of liberalism that portends to be supportive of inclusivity, and yet functions in an excluding manner not conducive to the furtherance of diversity and the public good, is critiqued. Stated differently, this chapter critiques generalisations by the judiciary pertaining to the boundaries of 'belief and the rational' or of 'belief and the irrational' which could be influential in how we may perceive the boundaries of the law itself to be and ultimately whether the inclusivity label attached to liberal democracies and the dominant constitutional jurisprudence emanating therefrom truly serves the progression of inclusivity; such progression being naturally linked to the aims of a liberal democracy. The boundaries of the irrational and the bizarre (including the potentiality thereof) should not be confined by the non-religious to meaning emanating exclusively from those who claim to be religious, but should also include meaning arising from non-religious sources that may seem irrational and bizarre from the point of view of the religious (even amongst the non-religious there may be instances where the other's views are thought to be irrational and bizarre). This chapter therefore aims at furthering the protection of religious interests and can consequently only be uplifting towards the progression of diversity.

2. The personifying of religion as nonsensical

As far back as 1943 we find in the judgment of *United States v Kauten*[9] the Second Circuit Court of Appeal in America stating, "Religious belief arises from a sense of the inadequacy of reason as a means of relating the individual to his fellow-men and to his universe ... It accepts the aid of logic but

---

tesque," *The Concise Oxford Dictionary of Current English*, R. E. Allen (ed.), 8th Ed., (Oxford: Clarendon Press, 1990), 112. 'Irrational' is defined as: "illogical; unreasonable, not endowed with reason", *The Concise Oxford Dictionary of Current English*, 627.

9   No. 134, Circuit Court of Appeals, Second Circuit, Feb. 8, 1943 (133 Federal Reporter, 2d Series).

refuses to be limited by it."[10] In the South African Constitutional Court case of *Prince v President, Cape Law Society, and Others*,[11] Justice Ngobo comments,

> Religion is a matter of faith and belief. The beliefs that believers hold sacred and thus central to their religious faith may strike non-believers as bizarre, illogical or irrational. Human beings may freely believe in what they cannot prove. Yet that their beliefs are bizarre, illogical or irrational to others, or are incapable of scientific proof, does not detract from the fact that these are religious beliefs for the purposes of enjoying the protection guaranteed by the right to freedom of religion.[12]

Justice Ngobo's view that "The beliefs that believers hold sacred and thus central to their religious faith may strike non-believers as bizarre, illogical or irrational" referred to above, may suggest that that which is non-religious is exempted from any sense of the irrational and the bizarre. Justice Sachs in the South African Constitutional Court judgment of *Christian Education v Minister of Education*[13] (against the background of explaining the challenges related to the balancing of competing rights) was of the view that "Religious conviction and practice are generally based on faith. Countervailing public or private concerns are usually not and are evaluated mainly according to their reasonableness,"[14] and shortly after this Justice Sachs speaks of the "weighing of considerations of faith against those of reason".[15] This implies that religion should be viewed as mainly based on faith whilst non-religion is usually not based on faith but on reason. This therefore

---

10 Par. 9, p. 708.
11 2002 (2) SA 794 (CC).
12 Par. 42. Also note in this quotation Justice Ngobo's reference to 'believers' and 'non-believers' which I assume was not intended to categorise 'the religious' as believers and 'the non-religious' as non-believers. Why do I say this? Simply because we are all believers whether religious or non-religious. Also, one may add to Justice Ngobo's comment, in the aforementioned, that "Religion is a matter of faith and belief" that "the non-religious also call upon faith and belief".
13 2000(10) BCLR 1051 (CC).
14 Par. 33.
15 Par. 34.

lends itself towards the labelling of religion as exclusively being prone to that which is not affiliated to reason. How can the "countervailing public or private concerns" that Justice Sachs refers to not be rested on some or other faith, albeit non-religious? In other words, religious claims frequently oppose non-religious claims (presented as 'public' or 'private' concerns) that are also based on moral views, such views also relying on arguments that are based on presuppositional points of departure that consequently cannot be demonstrated by a non-circular argument. What does Justice O'Regan mean when stating in the South African Constitutional Court case of *MEC for Education, KZN & Others v Pillay*, that "A religious belief is personal, and need not be rational …"[16] How about rephrasing this by stating that "A non-religious belief is personal, and need not be rational ..." What measure of rationality would Justice O'Regan use to distinguish the rational from the irrational? The assumption exemplified by O'Regan's is that it is especially religion that can be irrational. Surely it cannot be refuted that non-religious beliefs may also reflect irrationality.

Justice Cachalia, in the South African Supreme Court of Appeal judgment of *Kievits Kroon Country Estate v Mmoledi*[17] comments,

> Our courts are familiar with and equipped to deal with disputes arising from conventional medicine, which are governed by objective standards, *whereas questions regarding religious doctrine or cultural practice are not*. Courts are therefore unable and not permitted to evaluate the acceptability, logic, consistency or comprehensibility of the belief.

In *Steward v Botha*[18] the South African Supreme Court of Appeal was confronted with a delictual claim related to a person that was born with certain congenital defects that naturally arose before birth and this person wanted to claim damages for his birth being allowed to continue and consequently

---

16   2008 (1) SA 474 (CC), par. 146.
17   (875/12) [2013] 189 (ZASCA) (emphasis added).
18   (340/2007) [2008] ZASCA 84 (3 June 2008), par. 16.

for having to live a life with the said defects. The Court referred to the judgment of *Speck v Finegold*[19] where Justice Cercone stated,

> Whether it is better to have never been born at all rather than to have been born with serious mental defects *is a mystery more properly left to the philosophers and theologians, a mystery which would lead us into the field of metaphysics, beyond the realm of our understanding or ability to solve. The law cannot assert a knowledge which can resolve this inscrutable and enigmatic issue.*

and where Justice Spaeth stated,

> If it were possible to approach a being before its conception and ask it whether it would prefer to live in an impaired state, or not to live at all, none of us can imagine what the answer would be … *We cannot give an answer susceptible to reasoned or objective valuation.*

Here the judiciary emphasises its inability to solve the difficult analysis of determining whether it is better to have never been born at all rather than to have been born with serious defects. According to the Court, such a determination constitutes a mystery that should be left for investigation by philosophers and theologians and the judiciary's role is rather to provide an answer that is susceptible to reasoned or objective appraisal. Note here the judiciary's labelling of religion as overlapping with the mysterious and implying that the judiciary rather than religion should be understood as being associated with reasoned or objective assessment. This the Court says as if of the view that it can always provide an answer susceptible to reasoned valuation. Also, the Court says this as if of the view that it is always excluded from making decisions that do not depend on non-demonstrable assumptions freighted with metaphysics. The Court further emphasises that the transcendental should not be viewed as the domain of the judiciary, hereby implying that the judiciary is to be distinguished from the other-worldly, the spiritual, the mystical, the supernatural and all similar worlds that should

---

19   408 A 2d 496 at 508 para. 7 and 512. (emphasis added)

exclusively be left to the domains of philosophy and religion. This is similar to Justice Blackmun's view in the US Supreme Court judgment of *Roe v. Wade* decision that

> We need not resolve the difficult question of when life begins. When those trained in the respective disciplines of medicine, philosophy, and theology are unable to arrive at any consensus, the judiciary, at this point in the development of man's knowledge, is not in a position to speculate as to the answer.[20]

Here the Court, in dealing with the status to be awarded to the unborn, distances itself from the world of speculation, yet proceeds by taking a decision on the status of the unborn (or the foetus as some may wish to refer to). The end result in the *Roe* judgment is that the unborn should not be afforded protection in the first six months of pregnancy if the pregnant woman so prefers, hereby confirming the speculative route followed by the Court itself as to what the margins should be regarding the origin and meaning of human life. Consequently, this approach surely does not exempt the said Court's decision from being bizarre, irrational, strange, unreasonable and eccentric. A proper reading of the *Roe* judgment as well as of a plethora of scholarship critiquing the said judgment confirms that there are many, including legal scholars (whether religious or non-religious), who view this judgment as irrational and bizarre and that the arguments presented to indicate such irrationality and bizarreness seem quite rational to many.[21]

---

20   *Roe v. Wade*, 410 U. S. 113 (1973) cited in Louisell, "Does the Constitution Require a Purely Secular Society?", 27. This case gave rise to the legalisation of abortion in the United States of America and served as influential precedent for the legalisation of abortion in many countries around the world.

21   A similar approach was taken by the South African High Court in *Christian Lawyers Association of South Africa and others v Minister of Health and others* (1998 (4) SA 1113) where the plaintiffs sought an order declaring the *Choice on Termination of Pregnancy Act* (92 of 1996) (referred to as the *Choice Act*) unconstitutional and invalid. The plaintiffs pleaded that the life of a human being commences at conception, and that the *Choice Act* was in conflict with the right to life-clause of the Constitution of South Africa (Section 11 which states: "Everyone has the right to life") because it allows for the termination of human life at any stage between

The European Court of Human Rights referred to the following excerpt from the House of Lords judgment of R *(Williamson and Others) v. Secretary of State for Education and Employment,*[22]

> Typically, religion involves belief in the supernatural. It is not always susceptible to lucid exposition or, still less, rational justification … depending on the subject matter, individuals cannot always be expected to express themselves with cogency or precision. The language used is often the language of allegory, symbol and metaphor. Depending on the subject matter, individuals cannot always be expected to express themselves with cogency or precision.[23]

In this regard, religion is not only understood as belonging to the category of the irrational, but also to that of the supernatural – 'supernatural' is described as "attributed to or thought to reveal some force above the laws of nature; magical; mystical" and "occult, or magical forces, effects, etc"[24] or "matters and experiences connected with forces that cannot be explained by science".[25]

From the above it is clear that the courts have on occasion intimated that

---

conception and birth if the pregnant woman so wishes. The Court, in answer to the question whether the terms 'everyone' or 'every person' referred to in section 11 of the Constitution, applies to an unborn child from the moment of the child's conception, does not depend on either medical or scientific evidence and that it is not for the Court to decide the issue on religious or philosophical grounds. According to the High Court the issue is a legal one to be decided on the proper legal interpretation to be given to s 11, 1118 B-D. In similar fashion, the Canadian decision of *Tremblay v Daigle* [1989] 2 S.C.R. 530, 62 D.L.R. (4th) 634 was of the view that: "The Court is not required to enter the philosophical and theological debates about whether or not a foetus is a person, but, rather to answer the legal question of whether the Quebec legislature has accorded the foetus personhood … Decisions based upon broad social, political, moral and economic choices are more appropriately left to the legislature", cited in M. Shaffer, "Foetal rights and the regulation of abortion", *McGill Law Journal*, Vol. 39, 1(1994), 68.

22   [2005] UKHL.

23   As cited by the European Court of Human Rights in *Eweida and Others v. The United Kingdom* 2013 ECHR 37, par. 45. (emphasis added)

24   *The Concise Oxford Dictionary of Current English*, 1224.

25   *Cambridge International Dictionary of English*, Paul Proctor (Editor-in-Chief), (Cambridge: Cambridge University Press, 1995), 1463.

religion can potentially be viewed as irrational, bizarre, illogical, unreasonable, strange, eccentric, magical, mystical and beyond the confines of science. The concern here is not that that which seems nonsensical, strange
and defies the test of scientific scrutiny has no place within the category
of the religious; the concern is rather that that which may seem nonsensical, strange and beyond scientific explanation is perceived to be absent
from the non-religious. The judiciary's approach as reflected in the aforementioned represents a wrapping up of religion in the nonsensical and in
mystery and in the process ascribing to religion a sense of make-believe; of
being mythical, eccentric, potentially speculative; as something of attraction
to the imagination and prone to strangeness. This results in the debunking
of religion due to an inaccurate and unfair setting of the boundaries for
that which may be comprised of the irrational or the bizarre. Simply stated, these boundaries should be extended to non-religion as well. In other
words, it is not only the judiciary's view of religion as being potentially or at
times nonsensical and unusual that needs to be recognised but also religion's
view of the law as being potentially or, at times, unusual.

3. Towards the progression of diversity

This chapter is of relevance to Frederick Gedicks' comment that certain
liberals fail to see how thin the distinction is between knowledge and belief,
and that they seem to be ignorant of the possibility that religious claims
might be rational or that secular claims might be irrational.[26] In failing to
see how thin the distinction is not only between knowledge and religious
belief, but also between knowledge and non-religious belief, the judiciary in
liberal democracies participates in a form of exclusion. In this regard, there
is the exclusion of religious claims and interpretations from that which is

---

26   Frederick Mark Gedicks, "Public Life and Hostility to Religion", *Virginia Law
        Review*, Vol. 78, (1992), 694.

perceived to be rational by those who do not subscribe to religious convictions and which does not bode well for the protection of religious interests and, more ultimately, for the progression of diversity. It may be that religion harbours elements of mystery and strangeness for those on the outside. In fact, even the believer who strictly adheres to the doctrinal tenets of her religion may, even though not serving as impediments to her loyalty to such religion, find instances of irrationality or bizarreness within the religion that she adheres to. The concern, however, is the law's insinuations of religion as *exclusively* having the potential of being irrational or bizarre, which runs counter to an understanding of inclusivity that provides space for religion within the domain of the rational; approaches taken by the judiciary are not supportive towards the inclusion of religion into the domain of the rational or of non-religion into the domain of the irrational.

According to Stephen Carter,

> It is relatively easy ... to scoff at the idea that God's will is relevant to moral decisions in the liberal state, but the citizen who is religiously devout might ask why ... the will of the Supreme Court of the United ed States is more relevant to moral decisions than God's?[27]

Carter rightly comments that opinions stem from foundational beliefs, whether religious or not and liberal theory has, according to him, not presented a convincing answer to date.[28] The concern is the lack of liberal theory, in the sense that Carter refers to, in postulating a convincing explanation as to why a moral position taken from a position unrelated to the religious

---

27   Carter, "The Inaugural Development Fund Lectures: Scientific Liberalism, Scientistic Law", (Lecture Two: The Establishment Clause Mess), 523.

28   Stephen Carter comments that, "So, for example, Rawls' original position needs a justification apart from one flowing from the original position, Ackerman's neutral dialogue needs justification outside of neutral dialogue, and so forth", Stephen L. Carter, "The Inaugural Development Fund Lectures: Scientific Liberalism, Scientistic Law", (Lecture One: The Uses of Empiricism and the Use of Fanaticism), *Oregon Law Review*, Vol. 69, 3(1990), 480-481.

should reign supreme over a moral position taken from a position related to religion. Carter further observes (regarding the position in the US) that it is rather puzzling that a Communist or a Republican may try to have his worldview reflected in the nation's law, but that a religionist cannot,

> that one whose basic tool for understanding the world is empiricism may seek to have her discoveries taught in the schools, but one whose basic tool is Scripture cannot; that one whose conscience moves him to doubt the validity of the social science curriculum may move to have it changed, but one whose religious conviction moves her to doubt the validity of the natural science curriculum may not.[29]

As Alasdair MacIntyre has written, "the morality spoken of by contemporary liberal moral philosophers ... is constituted by a set of principles or rules to which any rational agent would assent ... *[N]o such set of rules has as yet been identified*".[30]

Regarding a contentious moral matter, the question can be asked as to what makes religious interpretations based on the wisdom and knowledge stemming from sacred texts and their overlap with science, informative and coherent argumentation as well as centuries of scholarship, less important than a modern-day Court's interpretations? In this regard, heed should also be taken of Craig Paterson's comment that it is erroneous to deduce that because some arguments presented by the religious are based on religious assumptions that all arguments presented by the religious must therefore be similarly compromised, or that any independent reappraisal of arguments presented by the religious based on religious assumptions is impossible to

---

29   Stephen L. Carter, "Evolutionism, Creationism, and Treating Religion as a Hobby", *Duke Law Journal*, Vol. 1987, 6(1987), 985-986. Also see Richard John Neuhaus, "A New Order of Religious Freedom", *George Washington Law Review*, Vol. 60, 3(1992), 621.

30   Alasdair Macintyre cited in Michael J. Perry, "A Critique of the 'Liberal' Political-Philosophical Project", *William and Mary Law Review*, Vol. 28, 2(1987), 218. (emphasis added)

be presented based on non-religious reason alone.[31] Why is it that religion is viewed as contributory when it comes to certain moral matters such as, for example, efforts at curbing slavery and racism, but when it comes to views on, for example, when human life begins and ends; the teaching in public schools of the source and development of the earth and humans; and views on marriage and acceptable forms of sexual conduct; it (religion) is marginalised or relegated to the private sphere?

J Budziszewski comments that, "... our various gods ordain not only different zones of tolerance, but different norms to regulate the dispute among themselves. True tolerance is not well tolerated ..."[32] Here we see that Budziszewski refers to "our various gods" that subscribe to different margins of tolerance[33] and in this, Budziszewski's reference to "gods" is most apt and accurate, implying the presuppositional points of departure regarding the setting of margins for tolerance that can only arise from belief and by this not only religious belief but non-religious belief is emphasised as well. This implies that the potentiality of being irrational and bizarre from the perspective of 'the other' also resides under the banner of non-religious belief, and therefore of non-religious sources pertaining to stances taken on matters of moral concern. This also sets the stage for a possible clash between the "gods" that Budziszewskii refers to, which provides the potentiality for the one believer, whether religious or non-religious viewing the other believer, whether religious or non-religious, as being affiliated with that which seems nonsensical and strange.

Surely there is much irrationality and strangeness in the eyes of many religious believers (and even from certain non-religious believers) when ob-

---

31   Craig Paterson, *Assisted Suicide and Euthanasia. A Natural Law Ethics Approach*, (Burlington: Ashgate Publishing Company, 2008), 42.
32   J. Budziszewski, *The Revenge of Conscience. Politics and the Fall of Man*, (Dallas: Spence Publishing Company, 1999), 53-54.
33   Ibid 53-54.

serving a certain non-religious believer's views that, for example, Intelligent Design theory should be excluded from public school education, or that abortion does not constitute the killing of human life or that an adult person who is experiencing pain and suffering should have the right to have his/her life terminated according to regulated medical procedures. It may even be that arguments in opposition to the above approaches and that emanate from those categorised as religious are accompanied by forms of reasoning that may even be convincing to believers outside the category of the religious.

Although there is a plethora of scholarship in support of the rationality of the possibility of Grand Design and that abortion and euthanasia constitute a grave violation of the right to life, it is important to briefly remind the reader of such rationality to emphasise the irrationality and bizarreness that may well be perceived to be present within non-religious circles. Regarding Grand Design theory, Iain Benson explains that "Both the atheist, committed (unscientifically) to there being no God is in the same position as the theist committed (also unscientifically) to the claim that there is a God. Science cannot help either of them since the key questions are non-empirical."[34] Benson adds that,

> Design, like the existence of God, love, human dignity or justice might well be beyond the proofs of science. But like justice and love, human dignity and God, or even the idea of chance itself, design cannot be disproven by science. We should introduce discussion about the possibility of "design" alongside "chance". Failure to note that there are competing theories for key notions such as origins, evolution, design, chance or intelligence show that a certain kind of arrogance, prejudice or fear are dominant and that scientism has trumped proper science.[35]

---

34   Iain T. Benson, "The Jurisdiction of Science: What the Evolution/Creation Debate is Not About", *Journal for Christian Scholarship*, Vol. 43, 3&4(2007), 3.
35   Ibid 26.

Regarding abortion, John Rawls comments that,

> Suppose that we consider the question in terms of three important
> political values: the due respect for human life, the ordered reproduc-
> tion of political society over time, including the family in some form,
> and finally the equality of women as equal citizens. *Now I believe any*
> *reasonable balance of these three values will give a woman a duly qualified right*
> *to decide whether or not to end her pregnancy during the first trimester. The reason*
> *for this is that at this early stage of pregnancy the political values of equality of*
> *women is overriding, and this right is required to give it substance of women and*
> *force.*[36]

In this regard, Paul Campos comments that it seems that for Rawls, reason
and the reasonable fill the lexical space that in many other discourses would
be filled by God, the Bible, or moral insight.[37] The concept of the reasonable becomes for Rawls what Kenneth Burke calls a "God term" and the
characteristics of this god remain, as perhaps befits its metaphysical status,
somewhat mysterious.[38] It does not take a leap of the imagination to infer
from this that Rawls' "reason" enters the realm of the irrational in the eyes
of many of those who have duly consulted religious texts together with
sources on science.

Pertaining to euthanasia, Craig Paterson rightly points out that rationality,

---

36 Rawls cited in Paul F. Campos, "Secular Fundamentalism", *Columbia Law Review*,
    Vol. 94, (1994), 1820.
37 Campos, "Secular Fundamentalism", 1820.
38 Campos, "Secular Fundamentalism", 1820-1821. Steven Tipton observes that
    Rawls seeks rational agreement on moral rules in the form of contractual prin-
    ciples of justice as fairness that can be justified without favouring any one of
    the conceptions of good that divide a society, "but such justification itself turns
    out to presuppose a particular conception of the person as prior to, rather than
    constituted by, his or her moral commitments", Steven M. Tipton, "Republic and
    Liberal State: The Place of Religion in an Ambiguous Polity", *Emory Law Journal*,
    Vol. 39, (1990), 194. According to Paul Campos, Rawls simply pronounces that
    some position is "reasonable" and then condemns opposing views for being not
    merely wrong, but contrary to reason. The term "reasonable", says Campos,
    therefore serves the same performative function in Rawls's theory as that served
    by the term "God" in dogmatic religious theory, Campos, "Secular Fundamental-
    ism", 1817. Also see Patrick Neal, "Rawls, Abortion, and Public Reason", *Journal
    of Church and State*, 346.

consciousness, self-awareness, moral agency, communication, emotionality and the capacity to feel pain as the selected criteria in deciding on death, result in a plethora of critical questions such, as for example: What is the degree of self-awareness that should be required? What does self-awareness really mean? Does loss of memory qualify the lack of critical awareness of the self? Which of the aforementioned criteria should enjoy prioritisation, or do they all carry the same weight?[39] In the words of Craig Paterson, "Threshold definitions of persons seem so contrived precisely because they do resort to such arbitrary and vague stipulations when seeking to 'pick' and 'select' features and levels for determining the category of persons from the category of non-persons."[40] These complexities result in drawbacks related to the arguments presented by proponents of euthanasia whilst equipping those who oppose euthanasia with credible arguments in support of the understanding that the mind and the biological make-up of the human being are not to be distinguished from each other. In this regard, Craig Paterson comments that quality-of-life concerns should always be focused on the ways and means in which humanitarian resources can be deployed to improve the health of patients and should not be conflated with attempts to assess the overall 'benefits of living' versus the 'benefits of death', as if the two can really be rationally weighed and compared to one another.[41] From the above it is clear that one needs to caution against allocating the irrational and bizarre to points of view that arise from those who are positioned within the category of religion.

The idea that we can be seated around the table and always find a uniform language to agree on approaches to challenges regarding substantive moral issues and the public good has ardently been critiqued over the past couple

---

39   Paterson, *Assisted Suicide and Euthanasia. A Natural Law Ethics Approach*, 134.
40   Ibid 35.
41   Ibid 107. Also see ibid., 51 & 38-139 and J. M. Finnis, *Human Rights and Common Good, Collected Essays: Vol. 3*, (Oxford: Oxford University Press, 2011), 239 & 247-248.

of decades. This also needs to be understood in the context of the clash between religious interests and the law in liberal societies. Of late, prominent theorists such as William Galston, Michael Walzer, Stephen Carter, John Gray, Peter Berkowitz, Alasdair MacIntyre, Michael Perry, Paul Horwitz, Stephen Smith, Stanley Fish and Amartya Sen have, in different ways, critiqued liberalism's idealistic pursuits towards the attainment of universal agreement. This has brought to light that consensualism has its limits and it is beyond these limits – away from consensualism – that discovering the strangeness in others lurks; it is here that we have in common, points of departure that resort under the transcendental and consequently the sharing in the possibility of the irrational or the bizarre. It is only fair and just that we do not marginalise the other by means of differences in labelling where such labelling rests on misconceptions; to do so would be contrary to the pursuit of the progression of diversity. Those insights and forms of meaning that emanate from those that are non-religious are in many instances viewed by the other, including the religious, as irrational or bizarre; just as perspectives arising from those loyal to a religion may at times be similarly viewed by the non-religious. The furtherance of tolerance and, coupled with this, the progression of diversity, will surely be assisted if we jettison a one-sided labelling of that which may seem irrational or bizarre.

In many instances, the perceived prudence of non-religious approaches by the law and the perceived irrelevance of religious approaches to the law become questionable, resulting in the realisation that one may doubt the prudence of non-religious approaches to law because they also have the potential of giving rise to that which is irrational or bizarre in the eyes of others. The grounding by the law of decisions related to deep moral concern and human rights protection rests on belief, which also includes non-religious beliefs. This opens the door to points of departure from the non-religious as potentially being viewed as irrational or bizarre from the point of view of those affiliated to a religion.

4. Conclusion

By critiquing the judiciary's labelling of religion as that which is prone to be nonsensical, irrational or even bizarre, this chapter brings to the fore a practice that questions the credibility of the interpretive world of religion and, in the process, questions expressed as well as inferred loyalties to inclusivity that we come across so often in the language of the non-religious, including the civil authorities, the courts and the law in general. This adds to the plethora of preceding scholarship that has addressed the paradoxes in liberal societies related to assumed inclusivity and by doing so hopefully assists in the furtherance of diversity.

It is the resorting to belief as ultimate qualifier for the taking of a moral stance that introduces the world of the transcendental and once we have entered this world, religion and non-religion are on the same plane. It is by eventually having to look outside of the concept itself so as to justify the concept that the potentiality of entering into the domain of the bizarre, the irrational and the supernatural are established. This implies that it is not only the justification of a principle or a concept that emanates from within the circles of the religious that may be strange to others but also the justification of a principle or concept that arises from within the circles of the non-religious that may be strange to others.

In bringing to the fore the realisation that the domain of the irrational is larger than exclusively from within religious circles, the furtherance of tolerance and consequently of diversity is hoped for. It is in the realisation that that which we originally understood only to have been a part of others also constitutes a part of ourselves that the potential for the progression of diversity arises. There is a liberalism that prides itself on the progression of diversity; yet such an endeavour leaves room for much improvement against the background of the protection of religious interests, especially taking into consideration the stifling of diversity by means of (as alluded to earlier) the law's monopolisation of meaning. This, together with the substantive separation of religion from the law,[42] does not bode well for the furtherance of diversity and labelling meaning arising from religious categories of belief as exclusively prone to being irrational or bizarre (and even being linked to the supernatural) is not helpful either. A liberalism that promotes diversity and by implication the protection of religious interests in both the private and public spheres is what requires emphasis. Peter Berkowitz rightly asks,

> But does liberalism ... require one to restrict one's gaze to specifically 'liberal' discontents, 'liberal' ideals, and 'liberal' virtues? Does liberalism demand that 'liberal' principles and 'liberal' norms exclusively define our hopes, our self-understanding, and our understanding of the world in which we dwell?[43]

Berkowitz adds,

> While declaring that human beings are equal in rights and equal before the law, liberalism does not compel us to ignore the respects in which people differ. Indeed, some of liberalism's specific virtues – its open-endedness, its skepticism, its reluctance to take sides on questions about fundamental conceptions of the best life – prepare it, as few rival political theories are prepared, to make room for sensibilities beyond the one it sustains and to recognize the discontent it engenders.[44]

---

42 It is this separation of law from religion that moves Stephen Carter to comment that the separation of law and religion "carries an implicit trivialization of religious faith, and a denigration of religion as against other ways of knowing", "The Religiously Devout Judge", *Notre Dame Law Review*, Vol. 64, (1989), 933.

43 Peter Berkowitz, "Liberal Zealotry" *The Yale Law Journal*, Vol. 103, (1994), 1380.

44 Ibid 1381. This is aligned with William Galston's opting for a liberalism that gives diversity its due rather than a liberalism that places the focus on autonomy or critical reflection as a point of departure, William A. Galston, "Two Concepts of Liberalism", *Ethics*, Vol. 105, 3(1995), 524. Eric Berger refers to Judge Learned Hand's comment that: "The spirit of liberty is the spirit which is not too sure that it is right"; rather than seeking to coerce fellow citizens, it "seeks to understand the minds of

The judiciary's approach to religion against the background of perceiving forms of meaning arising from the religious to be prone to that which is irrational, bizarre and even supernatural while not doing the same regarding non-religious, is reflective of the trivialization of religion by the judiciary and where something is deemed trivial one of the consequences is exclusion (or the establishing of the risk of excluding). Paul Horwitz's adept proposal towards the furtherance of the protection of religious freedoms by means of constitutional agnosticism is helpful in challenging the judiciary's labelling of religion as irrational or bizarre. Horwitz refers to the importance of the taking of an "imaginative leap into the mental space of religious belief and vice versa"[45] and that the judiciary must sincerely be interested in or empathetic towards religion.[46] The spirit of constitutional agnosticism is of such a nature that it is doubtful whether it is right and refrains from avoiding questions of religious truth.[47] Horwitz adds that constitutional agnosticism "attempts to meet religious claims from an internal and not external perspective".[48] This gains in understanding when considering that religion enjoys commitment from many and that such commitment in itself can be convincingly justified.[49] Eric Berger comments that, especially against the

---

other men and women", Learned Hand, "The Spirit of Liberty" in *The Spirit of Libert: Papers and Addresses of Learned Hand* cited in Eric Berger, "The Rhetoric of Constitutional Absolutism", *William & Mary Law Review*, Vol. 56, 3(2015), 755-756.

45   Horwitz, (n 5), xxviii.
46   Ibid 148.
47   Ibid 150-151, 153.
48   Ibid 151.
49   Michael McConnell comments that religious belief has been attested to by millions of seemingly intelligent and rational people over long periods of time, who report that they have experienced, in some way, transcendent reality. There is even a "large literature in Anglophone philosophy devoted to defending the rationality of religious belief", Michael W. McConnell, "Why Protect Religious Freedom?" (Review article on Brian Leiter's *Why Tolerate Religion?* by Brian Leiter), *Yale Law Journal*, Vol. 123, (2013), 789. Melissa Moschella states that, "I have argued here that, contrary to the views of many political and constitutional theorists, includ-

background of religious freedoms (and often in general discussions of judicial review), how courts speak to litigants, and the broader social, political
and cultural controversies they represent, can matter. According to Berger,
absolutist rhetoric by the judiciary hints that a given case's losers are not
just wrong, but fundamentally misguided about the country's core principles and, consequently, losing litigants are labelled as outsiders. In turn, this
may "inflict harms on constitutional losers that exceed the harm inherent
in losing a substantive constitutional argument".[50] The meaning of losing,
and its significance for our experience of autonomy, are profoundly affected by how we talk to one another in our deliberations.[51] Berger adds that
to the extent that one shares the proposition that courts (and other legal
decision-makers) should stay away from estranging legal and political losers,
as opposed to simply deciding against them, that proposition is especially
relevant to the argument that the general rejection of religious accommodation may fuel illiberalism rather than ease it.[52]

The labelling of liberal democracies as being inclusive and the law's expressed commitment towards inclusivity remain questionable when taking
into cognisance the substantive marginalisation of religion that takes place
in such societies. This chapter has brought to light one such practice that
results in the relegation of religion to a level that decreases its credibility and
competitiveness when compared to that of the non-religious. More specif-

---

ing Barry, Dworkin, Schwartzman, and Eisgruber and Sager, religion is
a distinct and architectonic human good that is recognizable as such by
reason, and that, given religion's special role in the well-being of both individuals and communities, it deserves special treatment in law", Melissa
Moschella, "Beyond Equal Liberty: Religion as a Distinct Human Good
and the Implications for Religious Freedom", *Journal of Law and Religion*,
Vol. 32, (2017), 17. Also see ibid., 4.

50   Eric Berger, "The Rhetoric of Constitutional Absolutism" cited in Paul
     Horwitz, "Against Martyrdom: A liberal argument for accommodation
     of religion", *Notre Dame Law Review*, Vol. 91, 4(2016), 140.
51   Ibid 140-141.
52   Ibid 141.

ically, it has been argued that it is imperative that the judiciary (and the law in general) refrains from exclusively labelling the religious as being prone to that which is irrational or bizarre in the eyes of the other as this would constitute a practice in opposition to that type of democratic liberalism that is committed to the furtherance of diversity.

Bibliography

Alexander L "Liberalism, Religion, and the Unity of Epistemology", *San Diego Law Review*, Vol. 30, (1993).

Benson IT "The Jurisdiction of Science: What the Evolution/Creation Debate is Not About", *Journal for Christian Scholarship*, Vol. 43, 3&4 (2007).

Berger E "The Rhetoric of Constitutional Absolutism", *William & Mary Law Review*, Vol. 56, 3 (2015).

Berkowitz P "Liberal Zealotry", *The Yale Law Journal*, Vol. 103, (1994).

Budziszewski J *The Revenge of Conscience. Politics and the Fall of Man*, (Dallas: Spence Publishing Company, 1999).

Cambridge International Dictionary of English, Paul Proctor (Editor-in-Chief), (Cambridge: Cambridge University Press, 1995).

Campos PF "Secular Fundamentalism", *Columbia Law Review*, Vol. 94, 6 (1994).

Carter SL "Evolutionism, Creationism, and Treating Religion as a Hobby", *Duke Law Journal*, Vol. 1987, 6 (1987).

Carter SL "The Inaugural Development Fund Lectures: Scientific Liberalism, Scientistic Law", (Lecture One: The Uses of Empiricism and the Use of Fanaticism), *Oregon Law Review*, Vol. 69, 3 (1990), 471-494.

Carter SL "The Religiously Devout Judge", *Notre Dame Law Review*, Vol. 64, (1989).

Carter SL "The Inaugural Development Fund Lectures: Scientific Liberalism, Scientistic Law", (Lecture Two: The Establishment Clause Mess), *Oregon Law Review*, Vol. 69, (1990), 495-525.

Finnis JM *Human Rights and Common Good, Collected Essays: Vol. 3*, (Oxford: Oxford University Press, 2011).

Fish S "Mission Impossible: Settling the Just Bounds between Church and State", *Columbia Law Review*, Vol. 97, 8 (1997).

Gedicks FM "Public Life and Hostility to Religion", *Virginia Law Review*, Vol. 78, (1992).

Horwitz P *The Agnostic Age. Law, Religion, and the Constitution* (Oxford: Oxford University Press, 2011).

Horwitz P "Against Martyrdom: A liberal argument for accommodation of religion", *Notre Dame Law Review*, Vol. 91, 4 (2016).

Moschella M "Beyond Equal Liberty: Religion as a Distinct Human Good and the Implications for Religious Freedom", *Journal of Law and Religion*, Vol. 32, (2017).

McConnell MW "Why Protect Religious Freedom?" (Review article on Brian Leiter's *Why Tolerate Religion?* by Brian Leiter), *Yale Law Journal*, Vol. 123, (2013).

Mendus S *Toleration and the Limits of Liberalism*, (Hampshire, London: Macmillan Education Ltd., 1989).

Neal P "Rawls, Abortion, and Public Reason", *Journal of Church and State*.

Neuhaus RJ "A New Order of Religious Freedom", *George Washington Law Review*, Vol. 60, 3 (1992).

Paterson C *Assisted Suicide and Euthanasia. A Natural Law Ethics Approach*, (Burlington: Ashgate Publishing Company, 2008).

Perry MJ "A Critique of the 'Liberal' Political-Philosophical Project", *William and Mary Law Review*, Vol. 28, 2 (1987).

Shaffer M "Foetal rights and the regulation of abortion", *McGill Law Journal*, Vol. 39, 1(1994), 58-100.

Smith SD *The Disenchantment of Secular Discourse*, (Cambridge, Massachusetts & London, England: Harvard University Press, 2010).

The Concise Oxford Dictionary of Current English, R. E. Allen (ed.), 8th Ed., (Oxford: Clarendon Press, 1990).

Tipton SM "Republic and Liberal State: The Place of Religion in an Ambiguous Polity", *Emory Law Journal*, Vol. 39, (1990).

3

JUDICIAL APPREHENSION OF RELIGIOUS BELIEF UNDER THE COMMONWEALTH RELIGIOUS DISCRIMINATION BILL

Mark Fowler

Abstract

Discrimination law has become one of the primary determinants of acceptable religious conduct within our community. Where religious discrimination protection or 'exemption' claims conflict with other interests or rights, discrimination law becomes either a vehicle of exclusion or of inclusion. The exact statutorily enshrined legal tests deployed to assess and then weigh conflicting claims within each jurisdiction can then determine the ability of the courts to assert common value and reconcile difference within our community. This article illustrates the significance of these propositions by considering their application to the Second Exposure Draft of the currently mooted Australian Commonwealth Religious Discrimination Bill. In so doing it considers how the liberal and existentialist philosophical traditions have helped to entrench the conscience as definitive of the Western tradition, and demonstrates how recent religious freedom decisions of the major Anglophone courts give effect to these traditions. When considered against this framework, the Bill is revealed as agitating complex themes that have long occupied judges endeavouring to dutifully maintain a liberal separation between church and state. By requiring judges to perform feats in the interpretation of religious belief that leading jurists around the world have overwhelmingly cautioned against, it delivers a salutary case study for legislators and drafters seeking to protect religious freedom.

Introduction

Discrimination law has become one of the primary determinants of acceptable religious conduct within our community. Where religious discrimination protection or 'exemption' claims conflict with other interests or rights, discrimination law becomes either a vehicle for exclusion or inclusion, the focus of these collected essays. A religious action that is protected from detrimental treatment, or which is the subject of an 'exemption', is accepted by the state as a legitimate expression, otherwise it is banished from our public life. As anti-discrimination law is largely a creature of statute, claims can stand or fall on precise statutory drafting. The exact legal tests employed to assess and then weigh conflicting claims within each jurisdiction can then determine the ability of the courts to assert common value and reconcile difference within our community.

This chapter illustrates the significance of these propositions by considering their application to the Second Exposure Draft of the currently mooted Religious Discrimination Bill 2019 (Cth) (the Bill). The Bill agitates complex themes that have long occupied judges endeavouring to dutifully maintain a liberal separation between church and state. By requiring judges to perform feats in the interpretation of religious belief that leading jurists around the world have overwhelmingly cautioned against, it delivers a salutary case study for legislators and drafters seeking to protect religious freedom. The first part of this chapter provides an analysis of the key provisions of the Bill. The second part considers how the liberal and existentialist philosophical traditions have helped to entrench the conscience as definitive of the Western tradition. The third part of this chapter demonstrates how recent religious freedom decisions of the major Anglophone courts give effect to these traditions. The chapter concludes with an analysis of the sufficiency of the Bill in light of those traditions and law.

Part I - Commonwealth Religious Discrimination Bill

In order to gain access to the protections of the Bill, an applicant or respondent must satisfy a judge that their conduct satisfies the following test: 'a person of the same religion as the first person could reasonably consider [the conduct] to be in accordance with the doctrines, tenets, beliefs or teachings of that religion'.[1] This test, which I will term the 'member alignment test', is the engine room of the Bill's protections. It must be satisfied by religious bodies seeking to defend a claim of religious discrimination under clause 11, by employees in respect of statements made outside of the workplace under subclause 8(3), by accredited professionals and tradespersons in respect of statements made outside the course of their employment under subclauses 8(4) and 32(6), by health practitioners seeking to assert a conscientious objection under subclauses 8(5), (6) and 32(7) and by a person seeking to defend a discrimination claim for a statement of belief that they have made under clause 42.

The accompanying Explanatory Notes clarify the drafter's intention is to require the judge to consider whether a 'reasonable' religious believer would 'reasonably consider that the [complainant or religious body's actions are] in accordance with the'[2] religion. The Explanatory Notes continue:

> This provision imports an *objective reasonableness test*. This will ensure that courts are not required to determine whether particular conduct

---

1   Religious Discrimination Bill 2019 (Cth) cl 5(1) (definition of 'statement of belief').

2   Explanatory Notes, *Second Exposure Draft of the Religious Discrimination Bill 2019* (Cth) [168] ('Explanatory Notes').

is in accordance with the doctrines, tenets, beliefs or teachings of a particular religion, but rather whether members of that same religion would reasonably consider that to be so. This recognises as a matter of general principle that courts are not well-placed to make decisions on matters of religious doctrine, and whether conduct conforms with such doctrine, and will avoid the need for courts to do so....

A person of the same religion for the purposes of this test is intended to be a person of the same religion, or relevant religious denomination, sect, stream or tradition, as the religious body. For example, *the relevant reasonable person* in relation to conduct engaged in by a Methodist church would be a Methodist person, rather than a Catholic person, or a Christian generally.[3]

We are told that the test provides religious bodies with a 'margin of appreciation', recognising 'that religious bodies implement the teachings of their faith in a variety of ways and should have the autonomy to do so'.[4]

Although the statement that 'courts are not well-placed to make decisions on matters of religious doctrine' appears intended to allay the concerns of religious people, on close analysis the Bill requires precisely such determinations; a judge must assess the doctrinal accuracy of a claim against the beliefs recognised by 'members of that same religion'. Where differing views are held among a religious community, the position of judge as declarant of doctrine is necessarily determinative.

On this point, the Bill clearly resists the consensus among leading Anglophone courts on preferred models for judicial engagement with assertions of religious belief. As I will argue, this consensus comprises:

a)   Regard to the 'genuineness' or 'sincerity' of a person's belief as the evidentiary standard for identifying belief;

b)   As a subcategory of the foregoing, an avoidance of tests that assess the validity of a religious belief against the consensus interpretations of other adherents to that belief;

c)   An avoidance of distinctions between valid 'core' and invalid pe-

---

3   Ibid [237], [239] (emphasis added).
4   Ibid [238].

ripheral religious belief; and

d)   That the foregoing conditions are necessary to:

     i.   ensure that the task of identifying religious be-lief does not become the back-door means by which limitations are imposed, and

     ii.   thus guarantee claimants subjected to limita-tions are given publicly available reasons deter-mined according to objective limitation stan-dards.

Notwithstanding the claims in the Explanatory Notes, when held against the light of this consensus it becomes evident that the Bill does in appli-cation require judges to make 'decisions on matters of religious doctrine'. Prior to embarking on that examination, my argument in support of the above judicial consensus and against the 'member alignment test' places that consensus within historical liberalism and liberalism's influential child, existentialist thought.

Part II – Liberalism, Existentialism and Sincerity

Liberalism defined

Liberalism is the preeminent philosophical tradition shaping (Western) mo-dernity. By way of definition, Jeremy Waldron writes:

> [l]iberals hold that political organisations are justified by the contri-bution they make to the interests of individuals … [t]hey reject both the view that cultures, communities and states are ends in themselves, and the view that social and political organisations should aim to transform or perfect human nature.[5]

Liberalism introduced to the Western tradition, first with Hobbes and then his successors Locke and Rousseau, the proposition that the foundations of political authority, and its subsequent edifices, originate in individual auton-

---

5   Jeremy Waldron, 'Liberalism' in Edward Craig (ed), *Concise Routledge Encyclopedia of Philosophy* (TJ International, 2000) 486.

omy. Where Rome was established on the myths of the sanctuary to crimi-
nals and brutal brotherly animosity,[6] liberalism's founding myth was that of
a social contract. In early modern liberal theory, the genesis of the political
is the act of the hypothetical individual in a state of nature freely laying
down their rights in exchange for the promise of security and prosperity.

The second core liberal notion, that of the conscience, was exemplified
in Locke's *Letter Concerning Toleration*.[7] There, Locke wrote: 'It is vain for
an Unbeliever to take up the outward shew of another man's Profession.
Faith only, and inward Sincerity, are the things that procure acceptance with
God.'[8] Locke's claim consistently applies his epistemology: sensate man is
the master of his perception. He is the author of 'complex ideas', including his moral understanding, constructed from sensation.[9] To compel a
person to act against conscience is tantamount to rupturing their formative
epistemological conceptions. Accordingly, Locke advocates the primacy of
persuasion over force in matters of conscience, for 'it is one thing to persuade, another to command; one thing to press with arguments, another
with penalties.'[10] Locke's epistemology flows from, and serves to cement, a
certain understanding of the nature of being human, an ontology of autonomy. The link between Locke's epistemology and liberal political philosophy
validates Carl Schmitt's claim that 'the metaphysical image that a definite
epoch forges of the world [as informed by its epistemology] has the same
structure as what the world immediately understands to be appropriate as a

---

6   Saint Augustine, *City of God* (Doubleday, 1958) bk 15, 5; see also Saint Augustine,
     City of God (Doubleday, 1958) bk 2.
7   John Locke, *Second Treatise of Civil Government and a Letter Concerning Toleration*
     (Basil Blackwell, 1948).
8   Ibid 141.
9   John Locke, 'Essay Concerning Human Understanding' in Robert Maynard
     Hutchins (ed), *Great Books of the Western World* (Encyclopaedia Brittanica, 1952)
     vol 35, bk 3, chs 5, 6; Pierre Manent, *The City of Man* (Princeton University Press,
     1998) 117.
10   Locke (n 7) 128.

form of political organisation'.[11]

However, from its earliest expressions, the experiment of founding a political order on the autonomous individual contended with two very simply defined, but intractable, challenges. First, when are limitations on individual autonomy legitimate? And second, in such an order, under what conditions may individuals be said to constitute a community? From Hobbes to Rawls a cornucopia of remedies have been prescribed for these two ills which follow, largely, from the liberal attempt to create order from a theorised denatured man in the state of nature.[12] While Hobbes imposed the totalising Leviathan,[13] Rousseau presented the all-commanding virtuous general will.[14] As a result, ever since the rapid movement from liberalism's first continental moment of political actualisation to bloodbath at the *Place de la Révolution*, it has continually heard from antiquity behind it the cries of Athens' neighbours: *'demos tyrannos!'* The long pall of the guillotine has in turn fuelled the counter-reaction that Christopher Insole has called 'the great liberal passion': the prevention of 'the potential tyranny of majorities over the liberties of individuals'.[15]

Plotting the Trajectory of the Conscience: Existentialism as a Paradox of Liberalism

The liberal understanding of the will as conscientiously exercised began the long traverse on the trajectory of equality to today's enfranchised democracy. This advance has, in turn, given birth to many counter-'isms', emana-

11   Carl Schmitt, *Political Theology: Four Chapters on the Concept of Sovereignty*, tr George Schwab (University of Chicago Press, 2005) 46.
12   Manent (n 9).
13   Thomas Hobbes, *Leviathan* (Penguin Books, 1968) ch 29-30.
14   Jean-Jacques Rousseau, *The Social Contract*, tr Maurice Cranston (Penguin Books, 2006) bk 1, ch 7; bk 2, chs 1, 3.
15   Christopher Insole, *The Politics of Human Frailty: A Theological Defence of Political Liberalism* (Canterbury Press, 2004) 18.

tions of what Charles Taylor has termed the 'supernova', whose white heat was first unleashed by modernity's unearthing of the secular.[16] Although its prevalence has waned from the heights of its influence during the twentieth century, existentialism has left an indelible impact on contemporary culture. Comprised of thinkers as diverse as Kierkegaard, Dostoyevsky, Nietzsche and Heidegger, existentialism contains within it both a hyper-effectuation of individual autonomy and a revulsed horror at the 'levelling' tendencies of liberal democracy. As I will show, for certain among them, such as Nietzsche, this recoil could express itself in decidedly anti-liberal sentiments.

Democracy's 'levelling' current was first perceived by a wide range of earlier thinkers, whose perception was perhaps enhanced by their residency in an age in which the fading glow of the ideal of nobility was still felt. Montesquieu could thus claim that in a democracy: 'each one there should have the same happiness and the same advantages, each should taste the same pleasures and form the same expectations'.[17] Tocqueville expressed the apprehension the existentialists would later diagnose as the cause of 'dread' or 'nihilism'. In democratic society, he warned, where all citizens are subjected 'indiscriminately to the details of a uniform rule', the sovereign descends 'to the side of each one of his subjects in order to rule over him and lead him',[18] and 'all fortunes are mediocre, passions are naturally contained, imagination limited, pleasures simple'.[19] As Manent acknowledges, even Rousseau 'calls into question the modern and bourgeois Hobbesian ideal of peace'.[20] Rousseau wrote: 'When all remain supine under the yolk, it is then that everything decays ... In ancient times, Greece flourished at the height of the

16   Charles Taylor, *A Secular Age* (Harvard University Press, 2007) pt 3.

17   Charles Louis de Secondat Montesquieu, *The Spirit of the Laws* (Cambridge University Press, 1989) bk 5, ch 3.

18   Alexis de Tocqueville, *Democracy in America, Vol. II*, tr James T Schliefer (Liberty Fund, 2012) vol 2, bk 4, ch 6.

19   Ibid.

20   Pierre Manent, *An Intellectual History of Liberalism*, tr Rebecca Balinksi (Princeton University Press, 1995) 69.

cruellest wars ... A little disturbance gives vigour to the soul'.[21] Analogously, the great liberal Burke considered democracy's tendency to nourish a desire for arbitrary power in the 'depraved taste of the vulgar' to be a great danger to liberalism – labelling it 'the most false, wicked, and mischievous doctrine that ever could be preached to [the people]'.[22]

Existentialism is thus revealed as a counter-revolution when observed in its temporal development consequent upon democratic liberalism and its equality revolution. Kierkegaard laments, 'whereas a passionate age *accelerates, raises up and overthrows, elevates and debases,* a reflective apathetic age does the opposite, it *stifles and impedes, it levels'.*[23] Existentialism diagnoses and stands against democracy as 'a passionless but reflective age'[24] characterised by mediocrity, pusillanimity, the valorisation of pity, the decline of eminence, collapsing ultimately in unbearable shallowness and meaninglessness. What unites existentialism's otherwise disparate ensemble of philosophers is the unmitigated grimace directed at the 'herd',[25] 'the mob' or 'rabble'.[26] So Kierkegaard writes:

> By seeing the multitude of people around it, by being busied with all sorts of worldly affairs, by being wise to the ways of the world, such a person forgets himself, in a divine sense forgets his own name, dares not believe in himself, finds himself too risky, finds it much easier and safer to be like others, to become a copy, a number, along with the crowd.[27]

---

21 Rousseau (n 14) bk 3, ch 9.
22 Edmund Burke, 'An Appeal from the New to the Old Whigs' in Edmund Burke (ed), *Further Reflections on the Revolution in France* (Liberty Fund, 1992) 158.
23 Søren Kierkegaard, *Two Ages: The Age of Revolution and the Present Age, A Literary Review,* tr Howard V. Hong and Edna H. Hong (Princeton University Press, 1978) 84 (emphasis in original).
24 Ibid 90.
25 Friedrich Nietzsche, *Thus Spoke Zaruthustra,* tr R. J. Hollingdale (Penguin Books, 1961) 63.
26 Ibid 121; Friedrich Nietzsche, *The Will to Power,* tr R. Kevin Hill and Michael. A. Scarpatti (Penguin Books, 2017) 864.
27 Søren Kierkegaard, *The Sickness Unto Death,* tr Alistair Hannay (Penguin Books, 1989) 36.

For Nietzsche, this concern led to a direct rejection of democracy: 'And I turned my back upon the rulers when I saw what they now call ruling: bartering and haggling for power – with the rabble!'[28] Existentialism's levelling critique burns clearly through the twentieth century in Heidegger's critique of the 'they'[29] and in Foucault's more recent conception of 'normalisation'.[30]

In their reaction to this democratic 'levelling', the existentialists were united in their hyper-vigilant awareness that existence is a thing genuine or authentic, inspiring a kind of dread at the immense consequence of our own agency, rendering our freedom a source of anguish. Tocqueville anticipated this existentialist dread in his analysis of the consequences of the liberalisation of religion: 'When no authority exists in matters of religion, any more than in political matters, men soon become frightened in the face of unlimited independence.'[31] Eliot gave expression to the dread that characterises an era where the tide of religion's counsel has withdrawn:

> Do I dare
> Disturb the universe?
> In a minute there is time
> For decisions and revisions which a minute will reverse...
> I have seen the moment of my greatness flicker,
> And I have seen the eternal Footman hold my coat, and snicker,
> And in short, I was afraid.[32]

However, to the extent that they can be said to seek to offer a cure to 'levelling', the existentialists refused to uncouple themselves from liberalism's fundamental tenet: individual autonomy. Whether in the form of Kierkegaard's 'knight of faith';[33] or Nietzsche's power-willing 'Übermensch', 'the

---

28   Nietzsche, *Thus Spoke Zarathustra* (n 25) 121; Taylor (n 16) 185.
29   Martin Heidegger, *Being and Time*, tr John Macquarie and Edward Robinson (Harper & Row, 1962).
30   Taylor (n 16) 634-5.
31   Tocqueville (n 18) vol 2, bk 1, ch 5.
32   T. S. Eliot, 'The Love Song of J. Alfred Prufrock' in M. J. Salter and J. Stallworthy M. Ferguson (eds), *The Norton Anthology of Poetry* (W. W. Norton, 5th ed, 2005).
33   Søren Kierkegaard, *Fear and Trembling*, tr Alistair Hannay (Penguin Books, 1985).

meaning of the earth!',[34] the 'sun' that shines against the slave morality of the Christians;[35] or the revulsion we are invited to feel at Dostoyevsky's Grand Inquisitor's cynical manipulation of the masses by morality,[36] above all else, we are aware that life is comprised in the authentic fulfilment of individual agency. As Nietzsche exclaimed:

> Souls that lack determination
>
> Rouse my wrath to white-hot flame.[37]

This radical individualism even calls into question universal moral principles. Against Kantian deontology, Nietzsche longs '[t]hat you might grow weary of saying: "An action is good when it is unselfish"'.[38] Rather, '[t]hat *your* Self be in the action, as the mother is in the child: let that be *your* maxim of virtue!'[39] In Kierkegaard's estimation, Abraham's willingness to murder his son positions him as a 'knight of faith'.[40]

For the existentialists, serious consequences entail for the citizen frustrated in the expression of this radical individuality. For Kierkegaard, the existential task of becoming an individual self is the task of attempting to stand in correct relation to the divine and to the temporal.[41] The person who fails to attain this self-realisation resides in '[d]espair…a disrelationship in one's inmost being; no fate or event can penetrate so far and so deep'.[42] Similarly, Nietzsche saves his most strident critique for Christianity *qua* slave morality,

---

34   Nietzsche, *Thus Spoke Zarathustra* (n 25) Prologue, ch 3.
35   Ibid 129-30; Friedrich Nietzsche, *The Genealogy of Morals*, tr Horace B. Samuel (Dover Publications, 2003).
36   Fyodor Dostoyevsky, *The Brothers Karamazov*, tr David McDuff (Penguin Books, 1993) 322.
37   Friedrich Nietzsche, *The Gay Science*, tr Thomas Common (Dover Publications, 2020) 234; Eugene G Newman, 'The Meta-Moralism of Nietzsche' (1982) 16 *Journal of Value Inquiry* 207, 217.
38   Nietzsche, *Thus Spoke Zarathustra* (n 25) 119.
39   Ibid 120 (emphasis in original).
40   Kierkegaard, *Fear and Trembling* (n 33).
41   Graham M. Smith, 'Kierkegaard from the point of view of the political' (2005) 31(1) *History of European Ideas* 35, 39, 45.
42   Søren Kierkegaard, *Works of Love*, tr Howard Hong and Edna Hong (Harper Collins, 1962) 54.

which, in repressing the will to power, gives rise to the 'great nausea, will to nothingness, and Nihilism'.[43] Although offering vastly differing perspectives on theology, the two are united in their diagnosis of the cause of the malaise: the emaciated, obstructed self.

Today we live in a society that has been dramatically shaped by the existentialist challenge: we are called to be defiantly all of who we are personally convicted to be in the face of our mortality. As Charles Taylor has termed it, we live in the Age of Authenticity.[44] The greatest sin remains inauthenticity to one's convictions, wherever they may fall, and in whatever temporality they may exist. In Taylor's 'supernova' of 'isms', it seems that Nietzsche's epistemic relativism has prevailed. There are no facts, 'only interpretations'.[45] The *pax postmoderna* offers the promise of peace by permitting each citizen to define their own truth according to self-referential determinants. These two major 'ideologies', liberalism and existentialism, have exercised momentous influence on contemporary ontological understanding, and from there (following Schmitt), our politics. The primacy of authentically aligning one's action with one's conviction is at the core of both movements. Having outlined this philosophical background, I now turn to assess the extent to which the Bill gives effect to, or alternatively, frustrates, the central concerns of these movements.

Part III - Stating the Problem: Exclusion Results from Conflating the Distinction between Defining and Limiting Beliefs

A strict distinction should be maintained between the task of identifying the content of a religious belief and the consideration of the limitations to be placed upon that belief. Without this division of judicial labour, a refusal to acknowledge a sincere belief as a correct interpretation could operate as a

---

43   Nietzsche, *The Genealogy of Morals* (n 35) bk 2, ch 24.
44   Taylor (n 16) 473-504.
45   Nietzsche, *The Will to Power* (n 26) ch 481.

limitation in the absence of a justification. Ahdar and Leigh thus argue for an 'approach [that] interprets the right quite broadly, then requires the state to justify the limitation; rather than the courts paring back the breadth of the right to begin with'[46] by refusing to acknowledge a belief *qua* 'religious belief'. In the latter case:

> An applicant may leave court either implicitly labelled as a hypocrite (for having made a false claim under cover of religion), or as having an inferior understanding of what he or she holds most dear (compared to the learned, amateur theologian—cum—judge).[47]

In the case of the Bill, this 'paring back' occurs in the assessment of whether 'a person of the same religion as the first person could reasonably consider' the impugned conduct accords with the relevant religion.

International law prescribes a circumscribed number of strictly articulated grounds for limiting religious manifestation.[48] Whether a claimant's beliefs align with the beliefs of other members of their religion is irrelevant to that assessment. It can then be said that, to the extent that the Bill fails to recognise legitimately held religious beliefs, it fails to acquit Australia's obligations under international law. It is difficult to comprehend what such a test adds to the Bill, other than seeking to provide a mechanism to winnow out sham claims. However, as will be seen, courts around the world have held that this is an end that is adequately met through a test that looks to the individual 'genuineness' of a religious belief, and which eschews conclusions as to the content of accepted religious belief.

---

46   Rex Ahdar and Ian Leigh, *Religious Freedom in the Liberal State* (OUP Oxford, 2nd ed, 2013) 192.

47   Ibid 167.

48   For Australia, the relevant obligation is found in art 18(3) of the *International Covenant on Civil and Political Rights 1966,* as applied in the jurisprudence of the United Nation Human Rights Committee: *International Covenant on Civil and Political Rights,* opened for signature 19 December 1996, 999 UNTS 171 (entered into force 23 March 1976).

'Genuineness' or 'Sincerity' Tests

To ensure judges avoid weighing matters of doctrine, the Australian High Court, House of Lords, the United States Supreme Court and the Canadian Supreme Court have all directed inferior courts to employ tests that have regard to the 'sincerity' (eliciting recollection of Locke's use of this term above) or 'genuineness' of a religious belief. Given the centrality of this law to this chapter's analysis of the Bill, and lest it be thought that this critique deploys novel arguments, the following section explicates the rationale for the sincerity test in the justices' own words. Against this backdrop of existing common law it is seen that the truly novel proposition is contained in the Bill's pivotal emphasis on the beliefs of a claimant's fellow-adherents.

Australia: 'Church of the New Faith v Commissioner for Pay-roll Tax' (Vic)

Amid the heralding of the widely accepted definition of 'religion' provided by Mason ACJ and Brennan J[49] and Wilson and Deane JJ[50] in *Church of the New Faith v Commissioner for Pay-roll Tax (Vic)* (*Church of the New Faith*),[51] it is often overlooked that, having defined the *boundaries* of religion, both judgements also establish a sincerity test for the determination of the *content* of distinct religious beliefs. Justices Wilson and Deane held:

> there was no suggestion made in the cross examination of Mrs. Allen and Mr. Cockerill that they were other than sincere in the beliefs they professed. Nor does the judgment of the learned trial judge contain any finding that any significant number of the more than 5,000 Victorian members of the applicant was other than genuine and sincere... the great majority of the Australian members of the applicant are sincere and genuine in their acceptance of current Scientology writings and practices.[52]

---

49   *Church of the New Faith v Commissioner for Pay-roll Tax (Vic)* (1983) 154 CLR 120, 129-30 (Mason ACJ and Brennan J) ('*Church of the New Faith*').
50   Ibid 174 (Wilson and Deane JJ).
51   Ibid.
52   Ibid 170 (Wilson and Deane JJ) (emphasis added).

In finding that Scientology comprised a religion, Mason ACJ and Brennan J determined that:

> the sincerity and integrity of the ordinary members of the Scientology movement were not in doubt…No attack was made upon the sincerity or integrity of the witnesses who stated what the general group of adherents believed and accepted.[53]

In many senses, this is the background Australian common law against which the Bill would operate, but for the member alignment test. Although the Explanatory Notes state 'the Act is informed by the approach taken by the High Court in *Church of the New Faith*',[54] in effect, the Bill displaces the High Court's jurisprudence by requiring a judge to objectively determine what conduct is sanctioned by a reasonable believer, regardless of the sincerely held convictions of the believer-claimant/respondent in question.

Canada: 'Syndicat Northcrest v Amselem'

Subsequently, in *Syndicat Northcrest v Amselem*[55] (*Amselem*), the Canadian Supreme Court required courts in that jurisdiction to apply a sincerity test that admits as religious acts that are 'neither fictitious, nor capricious, and [are] not an artifice'.[56] For Iacobucci J, with whom the majority of the Court agreed, this test flowed from key, foundational liberal precepts, including 'that society does not interfere with profoundly personal beliefs'[57] and, no less than, the modern separation between church and state:

> In my view, the State is in no position to be, nor should it become, the arbiter of religious dogma. Accordingly, courts should avoid judicially interpreting and thus determining, either explicitly or implicitly, the content of a subjective understanding of religious requirement,

---

53   Ibid 141 (Mason ACJ and Brennan J).
54   'Explanatory Notes' (n 2) [71].
55   (2004) 2 SCR 551.
56   Ibid.
57   Ibid [41], citing Dickson J in *R v Big M Drug Mart Ltd* [1985] 1 SCR 295, 346 (emphasis in original).

"obligation", precept, "commandment", custom or ritual. *Secular judicial determinations of theological or religious disputes, or of contentious matters of religious doctrine, unjustifiably entangle the court in the affairs of religion.*

That said, while a court is not qualified to rule on the validity or veracity of any given religious practice or belief, *or to choose among various interpretations of belief,* it is qualified to inquire into the sincerity of a claimant's belief, where sincerity is in fact at issue. It is important to emphasize, however, that sincerity of belief simply implies an honesty of belief...

the jurisprudence in this area evinces that inquiries into a claimant's sincerity must be as limited as possible... *"given the widening understanding of what constitutes religion in our society, the very rights ostensibly protected by the free exercise clause might well be jeopardized by any but the most minimal inquiry into sincerity"...*

the court's role in assessing sincerity is intended only to ensure that a presently *asserted religious belief is in good faith, neither fictitious nor capricious, and that it is not an artifice. Otherwise, nothing short of a religious inquisition would be required to decipher the innermost beliefs of human beings.* [58]

United Kingdom: R '(on the application of Williamson) v Secretary of State for Education and Employment'

In R *(on the application of Williamson) v Secretary of State for Education and Employment*[59] (*Williamson*) the House of Lords subsequently adopted Iacobucci J's articulation of the sincerity test, with Lord Walker citing *Church of the New Faith* as among the growing international acceptance of the rationale for a sincerity test. His Lordship held:

assuming for the moment that the issue is to be analysed in terms of (i) the existence of a belief, (ii) its manifestation, (iii) interference with the manifested belief and (iv) justification of the interference, *I doubt whether it is right for the court (except in extreme cases such as the "Wicca" case*

---

58   *Syndicat Northcrest v Amselem* (2004) 2 SCR 551, [50] (emphasis added) (citations omitted).
59   (2005) UKHL 15.

*mentioned below) to impose an evaluative filter at the first stage, especially when
religious beliefs are involved. For the court to adjudicate on the seriousness, cogency
and coherence of theological beliefs is (as Richards J put it in R (Amicus) v Secretary of State for Trade) to take the court beyond its legitimate role.* The High
Court of Australia expressed similar views in the *Church of the New
Faith case...* So did the Supreme Court of Canada in *Syndicat Northcrest
v Amselem.* [60]

Lord Walker condemns what Ahdar and Leigh term the 'paring back' approach, claiming the Australian High Court's seminal concern with sincerity
as commensurate with the 'proper role' of the courts within a liberal constitutional democracy.

United States: 'Employment Division, Department of Human Resources of Oregon v Smith'

Justice Scalia, delivering the opinion for the majority of the United States
Supreme Court in *Employment Division, Department of Human Resources of Oregon v Smith*[61] (*Smith*), articulated a similar warning against judicial assessment
of the correctness of a doctrinal position:

> *What principle of law or logic can be brought to bear to contradict a believer's
> assertion that a particular act is "central" to his personal faith? Judging the
> centrality of different religious practices is akin to the unacceptable "business of
> evaluating the relative merits of differing religious claims."* .... As we reaf-
> firmed only last Term, "[i]t is not within the judicial ken to question
> the centrality of particular beliefs or practices to a faith, *or the validity
> of particular litigants' interpretations of those creeds."* ... Repeatedly and in
> many different contexts, we have warned that courts must not pre-
> sume to determine the place of a particular belief in a religion or the
> plausibility of a religious claim. If the "compelling interest" test is
> to be applied at all, then, it must be applied across the board, to all
> actions thought to be religiously commanded.[62]

---

60   Ibid 267 (emphasis added) (citations omitted).
61   494 US 872 (1990).
62   Ibid 886-7 (Scalia J) (emphasis added) (citations omitted).

Each of the foregoing Courts have directed judges to adopt a (what might be characterised as recognisably Lockean) test of sincerity to avoid determinations of valid belief as a fundament of the liberal separation of church and state. As Julian Rivers helpfully summarises:

> Courts often remind themselves that it does not matter whether the litigant is part of a recognised religious community asserting a right on behalf of many others, or an individual with idiosyncratic views; each deserves respect.[63]

Conduct that people who hold the belief consider may be reasonably regarded as being in accordance with the belief

As will be apparent from the foregoing discussion, the direction from these senior Courts to not encroach upon matters proper to the religious domain contains within it the injunction to avoid any test that only recognises a person's religious beliefs where those beliefs are held by other persons of the same religion. This is often accompanied by related warnings cautioning against reliance on the testimony of experts.

In delivering the opinion of the US Supreme Court in *Thomas v Review Board of the Indiana Employment Security Division*,[64] Burger CJ stated:

> the guarantee of free exercise is not limited to beliefs which are shared by all of the members of a religious sect. Particularly in this sensitive area, *it is not within the judicial function and judicial competence to inquire whether the petitioner or his fellow worker more correctly perceived the commands of their common faith. Courts are not arbiters of scriptural interpretation.*[65]

Similarly, in *Amselem*, Iacobucci J held:

> *claimants seeking to invoke freedom of religion should not need to prove the objective validity of their beliefs in that their beliefs are objectively recognized as valid*

63   Julian Rivers, *The Law of Organized Religions, Between Establishment and Secularism* (Oxford University Press, 2010) 321.
64   450 US 707 (1981).
65   Ibid 715-16 (emphasis added).

by other members of the same religion, nor is such an inquiry appropriate for courts to make;... In fact, this Court has indicated on several occasions that, if anything, a person must show "[s]incerity of belief" and not that a particular belief is "valid"... "it is not the role of this Court to decide what any particular religion believes".[66]

Justice Iacobucci's admonition against judges interpreting doctrine applies to efforts to locate the true interpretation of a doctrine within a 'stream'. Such attempts breach a necessary component of separation between church and state:

This approach to freedom of religion effectively avoids the invidious interference of the State and its courts with religious belief. The alternative would undoubtedly result in unwarranted intrusions into the religious affairs of the synagogues, churches, mosques, temples and religious facilities of the nation with value-judgment indictments of those beliefs that may be unconventional or not mainstream..."an intrusive government inquiry into the nature of a claimant's beliefs would in itself threaten the values of religious liberty".[67]

For substantively the same reasons, Iacobucci J also cautioned against reliance on the testimony of 'experts':

The emphasis then is on personal choice of religious beliefs. In my opinion, these decisions and commentary should not be construed to imply that freedom of religion protects only those aspects of religious belief or conduct that are objectively recognized by religious experts as being obligatory tenets or precepts of a particular religion...

A claimant may choose to adduce expert evidence to demonstrate that his or her belief is consistent with the practices and beliefs of other adherents of the faith. While such evidence may be relevant to a demonstration of sincerity, it is not necessary. *Since the focus of the inquiry is not on what others view the claimant's religious obligations as being, but rather what the claimant views these personal religious "obligations" to be, it is inappropriate to require expert opinions to show sincerity of belief.*

---

66   *Syndicat Northcrest v Amselem* (2004) 2 SCR 551, [43] (emphasis added) (citations omitted).
67   Ibid [55].

> An "expert" or an authority on religious law is not the surrogate for
> an individual's affirmation of what his or her religious beliefs are.
> Religious belief is intensely personal and can easily vary from one
> individual to another. Requiring proof of the established practices of
> a religion to gauge the sincerity of belief diminishes the very freedom
> we seek to protect.[68]

This same approach has been adopted in the United Kingdom. As Lord
Nicholls, with whom the Court agreed, set out in *Williamson*:[69]

> emphatically, it is not for the court to embark on an inquiry into the
> asserted belief and judge its "validity" by some objective standard
> such as the source material upon which the claimant founds his belief
> or the orthodox teaching of the religion in question *or the extent to
> which the claimant's belief conforms to or differ from the views of others professing
> the same religion*. Freedom of religion protects the subjective belief of
> an individual. As Iaccobucci J also notes religious belief is intensely
> personal and can easily vary from one individual to another. Each
> individual is at liberty to hold his own religious beliefs, however irra-
> tional or inconsistent they may seem to some, however surprising.[70]

This is not to say that a claimant may not, of their own volition, lead evidence in support of their claim. However, as Ahdar and Leigh assert: 'It is
wrong to *insist* that expert evidence from religious authorities support the
claimant's case'.[71]

In interpreting the religious exemption in New South Wales anti-discrimination law in *OV & OW v Members of the Board of the Wesley Mission Council*,[72]
the New South Wales Court of Appeal applied substantively the same approach to a religious association contra the wider denomination in which it
was located:

> there is no basis in s 56 to infer that Parliament intended to exempt

68   Ibid [54].
69   R *(on the application of Williamson) v Secretary of State for Education and Employment*
      (2005) UKHL 15.
70   Ibid [22] (emphasis added) (citations omitted).
71   Ahdar and Leigh (n 46) 196.
72   (2014) 308 ALR 615; (2010) NSWCA 155.

from the operation of the Anti-Discrimination Act only those acts or practices which formed part (relevantly for present purposes) of the religion common to all Christian churches, or all branches of a particular Christian church (in the sense of denomination), to the exclusion of variants adopted by some elements within a particular Church, but not by others.[73]

The exemption 'section encompassed any body established to propagate a system of beliefs, qualifying as a religion'[74] and required regard to be had to the beliefs of the respondent organisation in question, not any other body.

As the history of the Church in the West attests, the sincerely held convictions of 'reasonable' people (leaving aside the unreasonable for the moment!) within the one tradition can differ on varying aspects of doctrine. However, history also demonstrates that religious unity can enfold internal difference, that certain distinctions need not preclude adherents from affirming each other as fellow-believers. In the face of this history, it is not too remote a possibility to contemplate that denominations contending with the member alignment test will feel impelled to define their position on previously 'contentious' matters as a means of protecting the actions of their adherents in the secular domain. If so, the Bill risks undermining the internal cohesion of religious denominations, causing them to depart from traditions that have previously allowed individual members to retain fellowship while holding their own sincerely held convictions on particular interpretations of religious texts.

The Risk of Disagreement among 'Reasonable' Believers

This accentuates a further practical evidentiary issue arising from the Bill's member alignment test. Surprisingly, given the centrality of this test, no guidance is given as to precisely who constitutes the 'members' qualified to

73   Ibid [41].
74   Ibid [50].

judge whether a claimant's views reasonably accord with the applicable doctrine, nor are we provided with any direction as to who may bring evidence
of the members' view. Are they religious leaders, experts external to the
tradition, a majority of fellow believers within the 'stream' or the prevailing
number of witnesses presented by the parties to litigation? These matters
are left to judicial discretion.

Where a range of views on a particular doctrinal matter exist within a 'religious denomination, sect, stream or tradition', how is a court to determine
which view is the correct one that would be adopted by a 'reasonable' religious believer? Where matters are contested, either the court will prefer one
view over another, or it will conclude that, given the array of views 'reasonably' held, the 'relevant reasonable person' need not hold the particular
asserted view. As such, it is not properly considered a belief characteristic
of that tradition and is thus lost to the Bill's protections. The concern is
only heightened when one contemplates the foreseeable alignment between
'contentious matters' over which fellow adherents 'agree to disagree' and
the kinds of beliefs that may incite a claim of discrimination. In this way,
the protections offered by the Bill are relegated to the lowest common de-
nominator, matters over which uniform agreement is held.

The Victorian Court of Appeal judgement in *Christian Youth Camps Ltd v
Cobaw Community Health Services Ltd*[75] (*Cobaw*) demonstrates that this is not
at all a remote possibility. There, the Court concluded that variation among
religious believers on sexual mores meant that there was no relevant central
(and thus protected) doctrine that was promulgated by the religion. President Maxwell held:

> The appeal submission for the applicants was that her Honour erred
> in viewing particular teachings and beliefs as applications of doctrine,
> rather than as doctrine in themselves. This conclusion was said not

---

75   (2014) 308 ALR 615; [2014] AVSCA 75 ('*Christian Youth Camps*').

to be open on the evidence. In my opinion, this submission must be rejected. On the evidence before her Honour, the distinction was inescapable…*there was even some diversity between Christian Brethren congregations as to which parts of the Bible were to be applied literally*. These were properly to be regarded as applications of doctrine, as her Honour found.[76]

The Court held that the central doctrines excluded the sincere religious assertions of the individual respondent, and in so doing, obviated the need to provide reasons for the limitation placed upon the believers in question. Religious movements, by their very nature, are collations, gradations in which internal partitions and commonalities, and their gravity differ according to historical, doctrinal and at times, cultural emphases. At best, the Bill clumsily engages with this reality, providing scarce practical direction to those who seek to come under its aegis and those genuinely desiring to meet its obligations.

Core v Peripheral Beliefs

The dictum of Scalia J in *Smith* extracted above contains a further, related direction that subordinate courts avoid any exercise in distinguishing between 'central' (protected) belief and peripheral (not protected) religious belief.[77] Similarly, in *Amselem*, Iacobucci J directed Canadian courts to avoid a doctrinal dichotomy between 'mandatory' conduct 'obligatory' for a religion (protected) and 'voluntary' conduct merely motivated by religious belief (not protected).[78] Again, *Cobaw* provides a useful case study in the disregard of such warnings. There, Maxwell P affirmed distinctions between conduct 'intimately or closely connected with belief, or of real significance to, the beliefs' and that which was not, and conduct that was 'required or

76   Ibid [277]-[279] (emphasis added).
77   *Employment Division, Department of Human Resources of Oregon v Smith* 494 US 872 (1990).
78   *Syndicat Northcrest v Amselem* (2004) 2 SCR 551, [47]-[49].

compelled by the doctrines' and that which was not in order to refuse the claim to an exemption.[79]

The Explanatory Notes to the Bill deploy similar distinctions. If these Notes are to provide any guidance, judicial application of the Bill's protections will be corralled towards 'conduct that has an intrinsically religious character or is fundamental to the practice of religion'.[80] As demonstrated above, the most senior Anglophone courts have been prompted to adopt the sincerity test in order to avoid just such exercises in determining doctrine.

Sham Religions and Illiberal Religious Acts

The most common, often instinctive, objection to a sincerity test is that it will protect sham religions. An analogous concern is that a sincerity test will permit religious believers to write themselves into law. Both concerns continue to press strongly in debates on the recognition of religious belief today. In their joint judgement Mason ACJ and Brennan J address the first demurral directly, promulgating the sincerity test alongside (or possibly as a means to) the lawful exclusion of 'sham' religion. The sincerity test:

> is not to deny that there are cases where what is put forward as being a religion cannot properly be so characterized for the reason that it is, in truth, no more than a parody of religion or a sham: the claimed religion of "Chief Boo Hoo" and the "Boo Hoos" in *United States v. Kuch* provides an obvious example of such a parody.[81]

As to the latter objection, at first it could seem that the Bill's 'reasonable religious believer' test adds a ground of refusal for anti-liberal religious beliefs. However, of itself, the test would not defeat the religious discrimination claim of the employee who is disciplined for their belief-based call to violence, where such violence is affirmed by their fellow adherents. The

79   *Christian Youth Camps* (n 75) [299].
80   'Explanatory Notes' (n 2) [240].
81   *Church of the New Faith* (n 49) 171 (Wilson and Deane JJ) (citations omitted).

limitation on such a claim of discrimination must be found elsewhere, for example in the reasonableness or comparator tests. In sum, a test of sincerity will not permit the automatic protection of sham or illiberal religious beliefs, and will not, in itself, limit the grounds that are otherwise available to defeat such claims.

In *Amselem*, Iacobucci J sought to provide practical evidentiary principles to guide the application of this test:

> Assessment of sincerity is a question of fact that can be based on several non-exhaustive criteria, including the credibility of a claimant's testimony, as well as an analysis of whether the alleged belief is consistent with his or her other current religious practices.[82]

Each of the markers asserted by Iacobucci J might also readily be applied to a religious body claimant/respondent by a statutorily articulated rule of attribution that requires regard to the credibility of the testimony of the relevant leaders of the institution, as well as consideration of whether the asserted belief is consistent with the conduct of the entity.

Inclusion

To conclude, I return to consider precisely how my support of a sincerity test is relevant to the theme of this collected works, 'inclusion'. To answer that question, I must return to Locke and existentialism. If Locke's epistemology is exemplary of modern liberalism, persuasion, not compulsion, defines the liberal ideal. The existentialists challenge us to face all of the terrible contingencies of our existence and then, above all, to act authentically on our individual convictions. The Bill defies both these traditions by blindfolding the judicial marksman given the task of assessing the protection of those convictions. To deploy existential parlance: the flight of the arrow is sublimated to the gravitational field of the denominational herd.

---

82   *Syndicat Northcrest v Amselem* (2004) 2 SCR 551, [53]; see also [56].

In failing to admit a sincerely held religious belief *qua* religious belief, the Bill excludes the applicant from the dignity enjoyed by those claimants whose religious convictions happen to align with their fellow-adherents. Those able to satisfy the member alignment test have the rationale for limiting their religious manifestation enunciated by judicial reasoning, whether it be for the reasons of maintaining public order, the countervailing rights of others or otherwise. However, for those failing to satisfy this test, the state abandons Locke's founding principle that, in matters of the conscience, persuasion is to be preferred over compulsion. For these citizens, the state eludes the Rawlsian obligation to provide publicly available reasons for limiting the conscience. The sole determinant for the failure of the religious applicants'/respondents' contentions is that certain other religious believers disagreed with their sincerely held conviction. This is a most radical, anti-liberal and anti-existentialist form of exclusion.

By precluding the applicant/respondent access to such reasons, the state withdraws any prospect that the believer may assess the legitimacy of the limitation, and thus denies the prospect (however remote) that the citizen-believer may contemplate acceptance of that limitation. Rather, the believer departs the courtroom with this sole judicial rationale for limiting her belief: you interpreted your religious beliefs incorrectly. These concerns are only enhanced where the 'believer' in question is a religious institution, who represents an association of believers within a tradition.[83]

I have presented existentialism as a reaction against democratic liberalism. Conversely, it shares with the philosophy that is the progenitor of its horror agreement on the primacy of individual autonomy, even hyper-activating it. The liberal and the existentialist thus share common agreement that failure

---

83   Mark Fowler, 'Identifying Faith-Based Entities for the Purpose of Anti-Discrimination Law' in Neville G. Rochow, Brett G. Scharffs and Paul T. Babie (eds), *Freedom of Religion or Belief: Creating the Constitutional Space for Fundamental Freedoms* (Edward Elgar Publishing, 2020)

to apprehend a person's conscientious convictions is the ultimate statement of exclusion. It denies their existence as an autonomous agent capable of formulating such convictions. Where the ultimate judicial determination limits their conscientious expression, it denies the means of existence resulting, in Kierkegaard's terminology, in 'despair', or in Nietzsche's 'ressentiment' collapsing into 'nihilism'.[84] By refusing to engage with the sincere convictions of the believer in the assessment of their actions, the Bill excludes them from the benefits enjoyed by other citizens – the fundaments of liberal/existential humanity are denied to such a person. In a community that assumes the form of a liberal democracy this is the ultimate statement of exclusion.

Conclusion

Where a religious believer is subjected to detrimental treatment as a consequence of their sincere religious expression, whether that expression is doctrinally correct according to the view of fellow believers should be irrelevant to the determination of whether the believer has been discriminated against. Similarly, the reliance of a body on an 'exemption' should not turn on a court's assessment of doctrinal correctness, whether by regard to fellow adherents or otherwise. Use of such means contemplate the possibility that a sincerely and genuinely held belief will be defeated as a belief that is not religious simply because of a dispute as to doctrinal interpretation. That is not necessary, when the ultimate question is whether the manifestation accompanying the belief is to be accommodated in a plural society. This chapter has shown that the member alignment test employed in the Bill runs contrary to the consensus among superior Anglophone courts. That consensus has settled on a sincerity test as a means to give effect to the separation of church and state in the functions of the judicial branch

---

84   Nietzsche, *The Genealogy of Morals* (n 35) bk 1, ch 10.

of government, and in order to avoid engaging the courts in unnecessary determinations of doctrinal disputes. It holds that wherever limitations are to be imposed upon the manifestation of religious beliefs, they should be imposed after the belief has been accurately evidenced, rather than, as is the approach in the Religious Discrimination Bill 2019 (Cth), through a refusal of a claim, or defence, as evidencing a proper assertion of religious belief.

References

Articles/Books/Reports

Ahdar, Rex and Ian Leigh, *Religious Freedom in the Liberal State* (OUP Oxford, 2nd ed, 2013).

Second Exposure Draft of the Religious Discrimination Bill 2019.

Burke, Edmund, 'An Appeal from the New to the Old Whigs' in Edmund Burke (ed), *Further Reflections on the Revolution in France* (Liberty Fund, 1992).

Dostoyevsky, Fyodor, *The Brothers Karamazov*, tr David McDuff (Penguin Books, 1993).

Eliot, T. S., 'The Love Song of J. Alfred Prufrock' in M. J. Salter and J. Stallworthy M. Ferguson (eds), *The Norton Anthology of Poetry* (W. W. Norton, Fifth ed, 2005).

Fowler, Mark, 'Identifying Faith-Based Entities for the Purpose of Anti-Discrimination Law' in Neville G. Rochow and Brett G. Scharffs Paul T. Babie (eds), *Freedom of Religion or Belief: Creating the Constitutional Space for Fundamental Freedoms* (Edward Elgar Publishing, 2020).

Heidegger, Martin, *Being and Time*, tr John Macquarie and Edward Robinson (Harper & Row, 1962).

Hobbes, Thomas, *Leviathan* (Penguin Books, 1968 ed).

Insole, Christopher, *The Politics of Human Frailty: A Theological Defence of Political Liberalism* (Canterbury Press, 2004).

Kierkegaard, Søren, *Works of Love*, tr Howard Hong and Edna Hong (Harper Collins, 1962).

Kierkegaard, Søren, *Two Ages: The Age of Revolution and the Present Age, A Literary Review*, tr Howard V. Hong and Edna H. Hong (Princeton University Press, 1978).

Kierkegaard, Søren, *Fear and Trembling*, tr Alistair Hannay (Penguin Books, 1985).

Kierkegaard, Søren, *The Sickness Unto Death*, tr Alistair Hannay (Penguin Books, 1989).

Locke, John, *Second Treatise of Civil Government and a Letter Concerning Toleration* (Basil Blackwell, 1948).

John Locke, 'Essay Concerning Human Understanding' in Robert Maynard Hutchins (ed), *Great Books of the Western World* (Encyclopaedia Brittanica, 1952).

Manent, Pierre, *An Intellectual History of Liberalism*, tr Rebecca Balinksi (Princeton University Press, 1995).

Manent, Pierre, *The City of Man* (Princeton University Press, 1998).

Montesquieu, Charles Louis de Secondat, *The Spirit of the Laws* (Cambridge University Press, 1989).

Newman, Eugene G., 'The Meta-Moralism of Nietzsche' (1982) 16 *Journal of Value Inquiry* 207.

Nietzsche, Friedrich, *Thus Spoke Zaruthustra*, tr R. J. Hollingdale (Penguin Books, 1961).

Nietzsche, Friedrich, *The Genealogy of Morals*, tr Horace B. Samuel (Dover Publications, 2003).

Nietzsche, Friedrich, *The Will to Power*, tr R. Kevin Hill and Michael. A. Scarpatti (Penguin Books, 2017).

Nietzsche, Friedrich, *The Gay Science*, tr Thomas Common (Dover Publications, 2020).

Rivers, Julian, *The Law of Organized Religions, Between Establishment and Secularism* (Oxford University Press, 2010).

Rousseau, Jean-Jacques, *The Social Contract*, tr Maurice Cranston (Penguin Books, 2006).

Schmitt, Carl, *Political Theology: Four Chapters on the Concept of Sovereignty*, tr George Schwab (University of Chicago Press, 2005).

Smith, Graham M., 'Kierkegaard from the point of view of the political' (2005) 31(1) *History of European Ideas* 35.

Taylor, Charles, *A Secular Age* (Harvard University Press, 2007).

Tocqueville, Alexis de, *Democracy in America, Vol. II*, tr James T Schliefer (Liberty Fund, 2012).

Waldron, Jeremy, 'Liberalism', *Concise Routledge Encyclopedia of Philosophy* (TJ International, 2000).

Cases

Christian Youth Camps Ltd v Cobaw Community Health Services Ltd (2014) 308 ALR 615; [2014] AVSCA 75.

Church of the New Faith v Commissioner for Pay-roll Tax (Vic) (1983) 154 CLR 120.

Employment Division, Department of Human Resources of Oregon v Smith 494 US 872 (1990).

OV & OW v Members of the Board of the Wesley Mission Council (2014) 308 ALR 615.

R (on the application of Williamson) v Secretary of State for Education and Employment (2005) UKHL 15.

R v Big M Drug Mart Ltd [1985] 1 SCR 295.

Syndicat Northcrest v Amselem (2004) 2 SCR 551.

Treaties

International Covenant on Civil and Political Rights, opened for signature 19 December 1996, 999 UNTS 171 (entered into force 23 March 1976).

Other

Explanatory Notes, *Second Exposure Draft of the Religious Discrimination Bill 2019 (Cth)*.

4

THE EXCLUSIVITY DEMANDS OF RELIGION MEET THE EXCLUSIVITY DEMANDS OF INCLUSION: THE CASE FOR A NEW APPROACH TO INCLUSION IN AUSTRALIA

Michael Quinlan

Abstract

Words matter and one word which has become particularly important in contemporary discourse is inclusion. Inclusion sounds like a very positive idea but it can actually be very divisive. This chapter argues for a new approach to inclusion in Australia. The chapter begins by considering the exclusive demands made by successful religious traditions in their doctrines, traditions and truth claims. It then considers the origins and meaning of the term 'inclusion' in the Western world and Australia, and how the term is currently employed. The chapter focusses on the business and workplace context. This is the context in which inclusion has been used to the detriment of some religious people in Australia, for example, to remove them from their employment and to disqualify them from their profession. The chapter concludes that the contemporary Australian approach to inclusion ignores the exclusive demands made by religions on their adherents. It argues that a new and broader meaning of inclusion is necessary in Australia to minimise conflict and to protect religious freedom.

Introduction

> [P]roclaim the message and, welcome or unwelcome, insist on it. Re-
> fute falsehood, correct error, give encouragement – but do all with
> patience and with care to instruct.[1]

This chapter argues for a new approach to inclusion in Australia. The chapter begins by considering the exclusive demands made by successful religious
traditions in their doctrines, traditions and truth claims. It then considers
the origins and meaning of the term 'inclusion' in the Western world and
Australia, and how the term is currently employed. The chapter focusses on
the business and workplace context. This is the context in which inclusion
has been used to the detriment of some religious people in Australia, for example, to remove them from their employment and to disqualify them from
their profession.[2] The chapter concludes that the contemporary Australian
approach to inclusion ignores the exclusive demands made by religions on
their adherents. It argues that a new and broader meaning of inclusion is
necessary in Australia to minimise conflict and to protect religious freedom.

1. The exclusive demands made by successful religious traditions

The High Court of Australia in the *Church of the New Faith v Commissioner
of Pay-Roll Tax (Vic)* ('*Church of the New Faith*') identified two criteria for a

---

1   2 Timothy 4:1-2 *New Jerusalem Bible* (Darton, Longman & Todd, 1994). Unless
     otherwise specified, all references to scripture in this chapter will be to the *New
     Jerusalem Bible* ('*NJB*').
2   Daniel Ramus, 'Israel Folau case exposes contradiction in ARU's inclusion pol-
     icy', *Sporting News (online,* 10 May 2018) <https://www.sportingnews.com/au/
     rugby/news/israel-folau-australia-rugby-union-inclusion-policy-saga-contradic-
     tion/1dc26kdcq68zp1qt432hyx7ufa>; Maani Truu, 'Academics sign open letter
     after law dean compares trans students to teens with eating disorders', *SBS News*
     (online, 19 September 2019) <https://www.sbs.com.au/news/academics-sign-
     open-letter-after-law-dean-compares-trans-students-to-teens-with-eating-disor-
     ders>; Human Rights Law Alliance, '"Jamie" - Protecting the Religious Beliefs
     of our Teachers', *Our Cases* (Web Page, 20 April 2017) <https://www.hrla.org.au/
     jamie>; Patrick Parkinson, 'Protecting Religious Freedom in An Age of Militant
     secularism' in Robert Forsyth and Peter Kurti (eds) *Forgotten Freedom No More* (Con-
     nor Court, 2020) 99, 106; Human Rights Law Alliance, '"Ryan" - Workplace Dis-
     crimination', *Our Cases* (Web Page, 10 June 2017) <https://www.hrla.org.au/ryan>.

religion to be recognised as such in Australia: 'first, belief in a supernatural Being, Thing or Principle; and second, the acceptance of canons of conduct in order to give effect to that belief'.[3] Alcorta and Sosis describe the following as traits which all religions share although they are expressed differently across cultures:[4] 'Belief in supernatural agents and counterintuitive concepts; [c]ommunal participation in costly ritual; -[s]eparation of the sacred and the profane; and [the] importance of adolescence as the life history phase most appropriate for the transmission of religious beliefs and values'.[5] In their view these traits act to maximise the retention and transmission of a religious faith and affective engagement with it.[6] Common to the High Court and to Alcorta and Sosis' description is the identification of religion with demands for adherents to subscribe to obligations of behaviour, be they embodied in doctrine or ritual, which are different to those of the general community. In other words, religions make exclusive demands on their adherents. The term 'exclusive' has many meanings but for this chapter the following will suffice:

1. not including or admitting of something else; incompatible
3. limited to a given object or objects
4. shutting out all others from a part or share
6. (of a club, group etc) having limited membership; elitist.[7]

Religions have their own rules about membership which usually involve ritual and assent or affirmation. In some traditions this assent or affirmation can, at least initially, be given by others on behalf of an infant.[8] Religions also have rules about those who can offer or lead certain rituals and sacra-

---

3   (1983) 154 CLR 120, 136.
4   Candace S Alcorta and Richard Sosis, 'Ritual, Emotion and Sacred Symbols: The Evolution of Religion as an Adaptive Complex' (2005) 16(4) *Human Nature* 323, 348.
5   Ibid 325.
6   Ibid.
7   *The Pocket Macquarie Dictionary* (2nd ed, 1989) 'exclusive' (def 1, 3, 4, 6) (examples omitted).
8   The Catholic Church, for example, practises infant baptism: see *Catechism of the Catholic Church* (St. Pauls, 1994) [1250]-[1252] ('*CCC*').

ments, who can hold certain positions or roles within the tradition and the circumstances in which access can be given to certain rituals or sacraments and to certain places.[9] In these ways religions exclude others from certain roles and participatory actions and they have a limited membership. Most religions are at least open to conversion by others to join them within their religious faith and some see this as a key part of their mission or their manifestation of faith.[10]

People who have lived within a particular religious tradition have always behaved differently to those around them who subscribe to a different or to no religious tradition.[11] Participation or manifestation of the "canons of conduct" of religious belief by action is in fact a fundamental feature of a religion. Knowledge of the longevity of religious belief in human history is founded on the evidence of human beings acting on their religious faith by doing things such as creating art, creating places of worship and burying their dead in particular religious ways. Religions make demands on their followers, they impose duties, they have their own doctrines and moral codes of behaviour which their believers follow. Religious people are, in other words, called on by their religious faith to think and to behave differently to other people. This is at the core of religion and at the heart of being a person of religious faith. Many examples could be provided but the example of the behaviour of the early Christians will suffice to make good this point. The early Christians stood out from others around them in the

---

9   In the Catholic Church, for example, only validly ordained priests can preside at the sacrament of the Eucharist and only Catholics who are in 'the state of grace' can receive communion: Ibid [1411], [1415]. In the Church of Jesus Christ of the Latter-day Saints rules govern entry to the Temple: see Julie Zauzmer, 'The public will be allowed to visit the Mormon temple on the Beltway for the first time in 46 years', *The Washington Post* (online, 16 August 2017) <https://www.washingtonpost.com/news/acts-of-faith/wp/2017/08/16/the-public-will-be-allowed-to-visit-the-mormon-temple-on-the-beltway-for-the-first-time-in-46-years/>.

10   In the Catholic Church, for example, each Catholic is called upon to lead others to join that religious tradition: see *CCC* (n 8) [904].

11   See, eg, 1 Maccabees 10-15, 41-43, 54-57, 62-64; 2 Maccabees 6:18-31, 7:1, 20-31.

Roman Empire for the very reason that they did not behave as the Romans did. Unlike those around them,[12] the early Christians did not worship the Roman Gods; they married, they did not practice infanticide, contraception or abortion and instead had and nurtured their children in families.[13] They did not engage in the sexual behaviours common in the Empire and they cared for the sick and the poor.[14]

As Vardy has described it, 'a general feature of belonging to a religion is the need for conformity and loyalty, which can bind a community into a whole greater than the sum of its parts.'[15] Through their exclusive canons of conduct, their exclusive beliefs in particular counter-intuitive concepts and through their particular rituals, religions create a group of believers with shared religious beliefs and a shared sense of duty and belonging. As Baker observes: '[s]trictness leads to a higher level of attachment, affiliation and buy-in to the group which creates commitment among members'.[16] This can be seen by comparing the success of contemporary churches which share the basic features of religion described by Alcorta and Sosis with those which do not or which do not do so as comprehensively. The churches which are more exclusive, by making stricter or more costly demands on their followers, and those that more clearly separate the sacred from the profane, are prospering in United States and Canada.[17] Examples of

12   Anthony Percy, *The Theology of the Body made Simple* (Pauline Books and Media, 2005) 12.
13   Allan Carlson, 'Family and Society the End of Liberalism', *News Weekly* (Web Page, 23 February 2019) <http://www.newsweekly.com.au/article.php?id=58435&s=ddUIaM>.
14   Ibid.
15   Peter Vardy, *Good & Bad Religion* (SCM Press, 2010) ix.
16   Joseph O Baker, 'Social Sources of the Spirit: Connecting Rational Choice and Interactive Ritual Theories in the Study of Religion' (2010) 71(4) *Sociology of Religion* 432, 452.
17   Laurence R Iannaccone, 'Why Strict Churches Are Strong' (1994) 99(5) *American Journal of Sociology* 1180; Kevin N Flatt, D Millard Haskell and Stephanie Burg, 'Secularization and Attribution: How Mainline Protestant Clergy and Congregants Explain Church Growth and Decline' (2018) 79(1) *Sociology of Religion* 78, 79-80; Anna Grzymala-Busse, 'Good Clubs and Community Support:

such churches are the Amish, Church of Jesus Christ of Latter-Day Saints (LDS), Jehovah's Witnesses, Orthodox Jews and to a lesser extent pre-Vatican II Catholics.[18] Anna Grzymala-Busse has observed:

> [T]hese religions have grown over time, without significant doctrinal transformations or attempts to loosen theological strictures on beliefs and practices of their members. Moreover, these strict denominations have grown at higher rates than their mainstream counterparts … Retention rates for the Amish and Mormons in the United States, for example, are in the 80-90 per cent range and remain considerably higher than for mainline denominations.[19]

Even in mainline Protestant churches those which are more conservative are growing whilst their more liberal counterparts decline. In Flatt, Haskell and Burgoyne's 2018 study of 22 clergy and 128 congregants from 21 mainline Protestant churches, including 13 with declining and 8 with growing congregations, the clergy and congregants of growing churches were all more theologically conservative than their counterparts in declining churches.[20] Theological conservatism here was assessed by belief in the literal resurrection of Christ and in the active participation of God in the world and disagreement with theological liberal beliefs such as the view that some of the teachings of the Bible are misguided or wrong.[21] Clergy and congregants in the growing churches in Flatt's study also read the Bible and prayed more often than their counterparts in declining churches.[22]

In Australia the proportion of Australians identifying as Catholic,[23] Angli-

---

Explaining the Growth of Strict Religions' (2014) 56(2) *Journal of Church and State* 269; Jeremy N Thomas and Daniel V A Olson, 'Testing the Strictness Thesis and Competing Theories of Congregational Growth' (2010) 49(4) *Journal for the Scientific Study of Religion* 619; Baker (n 16).

18   Grzymala-Busse (n 17) 270.
19   Ibid.
20   Flatt, Haskell and Burgoyne (n 17) 87.
21   Ibid.
22   Ibid.
23   25.3% to 22.6%: Australian Bureau of Statistics, '2016 Census data reveals "no religion" is rising fast', *2016 Census: Religion* (Web Page, 27 June 2017) <https://www.abs.gov.au/AUSSTATS/abs@.nsf/mediareleasesbyRelease-

can[24] and as members of the Uniting Church[25] all fell significantly between 2011 and 2016. Whilst particularly the Catholic Church does have a clearly enunciated record of the canons of conduct which it expects its believers to adhere to,[26] and many of those doctrines and demands are significantly different to behaviours in the general population, there is a wide range of commitment among Catholics to those doctrines. Many examples could be given to make good this point, but mass attendance is a clear example. There is a clear obligation for all Catholics to participate in a Catholic mass every Sunday and on other holy days of obligation.[27] Unless there is a serious reason such as illness or the care of children it is a grave sin for a Catholic not to go to mass on any of those days.[28] Despite this obligation, and the clarity of its teaching in the official documents of the Catholic Church, the vast majority of Catholics do not go to mass as mandated. In Australia and New Zealand for example, the percentage of people who continue to self-identify as Catholics attending weekly mass has fallen from 28% in the 1990s to 21% from 2010 to 2012.[29] Although this canon of conduct usually involves only one hour per week of communal participation in a ritual involving the separation of the sacred and the profane, it is a commitment which the vast majority of Catholics are not prepared to make. The commitment to other teachings of the Church of those who consider themselves to be Catholics is even lower than the commitment to weekly mass attendance. Even among Catholics who do attend church regularly and do so by attending mass in the vernacular of the people in the most commonly

---

Date/7E65A144540551D7CA258148000E2B85>.

24   17.1% to 13.3%: ibid.

25   5.0% to 3.7%: ibid.

26   In documents such as the *CCC* (n 8).

27   Ibid [2180], [2192]-[2193].

28   Ibid [2181].

29   Center for Applied Research in the Apostolate, 'Global Catholicism: Trends & Forecasts' (Report, 4 June 2015) 41 <https://cara.georgetown.edu/staff/web-pages/global%20catholicism%20release.pdf>.

used form of service today - the Novus Ordo Mass (NOM)[30] – the majority reject that Church's official teaching against contraception, abortion, same sex marriage and the obligation to confess serious sins at least once a year within the sacrament of confession.[31]

So whilst the Catholic Church might have strict rules, it is not as a whole appropriately considered to be a strict church in the sense that the majority of its followers sacrifice pleasures, give up opportunities and risk or invite social stigma by their commitment to following their religious faith.[32] The Anglican and United Church are similar in this regard although some parts of those churches are considerably more liberal on social and moral matters than the official position of the Catholic Church. Like the Episcopal, Methodist, Presbyterian and United Church of Christ in the United States, the Anglican (perhaps with the exception of the Sydney Archdiocese) and Uniting Church in Australia might be considered as the least distinctive in terms of lifestyle or morality from the Australian mainline lifestyle in these respects.[33]

Stricter churches make more demands on their followers and might be considered to be less likely to grow or to maintain followers than the less strict. There is a tension between the binding quality of exclusive doctrines and canons of conduct, and the desire to share the views of the majority. As Indermaur has noted: '[m]ost people, it seems, want to have an opinion that is in keeping with the majority, particularly in relation to subjects where there is a risk of social isolation from proclaiming an unfashionable or un-

---

30   Donald Kloster, 'Traditional Latin Mass National Survey', *Liturgy Guy* (Web Page, 24 February 2019) <https://liturgyguy.com/2019/02/24/national-survey-results-what-we-learned-about-latin-mass-attendees/?fbclid=IwAR3u9tQDjUt-p4zYZnv9GKE4Bmsa5Bdb-fZ8_INYlxj2b346_QdvSOM_2iBc>;   Grzymala-Busse (n 17) 277, 286-7.

31   Kloster (n 30).

32   Iannaccone (n 17) 1182.

33   Ibid 1190.

palatable view'.[34]

For successful religions and committed religious believers, this risk of so-cial isolation is offset by the social cohesion and relationships and other spiritual benefits which are to be found within religious communities. Baker observes that:

> Beyond buying into a more exclusive claim to truth and the potential for eternal reward in the case of religion, the value of a collective good increases because those involved draw higher levels of emo-tional energy, satisfaction and a sense of identity from group partici-pation. A stronger sense of attachment to an exclusive group – which is reinforced through collective symbols and rituals – ultimately pro-duces members who exhibit more commitment to the collectivity. Committed members hold strong affinities for the group and bring emotional force to gatherings, particularly during rituals involving shared symbols and focus. [35]

This explains why it is that the presence of and the commitment of reli-gious believers to the demands of their religion – and the existence of real demands to act in ways which are outside those of the balance of the society – are indicators of the likelihood of a religion surviving and prospering.[36]

As might be predicted from this analysis, this is found within the stricter churches in Australia. Unlike the decline which is being experienced by the less strict churches stricter churches are not losing followers. The Latter-day Saints,[37] Seventh-day Adventists,[38] Jehovah's Witnesses,[39] and Pentecostals[40] have all maintained a stable percentage share of the Australian population.[41]

---

34   David Indermaur, 'Contemporary Attitudes to the Death Penalty: An Australian Perspective' (2006) 17(3) *Current Issues in Criminal Justice* 444, 446.
35   Baker (n 16) 437.
36   Iannaccone (n 17) 1204-5.
37   0.3%: Australian Bureau of Statistics (n 23).
38   0.3%: ibid.
39   0.4%: ibid.
40   1.1%: ibid .
41   Ibid. From 2011 to 2016 the proportion of Australians identifying as Catholic (25.3% to 22.6%), Anglican (17.1% to 13.3%) and the Uniting Church (5.0% to 3.7%) all fell. In the same period, the numbers of Latter-day Saints (0.3%), Sev-

Worshippers within these traditions are called upon by the moral positions of their religious faith to live differently to the majority of the population. Mormons are forbidden from drinking alcohol or coffee and from smoking. Seventh Day Adventists may not eat certain meat. Jehovah's Witnesses may not receive blood transfusions and have obligations to train in doctrine and engage in missionary activities.[42] Pentecostals are called upon to believe that the Holy Spirit makes gifts such as healing and prophecy available to them; to worship in a style which values spontaneity and authenticity and involves the lifting of arms in praise; the laying on of hands for healing; speaking in tongues and singing; regularly attend Sunday services with a duration of several hours, often attend at least another service each week and are regularly involved in home worship; Bible study; tithe; and volunteer their time for church offices and evangelisation.[43] Each of the traditions which are described in this chapter as strict have their own specific characteristics and expectations of their followers – each is a religious faith after all. Some focus more directly on strict adherence and support for doctrine and more clearly separate the sacred from the profane. Each is however properly characterised as strict in being more exclusive, by making stricter or more costly demands on their followers. Statistically, followers of these traditions abide by their demands.[44] Their members sacrifice pleasures and opportunities and risk social stigma due to their difference in behaviours and attitudes.[45]

The more demanding and more exclusive religious traditions are more regular church goers, give more, have stronger religious beliefs, participate in more faith-based groups and are more likely to identify as being strong

---

enth-day Adventists (0.3%), Jehovah's Witnesses (0.4%) and Pentecostals (1.1%) remained stable.

42   Iannaccone (n 17) 1182; Baker (n 16) 451.
43   Joel Robbins, 'Pentecostal Networks and the Spirit of Globalization: On the Social Productivity of Ritual Forms' (2009) 53(1) *Social Analysis: The International Journal of Social and Cultural Practice* 55, 56-8, 61; Baker, (n 16) 441.
44   For Pentecostals, see Robbins (n 43) 57.
45   Iannaccone (n 17) 1182.

members of their faith.[46] They are less likely to drink alcohol, to engage in pre-marital sexual activities or to experiment with 'new age' or alternative religions. These stricter and more exclusive churches demand more from their congregations than some other religious faiths. Iannaccone argues that it is the very existence of these demands which explains the success of these stricter religions. He says that 'strict demands "strengthen" a church in three ways: they raise overall levels of commitment, they increase average rates of participation, and they enhance the net benefits of membership'.[47]

Whilst Pentecostals might not subscribe to a clear separation of the sacred and profane, they are justifiably considered strict in this analysis because they are strong on moral strictness and certainty, and make costly demands on their followers as outlined above.[48] Whilst Pentecostals in Australia may use contemporary music styles and less distinctive forms of architecture for their buildings and dress for their pastors, they are strongly 'counter-cultur-al' in their views of sexuality and marriage.[49] Whilst only 9% of Australians consider that sexual relations before marriage is always wrong this is the view of 78% of Pentecostals.[50] This can be contrasted with the views on this subject of those who identify as members of the Uniting Church or as Anglicans. Only 8% and 4% respectively of those less strict denominations consider sexual relations outside marriage to always be wrong.[51] Those views are reflected in the marriage rates of adherents to these different traditions, which in the 20 to 24 age group, is 15% for Pentecostals but 6% of the population and just 5% of Uniting Church members and 4% of Anglicans.[52]

The growth of worshippers within the Catholic Church choosing parishes

46   Ibid 1190, 1194, 1197, 1205.
47   Ibid 1183.
48   Robbins (n 43) 59-60, 63.
49   Philip Hughes, 'The Multi-Dimensional Issue of Culture and Christian Ministry' (2015) (1) *Journal of Contemporary Ministry* 6, 12, 14.
50   Ibid 12.
51   Ibid.
52   Ibid.

which celebrate the Traditional Latin Mass rather than using the NOM in the vernacular is another example of the phenomenon identified by Alcorta and Sosis and Iannaccone. It is parishioners who choose to attend worship celebrated in the ancient Church language of Latin who most conform their behaviour to the official teachings of the Catholic Church. This is in stark contrast to Catholics worshipping in parishes whose priests use the vernacular in the mass.[53] Traditional Latin Mass goers almost uniformly attend weekly mass[54] and at least annual confession as mandated by their Church[55] and disapprove of contraception,[56] abortion[57] and same sex marriage.[58] They also have more children[59] and donate more of their income[60] than other Catholics.[61] This form of worship has experienced substantial growth in Italy and the United States.[62] This growth has occurred in those parishes which make the most demands on their parishioners in the form of worship which they have chosen. Rather than the liturgy being celebrated in the common language that would be understood by all attending, these parishes choose to worship in an ancient language which is rarely used outside of the liturgy and official church documents. In this way they separate the sacred from the profane.

In summary then, religion, and certainly successful religions, make demands of exclusivity of their adherents and their adherents respond to these demands positively. It is in the nature – the substance – of a religion for it

---

53   Kloster (n 30).

54   99%: ibid.

55   98%: ibid.

56   98%: ibid.

57   99%: ibid.

58   99%: ibid.

59   A fertility rate of 3.6%: ibid.

60   6% of their income: ibid.

61   Ibid.

62   Anon, 'The Growth of the Latin Mass', *The Saint's Pub* (Web Page, 7 November 2016) <https://thesaintspub.wordpress.com/2016/11/07/the-growth-of-the-latin-mass/>; AP, 'The current situation for the TLM in Italy' (Blog Post, 23 February 2010) <https://rorate-caeli.blogspot.com/2010/02/current-situation-for-tlm-in-italy.html>.

to demand different behaviours – different doctrines – to those by which the balance of the population are guided. Difference can create misunderstanding, conflict and unfair or unjust treatment of others where their differences are not respected. This is a particular risk in a multi-faith society where divergences between the beliefs, ideals and behaviours of the bulk of the population and those of religious groups may be most variegated. These differences are likely to be largest for minority religions and serious and committed believers with a deeper commitment to their religious faith than others within their tradition. This is why respect for religious freedom in international covenants such as art 18 of the *International Covenant on Civil and Political Rights*[63] ('*ICCPR*') is such an important means of minimising conflicts and disputation. The *ICCPR* recognises that the right to religious freedom is derived 'from the inherent dignity of the human person'.[64] As a consequence, the *ICCPR* calls on States to respect the dignity of each person to hold and manifest their religious beliefs including as manifested through action. As noted earlier, action is – and it has always been – a fundamental feature of a religion.

A particular obligation that many religions impose on their followers, which can cause friction in its manifestation, is the demand that they let other people know about their faith. Christians are, for example, called to 'proclaim the message and, welcome or unwelcome, insist on it. Refute falsehood, correct error, give encouragement – but do all with patience and with care to instruct'.[65] In this expression of the call to share that religious faith might be seen the basis of claims that religious believers are judgmental and that

---

63   *International Covenant on Civil and Political Rights*, G.A. Res 2200A (XXI), U.N. GAOR, 21st Sess., Supp.No.16 U.N. Doc.A/6316 (16 December 1966, entered into force on 23 March 1976) art 18.1 ('*ICCPR*'). Everyone shall have the right to freedom of thought, conscience and religion. This right shall include freedom to have or to adopt a religion or belief of his choice, and freedom, either individually or in community with others and in public or private, to manifest his religion in worship, practice and teaching.
64   Ibid Preamble.
65   2 Timothy 4:1-2.

they are not inclusive. If those terms are used to mean accepting, agreeing with and endorsing other people's ways of living, then the charge may be accurate. However, the making of such charges in itself betrays a lack of understanding of the exclusiveness which is inherent in religion. Such complaints are at their core complaints about the very existence of religions. Evangelisation is but one demonstration of how the differences intrinsic to religious traditions may create tensions.

Many religions have theological and moral positions on matters which are not shared by significant proportions of the population. These include views on such matters as abortion, confession, marriage, the roles of the sexes, styles of clothing, sexual activity outside traditional marriage, adultery and on the ethical and appropriate moral response to sexual orientations other than heterosexual and to gender dysphoria. These positions may have developed or been extant for centuries or longer within some religious traditions. Whilst the community's attitudes towards such matters may increasingly vary from the doctrines and tenets governing some religious traditions, this provides no foundation for reducing or interfering with the State's recognition of freedom of religion for religious believers or religious organisations. Nor does it warrant workplaces or societies excluding religious believers because they are religious. If anything, such changes in community standards make the continuation of protections for religious believers and organisations even more pressing and acute than may have been the case when the doctrines and tenets of mainstream Christianity more closely aligned with the moral zeitgeist. As Laycock and Berg have observed:

> [C]ommitted religious believers argue that some aspects of human identity are so fundamental that they should be left to each individual, free of all nonessential regulation, even when manifested in conduct. For religious believers, the conduct at issue is to live and act consistently with the demands of the Being that they believe made us all

and holds the whole world together.[66] No religious believer can change his understanding of divine command by any act of will … Religious beliefs can change over time … But these things do not change because government says they must, or because the individual decides they should … [T]he religious believer cannot change God's mind.[67]

Whilst Murray makes this observation more generally about contemporary Western society, it is apposite here:

> As anyone who has lived under totalitarianism can attest, there is something demeaning and eventually soul-destroying about being expected to go along with claims you do not believe to be true and cannot hold to be true. If the belief is that all people should be regarded as having equal value and be accorded equal dignity, then that may be well and good. If you are asked to believe that there are no differences between homosexuality and heterosexuality, men and women, racism and anti-racism, then this will in time drive you to distraction.[68]

As the above analysis demonstrates, religions, and certainly successful religions and religious believers, are very likely to be judgemental and non-inclusive in this sense due to the very nature of religion. Individuals can choose whether or not they wish to participate in any religion or in any particular religion. As Mascareno and Carvajal observe:

> Those who consider themselves non-believers – 36% worldwide, including the non-religious and atheists – allow themselves self-exclusion from religious practice which, nevertheless, remains available for future inclusions … [T]he possibility of reverting self-exclusion through self-inclusion is always available: people can believe again or believe for the first time.[69]

Religious believers within a particular tradition may consider those who reject their religious tradition as nevertheless being included in some sense

66   Douglas Laycock and Thomas Berg, 'Same-Sex Marriage and Religious Liberty' (2013) 99(1) *Virginia Law Review* 1, 3.
67   Ibid 4.
68   Douglas Murray, *The Madness of Crowds* (Bloomsbury Continuum, 2019) 9.
69   Aldo Mascareño and Fabiola Carvajal, 'The Different Faces of Inclusion and Exclusion' (2015) 116 *CEPAL Review* 127, 134.

as a brother or sister, a neighbour or a child of God.[70] They may look to include them in their religion through evangelisation.[71] Joining or rejecting any religious faith but particularly a strict religion has implications. A religion's 'canons of conduct' are most unlikely to be a repetition of the laws and moral codes of the majority of a State's population. A religion which did not have 'canons of conduct in order to give effect to [its beliefs]' would cease to be a religion within the meaning of religion expressed by the High Court of Australia in *Church of the New Faith* as set out above. In the circumstances, religious believers are not likely to be able to conform their beliefs to align with beliefs mandated by the State or by their employer. With this understanding of the exclusive demands of religion in mind, this chapter now turns to consider what this means for what should happen when these exclusivity demands of religion meet the exclusivity demands of inclusion. Answering this question first requires a consideration of the meaning of the term 'inclusion' in Australia.

2. The origins and meaning of the term 'inclusion' and current usage

The term inclusion is in common use today in Australia but it 'is a heavily politicised (and admittedly quite fuzzy) term'.[72] It is a vague and imprecise term with a fluid and changing meaning particularly when applied in a business or political context. According to the Macquarie Dictionary 'include' means:

1.   to contain, embrace or comprise

2.   to place in a group, class etc

---

70   Ibid.
71   Ibid.
72   Arthur J Cockfield, 'Limiting Lawyer Liberty: How the Statement of Principles Coerces Speech' (Research Paper No 2018-100, Queens Law Research Paper Series, 15 March 2018) 23 <https://papers.ssrn.com/sol3/papers.cfm?abstract_id=3141561>.

3.   to contain as a smaller element within something larger.[73]

and 'inclusion' means:

1.   the act of including

2.   the condition of being included.[74]

As should be evident from these definitions, whether or not 'inclusion' is necessarily a good thing or not and whether it is or is not a morally good thing to 'include' something is not a matter which can be addressed in the abstract. The answer will always depend on the context. For example, putting a lamb in a lion's cage may be a good thing if the intention is to feed starving lions and there is a perceived benefit in them capturing and killing their prey to simulate nature. This approach to inclusion might be less of a good thing from the lamb's perspective and if the objective is to minimise animal suffering. Similarly, if one wishes to obtain medical or legal advice for a health or legal problem it might be dangerous for those without the requisite skills, education and qualities to be included in the category of doctor or lawyer and appropriate for them to be excluded.[75] However, it might not be a good thing if those who had fulfilled the specific skill and educational requirements were excluded from admission to the relevant profession due to some character irrelevant to their ability to perform the role. As will be evident from the discussion below, in contemporary Australia the term, particularly when used in a business context, is regularly used to have a meaning which is closer to prefer, or to positively discriminate in favour of, than to the dictionary definitions set out above.

The sociologist and anthropologist David Pocock suggested that practices of inclusion and exclusion were features of all hierarchies more than 60

---

73   *The Pocket Macquarie Dictionary* (n 7) 'include' (def 1, 2, 3).
74   Ibid 'inclusion' (def 1, 2).
75   Werner Schirmer and Dimitris Michailakis, 'The Luhmannian Approach to exclusion/inclusion and its Relevance to Social Work' (2015) 15(1) *Journal of Social Work* 45, 54.

years ago.[76] The terms inclusion and exclusion have been widely applied in France since the 1970s having entered public discourse through the work of Rene Lenoir.[77] The term inclusion has also been used in a business context since at least the 1970's. It gained popularity during the 1990's in public policy and practice.[78] In an employment context in 1971, Schein described it as the degree to which an employee was an 'insider' within an organisation.[79] In 1998, Mor-Barak and Cherin referred to decades of research which had demonstrated the business benefits to be derived from increasing the level of commitment that employees feel towards their employer and the positive impact that feeling accepted by an organisation had on commitment levels.[80] They provided a definition of the concept of 'inclusion-exclusion' as follows: '[w]e define inclusion-exclusion as a continuum of the degree to which individuals feel a part of critical organizational processes such as access to information and resources, involvement in work groups and ability to influence the decision making process'.[81]

The identification of interpersonal differences relevant to Mor-Barak and Cherin's analysis was confined to 'race, gender, age and ethnicity' and omitted any specific identification or consideration of religion or religious belief. [82] They argued that due to overt or covert discrimination including racism, sexism and ageism, women, the aged and people from different cultural and ethnic groups are often excluded from information and opportunity. [83] The identification of a limited group of characteristics, which omit religion

---

76   Dan Allman, 'The Sociology of Social Inclusion' (2013) 3(1) *SAGE Open* 1, 1.

77   Mascareño and Carvajal (n 69) 132; Ibid 7-9.

78   Mascareño and Carvajal (n 69) 128.

79   LH Pelled, GE Ladford Jr and SA Mohrman, 'Demographic dissimilarity and workplace inclusion' (1999) 36(7) *Journal of Management Studies* 1013, 1014.

80   Michal E Mor-Barak, and David A Cherin, 'A Tool to Expand Organizational Understanding of Workforce Diversity' (1998) 22(1) *Administration in Social Work* 47, 48.

81   Ibid.

82   Ibid.

83   Ibid 50.

or religious belief, in discussions about discrimination and inclusion is not uncommon but it is regrettable. The failure to focus on this characteristic leads to widespread discrimination or failure to accommodate religious differences in the workplace.[84] A 2014 study found that 36% of Americans, which is 50 million people, had witnessed or experienced workplace religious discrimination of a failure to provide religious accommodation.[85] In 2018 in the United States, for example, a thousand more complaints of religious discrimination were made to the Equal Employment Opportunity Commission ('EEOC') than those for sexual orientation discrimination.[86] This demonstrates that religious inclusion is not a focus for most companies.[87] The significance of religious diversity and inclusion to businesses is not something about which most leaders and mangers in business have received much, if any, education.[88] This results in an absence of appropriate practices, protocols and human resource policies which accommodate religious difference.[89]

Religious beliefs are not properly subsumed within the identification of culture or ethnicity. They are complex and variegated in their own right as is

---

84   Religious Freedom and Business Foundation, 'Business Case For Workplace Religious Diversity & Inclusion' (Web Page) <https://religiousfreedomandbusiness. org/business-case-for-workplace-religious-diversity-and-inclusion> ('Diversity & Inclusion').

85   Religious Freedom and Business Foundation, 'Workplace Religious Discrimination Encountered by 1-in-3' (Web Page, 11 August 2014) <https://religiousfree-domandbusiness.org/business-case-for-workplace-religious-diversity-and-in-clusion>, citing Tanenbaum Center for Interreligious Understanding, 'What American Workers Really Think About Religion: Tanenbaum's 2013 Survey of American Workers and Religion' (Report, 2013) 4 <https://tanenbaum.org/wp-content/uploads/2014/02/Tanenbaums-2013-Survey-of-American-Work-ers-and-Religion.pdf>.

86   Religious Freedom and Business Foundation, 'Religious Freedom Helps Businesses & Economies Grow' (Web Page, 6 May 2019) <https://religiousfreedo-mandbusiness.org/religious-freedom-helps-businesses-economies-grow> ('Religious Freedom Helps').

87   Diversity & Inclusion (n 84).

88   Ibid.

89   Ibid.

the experience of religious persecution and discrimination in Australia.[90] Catering for the full range of religious sensitivities is not easy but disregarding them entirely cannot properly be characterised as an inclusive approach. Some people have religious beliefs which preclude them from working on certain days or times of day and they can be offended by emails or phone calls made to them during those times. Some people have religious beliefs which preclude them from eating certain foods and they can be offended if those foods are offered to them at a business function or meeting. Some people have religious beliefs which make offering a handshake inappropriate. Some people may, due to religious beliefs about sex or for other reasons, be deeply offended if they were asked to identify their preferred pronouns or to participate in some way in a same sex wedding or in medical procedures such as abortion or euthanasia. Some employees may be deeply offended if they are asked not to attend a meeting or to be involved on a project because a client – or other member of staff – prefers to deal with persons of a sex which is not that of that employee – whether that is on cultural or religious grounds or because the client is simply an unreformed sexist. Some employees, because of their deeply held religious beliefs, may not be able to refer to a client by their preferred pronoun where that is other than their birth sex. As noted earlier, some people feel obliged by their religious beliefs to share their religious faith with others. If religious belief is simply excluded from the category of inclusion there is little hope for the development of any understanding let alone tolerance of religious behaviours by those outside a particular religious tradition.

In 1994, O'Hara, Beehr and Colarelli described inclusion as the 'degree of acceptance one has by other members of the work system'.[91]   They

---

90   See Michael Quinlan, 'Born (Again) This way: Why The Inherent Nature of Religiosity requires A New Approach to Australia's Discrimination laws' in Augusto Zimmermann (ed), *A Commitment to Excellence* (Connor Court, 2018) 96, 131, 139-41.

91   KB O'Hara, TA Beehr and SM Colarelli, 'Organizational centrality: a third dimen-

considered that an employee's access to sensitive information and decision making influence were two important indicia by which inclusion could be evidenced.[92] In 1999, Pelled, Ladford Jr and Mohrman added job security to that list of criteria.[93] By 2006, Robertson was describing inclusion as focussing on removing 'obstacles to the full participation and contribution of employees in organizations'.[94] In the same year in her systematic blueprint for energising and utilising universities as a means to develop an 'architecture of inclusion', Sturm argued that:

> The project of achieving inclusive institutions is not only about eliminating discrimination or even increasing the representation of previously excluded groups. *It is about creating the conditions enabling peoples of all races and genders to realize their capabilities as they understand them.* All institutional citizens should be able to realize their potential and participate fully in the institution.[95]

In her paper, Sturm called specifically for universities to use their position of power to bring about inclusion within this sense.[96] Writing in an American context in 2001, Prasad provided this description:

> workplace inclusion/empowerment in today's organizational society is an integral part of the overall agenda for social welfare and reform and, hence, too important a project to be left completely (or even mostly) to the inclinations and preferences of individual organizations. This discursive theme, thus, would appear to be more conscious of the totality of issues at stake. Such consciousness of totality is linked, in part, to this theme's active historical memory, with the result that *inclusion and empowerment of marginal groups is seen as an important step towards undoing the historical wrongs suffered by persecuted and*

---

sion of intraorganizational career movement' (1994) 30(2) *Journal of Applied Behavioural Science* 198, 200, quoted in Pelled, Ladford Jr and Mohrman (n 79) 1014.

92   Pelled, Ladford Jr and Mohrman (n 79) 1014-5.

93   Ibid 1015.

94   Quinetta M Robertson, 'Disentangling the Meanings of Diversity and Inclusion in Organization' (2006) 31(2) *Group & Organization Management* 212, 217.

95   Susan P Sturm, 'The Architecture of Inclusion: Advancing Workplace Equity in Higher Education' (Research Paper No 06-114, Columbia Law School, 2006) 4 (emphasis added).

96   Ibid 6.

oppressed groups, for example, African-Americans. [97]

It is this far broader conception of inclusion which has gained currency and become broader again in contemporary Australia. In this formulation, inclusion is not simply about providing staff with equal opportunities in the workplace. It is about creating not just inclusive workplaces, but transforming society. It takes a holistic and more integrated approach seeking to reach beyond the boundaries of business to achieving a society which is supportive of particular minority groups and behaviours. Tensions can be exacerbated when this approach to inclusion involves – at least a perception if not a reality of – promoting behaviours which are contrary to the moral traditions of religions. This approach to inclusion is about separating those who are inclusive – willing and able to embrace new moral codes and mores – from those who resist and are not inclusive. In this approach, using language which might be perceived as presenting anything other than a positive endorsement of those with certain identified characteristics or behaviours or self-identification categories, is contractually and/or legislatively proscribed.

The Folau Affair as an example of exclusionary inclusion

A risk in the contemporary approach to inclusion is that certain minority characteristics and behaviours but not others are identified as deserving of inclusion. This can result in at least the ignoring of – if not the punishment of – people with other characteristics and attitudes towards the now lauded behaviours even though, as the *ICCPR* expressly recognises, these people, like all people, are themselves worthy of consideration and respect for their human dignity. Corporations continue to overlook religious inclusion while

---

97   Anshuman Prasad, 'Understanding Workplace Empowerment as Inclusion: A Historical Investigation of the Discourse of Difference in the United States' (2001) 37(1) *The Journal of Applied Behavioural Science* 51, 66 (emphasis added).

emphasising other diversity classifications by a factor of 34-to-1.[98]

It is this way of thinking which led to the Australian Rugby Union (ARU) decision to terminate the four year $4 million playing contract of star international rugby player, Israel Folau. His case provides a clear example of the conflict between contemporary inclusion and the exclusive nature of religious belief. Folau is a serious and committed member of, and sometimes preacher at, a Church established by his father Pastor Eni, in the Sydney suburb of Kenthurst.[99] His Church has about 30 members and is called The Truth of Jesus Christ Church.[100] Like all religions, it has its own doctrines. It is reported to reject the Trinity, baptise only in the name of Jesus and believe that it is necessary to be 'born again' in 'the name of Jesus' to be saved.[101] Many Christians would argue that belief in the Trinity is an essential element of Christianity.[102] Given these doctrinal divergences from mainstream Christianity, some have argued that The Truth of Jesus Christ Church is not a Christian church and others have labelled it a 'sect'.[103] Folau operated an Instagram account and used this account to post his religious perspectives of life, which included a summary of what he took from Galatians 5:19-21 as follows:

98   Religious Freedom and Business Foundation, 'Measuring the Fortune 100's Commitment to Religious Inclusion' (Report, 2020) 5 <https://religiousfreedomandbusiness.org/wp-content/uploads/2020/02/RE-DI-Index-2020-FINAL.pdf> ('Fortune 100's Commitment').

99   John Tait, 'Did Israel Folau actually misquote the Bible? Hell, yes', *Sydney Morning Herald* (online, 17 July 2019) <https://www.smh.com.au/national/did-israel-folau-actually-misquote-the-bible-hell-yes-20190717-p5281z.html>.

100   Kate McClymont and Julie Power, 'Folau's group far from mainstream Christianity, leaders say', *Sydney Morning Herald* (online, 20 July 2019) <https://www.smh.com.au/national/nsw/folau-s-group-s-far-from-mainstream-christianity-leaders-say-20190720-p5292n.html>.

101   Ibid.

102   Josh McDowell and Don Stewart, *Answers to tough questions about the Christian faith* (Authentic Media, 2006) 21-33; see also ibid.

103   McClymont and Power (n 100).

Warning. Drunks, homosexuals, adulterers, liars, fornicators, thieves, atheists, idolators. Hell awaits you. Repent. Only Jesus saves. Those that are living in sin will end up in hell unless you repent. Jesus Christ loves you and is giving you time to turn away from your sin and come to him.[104]

The ARU's position was that Folau breached its code of conduct by publishing this post. However, as is clear from this post, Folau was not condemning all same sex attracted persons to hell. Any fair reading of his post reveals that he was calling on all who drink to excess, all who engage in sexual activities outside traditional marriage, all who steal, all who deny the existence of God and all who worship idols to change their behaviours for religious reasons. The ARU acknowledged in subsequently settling a claim for unfair dismissal commenced by Folau that '[t]he Social Media Post reflected Mr Folau's genuinely held religious beliefs, and Mr Folau did not intend to harm or offend any person when he uploaded the Social Media Post'.[105]

Whilst the claim was settled, Folau was not offered a new playing contract with the ARU. His playing contract was terminated for breaching what the Chair of the ARU, Raelene Castle, described as 'the very, very, very key value of inclusiveness'.[106] Folau's post now acknowledged to be a statement of his 'genuinely held religious beliefs' also led then Australian Rugby League Commissioner Peter Beattie and current chairmen Peter V'landys to state that Folau would not be welcome to play rugby league in Australia because his 'non-inclusive attitudes are not welcome in the

---

104   Tait (n 99).

105   Ian Payten, 'Ugly Folau saga finally ends after sacked star settles with Rugby Australia and NSW Rugby', *News* (Web Page, 4 December 2019) <https://www.rugby.com.au/news/2019/12/04/israel-folau-mediation>.

106   Janet Albrechtsen, 'Woke hypocrites humiliated as Folaus bask in apology', *The Australian* (online, 6 December 2019) <https://www.theaustralian.com.au/inquirer/woke-hypocrites-humiliated-as-folaus-bask-in-apology/news-story/400a6e9c1d433eafff7ec01f7856b3f3>.

game'.[107] Folau is therefore unable to play rugby union or rugby league in Australia because his genuinely held religious beliefs are not 'inclusive'.

The logical deficiency of inclusion

Somek has identified an underlying logical deficiency in the principle of 'inclusion' as a governing or substantive concept for business or policy: '[a]s a principle, inclusion is governed by a recursive logic. Once one factor of exclusion has been eliminated – for example, discrimination on the grounds of nationality – the focus can move on to remaining factors, such as race and gender'. [108]

There are an unlimited number of minorities which can be identified for inclusion and so inclusion can never be fully realised. Not only is Folau a member of a very small and new Church, he is also is a member of Australia's growing Tongan community. Like other groups sharing a Pacific Islander heritage, this is a disadvantaged group in Australian society on many indicia.[109] If 'inclusion' were to operate to protect disadvantaged minorities on this view, Folau ought to qualify for beneficent treatment. People are much more complicated than labelling according to certain characteristics or behaviours allows. People have a wide range of characteristics which can be very important to their self-perception and their behaviours, and which can be more or less important to them over their lifespan. Mentioning some but not other characteristics is problematic.

---

107   Danny Weidler, 'Broncos put the feelers out for Folau', *The Sun-Herald* (Sydney, 8 December 2019) 2.

108   Alexander Somek, 'From Workers to Migrants, from Distributive Justice to Inclusion: Exploring the Changing Social-Democratic Imagination' (Research Paper, University of Iowa College of Law, December 2012) 18 <http://ssm.com/abstract=2172475>.

109   Jioji Ravula, 'Pacific Communities in Australia' (Research Paper, University of Western Sydney, 2015) <https://www.uws.edu.au/__data/assets/pdf_file/0006/923361/SSP5680_Pacific_Communities_in_Aust_FA_LR.pdf>.

3. The need for a new approach

Exclusionary Inclusion

As the Folau example demonstrates, practices of inclusion which operate to exclude people with some characteristics which might not be perceived as being supportive of or which might contrast with those within a group identified as warranting inclusive recognition, may operate effectively to exclude those with those characteristics which are not considered to be worthy of inclusive recognition and treatment. This approach is more appropriately described as an exclusionary rather than inclusive approach. This is not to suggest that the ARU was not trying to be 'inclusive' when it terminated Folau's contract. Instead, what might have occurred may have been a consequence of the management of a workforce in whole or by majority sharing the same perspectives and so being unable to empathise with the consequences of their own behaviours on others. As Pelled has observed, 'people's backgrounds tend to shape what they notice and what they perceive to be important or interesting'.[110] In what is a very pertinent passage to consider in the context of current approaches to and application of practices and policies of 'inclusion', in 1998, Mor-Barak and Cherin observed that:

> [P]eople tend to feel more comfortable with others with whom they share important characteristics, strengthening in-group/out-group perceptions and creating exclusionary behaviours. Perception patterns of in-group/out-group variability contribute to attitudes that close opportunities to those who are different. These processes increase the likelihood of exclusion of those who are different i.e. women, ethnic and racial minorities and members of groups that may be defined or labelled different.[111]

In contrast, people who do not fit or are not liked by their peers are often pressured to leave.[112] Even if in practice workers who are unable or refuse

---

110   Pelled, Ladford Jr and Mohrman (n 79) 1017.
111   Mor-Barak and Cherin (n 80) 50.
112   Pelled, Ladford Jr and Mohrman (n 79) 1016.

to conform their moral positions to those of their employer or to participate in activities which they are called upon to support are not treated less
favourably, if they do decline to publically endorse those behaviours, they
may not only be 'driven to distraction', (to use Murray's formulation quoted
in part 1 above) they may feel that they are less valued. As Bond and Haynes
note:

> A person does not have to directly experience bias or even be directly
> reminded about stereotypical expectations: rather, qualities of set-
> tings have the power to signal whether or not someone can anticipate
> that their social identity will place them at risk of differential treat-
> ment. People look for environmental cues, like organization values,
> for diversity and the availability of co-workers who share one's so-
> cial identity, to assess whether they will or not be safe [from stereo-
> type-based biases in the workplace].[113]

As noted in part 2 above, religious faith is often overlooked in discussions
of inclusion.[114] However, whilst the number of Australians who now identify in the census as having 'no religion' is growing significantly, it was still
only 30% of the population in 2016.[115] This means that the vast majority
of Australians continue to identify with a religious tradition.[116] As noted in
part 1 above, central to religion is a set of doctrines and a moral code which
leads religious believers to manifest their faith through their actions. As
also noted in part 1 above, some religious believers will have stronger held
beliefs and a deeper commitment to their faith than others. To ignore this
reality is to disregard an aspect of most people's lives which is of central
importance to some. If a workforce or its management does not understand
religious worldviews, employees with those worldviews may be ignored,

---

113   Meg A Bond and Michelle C Haynes, 'Workplace Diversity: A Social-Ecological
      Framework and Policy Implications' (2014) 8(1) *Social Issues and Policy Review* 167,
      181.
114   See also Francesca Fontana, 'Have faith in your workforce', *Weekend Professional*,
      Weekend Australian (Sydney, August 2017) 5-6.
115   Australian Bureau of Statistics (n 23).
116   Ibid.

overlooked or marginalised in various ways despite inclusion policies. This may be deliberate or inadvertent. As Bond and Haynes note:

> Ignoring differences neither makes them disappear nor renders them irrelevant: philosophies that recognize and value differences tend to have more positive effects on reducing bias and other barriers to the inclusion of diverse group numbers ... Organizations can promote the full inclusion of diverse members, and mitigate the potential negative repercussions that may accompany diversity, in a wide range of ways – by signalling acceptance/safety for members of minority groups; by increasing the sense that the organisation considers diversity as asset; by disrupting the negative consequences of social categorization; by confirming clearly that discriminatory behaviour is not acceptable, and/or by establishing practices that communicate the importance of both a shared mission and a collective value for contribution of diverse others.[117]

Real Diversity and True Inclusion

The extent to which employees should conform to their employer's demands to behave in what the employer considers to be an inclusive manner when those demands put the employee in conflict with his or her conscience, religious beliefs or cultural background is a complex question. It should at the very least be considered in the application of policies of inclusion. It may be far from inclusive for an employer to demand that every employee should always conform to their employer's notion of inclusivity or their client's wishes or expectations. The issue becomes even more intrusive on religious freedom where the State makes these demands of conformity on its citizens.

A truly inclusive workplace is one which should at least recognise the very complex issues presented by the need to attract employees who are representative of the multifaith, multiracial, multicultural and pluralist Australia

---

117   Bond and Haynes (n 114) 183-4.

of today, and to recognise the irony and error of employees being asked
(or worse expected and required by their employer) to subjugate their own
characteristics in favour of those of their employer or of prospective or
actual clients or sponsors. Lalich describes the importance of diversity as
follows:

> The importance of diversity in the workplace is that it encourages peo-
> ple to be themselves at work, so you get more out of them. ... Employ-
> ees who are more comfortable being themselves in the workplace are
> going to be mentally more 'at' the workplace, and you're also less likely
> to lose good talent if people feel comfortable at the workplace.[118]

This portrayal of diversity, which we might call real diversity, ought to be the
goal of any policy of inclusion, which we might call policies of true inclusion. Similarly, a truly inclusive society is one which recognises the multiplicity of differences between people and seeks to understand, rather than to
ignore those differences, and to accommodate them. Real or true inclusion
requires a much more nuanced and careful response to some aspects of
culture, gender, religious and other differences than the contemporary approach to inclusion allows. Achieving real diversity or true inclusion of this
type is not easy. It involves seeking to create 'an organizational context in
which everybody feels an insider'.[119] This is not an approach which focusses
only on work-related indicators such as access to information, control over
decisions and job security but which also looks to a relational dimension of
inclusion where individuals actually interact. This is not just interaction at
the management level but wherever and at whatever levels people are at in a
workforce.[120] Collaborative work arrangements and conflict resolution pro-

---

118   The Law Society of New South Wales, 'The Flip Report 2017' (Report, 2017) 89
      <https://www.lawsociety.com.au/sites/default/files/2018-03/1272952.pdf>.
119   Maddy Jannsens and Patrizia Zanoni, 'What Makes an Organization Inclusive?
      Organizational Practices Favoring the Relational Inclusion of Ethnic Minori-
      ties in Operative Jobs' (Conference Paper, International Association for Conflict
      Management, 9 November 2008) 2.
120   Ibid 2.

cesses are required to build such a truly inclusive workforce.[121] Unlike the contemporary approach to inclusion, which sees inclusion in terms of seeking to remedy past attitudes and behaviours by preferring some attitudes over others, this approach seeks to treat the majority and minority the same by respecting their differences.[122] This means the creation of clear, explicit and transparent performance based standards with clear evaluation criteria for all and applying those standards on merit.[123] It means emphasising a clear collectivist superordinate objective or identity for the enterprise – such as winning the Rugby World Cup or becoming the number 1 supplier of widgets in the country – so that there is an overarching goal or objective to which all employees can aim which is not based on any majority norm but is open to and respectful of difference.[124] It means creating a culture and logic of 'employee care' within organisations in which employees are treated with care and with a recognition of their differences and needs.[125]

In this approach, ethnic minorities, for example, maintain their distinctive cultural and religious identities and behaviours in the workforce.[126] For this to be achieved successfully, the majority need to care enough about the other people they work with that they show an interest in the culture, language and religion of minorities.[127] In Jannsens and Zanoni's study, for example, an employee who was not from a Muslim background voluntarily fasted during Ramadan to share that experience with colleagues from the Islamic tradition.[128] The successful achievement of this sort of inclusion requires sensitivity and respect among colleagues. In a workforce which is not itself operating within a particular religious tradition, where respect for that tra-

---

121   Ibid 5.
122   Ibid 6-7.
123   Ibid 17.
124   Ibid 26.
125   Ibid 19-20.
126   Ibid 7.
127   Ibid 15.
128   Ibid.

dition may necessitate behaviours in a workplace which are consistent with a particular religious context, inclusion should be evident in respect for religious practice. This might be evident in permitting the wearing of religious attire such as headscarves or crosses, or proving employees with time to pray. Where the workplace is able to provide work scheduling flexibility it is important that this is a general policy which is not only available to those who are from a particular religious tradition which might, for example, prefer to have time to eat at times other than those of the majority during Ramadan.[129] Jannsens and Zanoni:

> consider the presence of such cultural practices to be a clear sign of inclusion, especially as in Europe they are often judged inappropriate in public spaces. It suggests that ethnic minorities are not forced to choose between being loyal to either their own culture or the majority's culture to be considered full members of the organization, and that they are accepted by the majority as they are.[130]

True inclusion requires sensitivity to the need to allow for differences in motivations and understandings of the world, not just among colleagues but among employees, clients and those with whom people interact. This requires recognition not only of the characteristics of employees and also of clients with whom they interact. Making the client feel at ease at the expense of the ease of the employee involved might not always be the best approach. True inclusion is not a feature of the contemporary West or today's Australia. In Australia, for example, '[l]awyers continue to be held back from full participation due to a variety of factors including gender, disability, family status, faith and cultural identity.'[131] The same is true across the broader Australian society.

---

129   Ibid 2.
130   Ibid 15-6 (citations omitted).
131   The Flip Report 2017 (n 119) 89.

The Economics of Real Diversity and True Inclusion

It is not only contrary to the inherent dignity of religious believers for employers or the State to ignore – or worse belittle and punish – their perspectives on contested moral and ethical questions, it is poor business judgment. Lalich's view that encouraging people to be themselves and to feel comfortable at work produces better retention and more productive workers is shared by Bond and Haynes.[132] They consider that along with increased productivity, reduced absenteeism and turnover of staff, such employers can witness improvements in their staff commitment to them.[133] In turn, this can lead to employers having a workforce which is representative of the community and of their client base.[134] In contrast, a workforce which is homogenous may discourage clients and staff with different characteristics from hiring the business to work for them or from seeking employment there.[135] There are also economic benefits for employers who specifically respect religion. Employers with religious non-discrimination policies are likely to have better retention of religious staff and those who accommodate religious staff with flexible hours to enable them to meet their obligations of religious observance are twice as likely to have staff who enjoy their work.[136]

The economic benefits to be derived by businesses seeking to attract a variegated workforce and to respect the differences of workers are such that, as Prasad observes, it might be argued that 'smart and visionary companies will automatically take serious efforts to include a wide range of difference in their workforces and that those companies that fail to do so will be disciplined by the market because their performance will inevitably suffer'.[137]

---

132   Bond and Haynes (n 114) 167, 170 (citations omitted); Diversity & Inclusion (n 84).
133   Bond and Haynes (n 114) 167, 170.
134   Ibid 167, 175.
135   Ibid.
136   Francesca Fontana (n 115).
137   Prasad (n 97) 64.

The Religious Freedom and Business Foundation ranked Fortune 100 companies by reference to their accommodation of religious believers in a Corporate Religious Equity, Diversity & Inclusion ('REDI') Index. Companies which publicly acknowledged religion achieved better results on all seven of the EEOC diversity categories than those which failed to do so.[138] For example, companies which accommodated religious difference achieved significantly higher scores on age inclusion (69% higher), veterans/military inclusion (63% higher), disability inclusion (60% higher), race/ethnicity inclusion (47% higher), women/gender inclusion (35% higher), family inclusion (31% higher) and sexual orientation inclusion (4%).[139] The benefits of accommodating religious belief is not limited to individual businesses but extends to nations, as governments which respect religious freedom enjoy superior economic growth.[140] Countries with higher levels of religious freedom also provide a better environment for people who are same sex attracted, bisexual or transsexual.[141]

The risk of reducing True Inclusion to economics

Whilst economic benefits of true inclusion might persuade some businesses to treat each employee as an individual worthy of respect with the characteristics that they have as a person, this chapter does not argue for a new meaning and a new approach to inclusion purely on economic grounds. It argues for true inclusion as a means of respecting human dignity. This

---

138   Fortune 100's Commitment (n 98) 5.
139   Ibid 5-6.
140   Religious Freedom Helps (n 86); Religious Freedom and Business Foundation, 'Religious Freedom Linked to Economic Growth, Finds Global Study' (Web Page) <https://religiousfreedomandbusiness.org/religious-freedom-business>; Brian J Grim, Greg Clark and Robert Edward Snyder, 'Is Religious Freedom Good for Business?: A Conceptual and Empirical Analysis' (2014) 10 *Interdisciplinary Journal of Research on Religion* 1; Brian J Grim and Melissa E Grim, 'The Socio-Economic Contribution of Religion to American Society: An Empirical Analysis' (2016) 12 *Interdisciplinary Journal of Research on Religion* 1.
141   Fortune 100's Commitment (n 98) 5-6.

'means acknowledging, understanding and appreciating difference'.[142] This core justification may be lost if inclusion is seen purely in economic terms. Prasad makes this observation:

> By presenting difference as a dimension of human capital and there-fore as a source of competitive advantage this theme seemingly holds the hope of greater inclusion of different individuals in today's or-ganizations. However by stressing the economic value of difference, it also converts difference into a commodity that has exchange value *but little intrinsic human worth*. In other words, according to this scheme of things, difference is not valued outside its potential to enhance an organization's economic and instrumental performance.[143]

Does True Inclusion Ignore Historic Injustices?

In Australia and the West more generally, inclusion has become increasingly associated with approaches to sex, sexual orientation and gender identity.[144] Some argue that this is appropriate and that broadening the approach to include other categories of difference is inappropriate. As Prasad explains:

> [B]y widening the categories of difference to include personality styles, personal experiences, and so on, the theme of diversity also removes the focus that the themes of discrimination ensured on the exclusion of historically disadvantaged groups based on race, sex and ethnicity. Indeed, by popularizing a wide range of less excluded dif-ferences, the current themes of diversity seems to trivialize (to some extent at least) the more serious consequences of historical disadvan-tage that are still experienced by women, certain minorities and races and those with alternate sexual preferences.[145]

Proponents of this approach argue that there is a need to focus on histor-

---

142   David Jamieson and Julie O'Mara, *Managing workforce 2000: gaining the diversity ad-vantage* (Jossey-Bass, 1991) 3, quoted in Prasad (n 97) 64.

143   Prasad (n 97) 65 (emphasis added).

144   See, eg, Melissa Coade, 'BigLaw and LGBTQI rights: A law firm partner re-flects', *Lawyers Weekly* (online, 22 May 2018) <https://www.lawyersweekly.com.au/biglaw/23284-biglaw-and-lgbtqi-rights-a-law-firm-partner-reflects>.

145   Prasad (n 97) 65. Whilst this comment is made in relation to diversity, the logic of the argument applies equally to inclusion.

ically disadvantaged groups in applying policies of inclusion and diversity. This approach to inclusion is evident in the ARU's approach to the Folau matter discussed in part 2 above notwithstanding the inclusion of religion in the relevant ARU codes of conduct.

Why the "Historic Injustices" Argument for Limited Inclusion Ought Be Rejected

Remembering the logical deficiency of inclusion

Identifying the victims of historical disadvantage by reference to sex, sexual orientation and gender identity involves the identification of a small subset of the characteristics and behaviours which are important to people and a small subset of characteristics and behaviours which have attracted and continue to attract disadvantage and abuse. The approach to inclusion which seeks to preference people with certain identified characteristics above others suffers from the logical deficiency identified by Somek and discussed in part 2 above. There will always be a class of people who have suffered historic disadvantage who are yet to be relevantly included. There is no doubt that small and emerging religions and religions characterised as 'cults' have been victims of historic discrimination in Australia[146] as have Pacific Islanders.[147] If the focus is on the inclusion of minorities by reference to sex, sexual orientation and gender identity, as the Folau affair demonstrates, persons with those characteristics will be privileged where a competition arises with a person seeking to manifest their right to freedom of religion. This will be so even if that person is from a small minority (and arguably heretical if viewed against mainstream Christian theology)[148]

146   See, eg, Bernard Doherty and James T Richardson, 'Litigation, liberty, and legitimation: The experience of the Church of Scientology in Australian law' [2019] (March) (247) *St Mark's Review* 61.

147   Ravula (n 110).

148   McClymont and Power (n 100).

offshoot of a recognised tradition by a group from a disadvantaged racial and cultural group. This prioritising of one group over another is subject to change if and when other minority characteristics are relevantly 'included' in the future.

An approach which is atomising rather than holistic

This approach fails to treat people holistically. When people are slotted into particular categories, rather than considered holistically, categorisation errors can occur. Douglas Murray is critical of this practice as embodied in 'identity politics' but his criticism of that approach has broader application to contemporary approaches to 'inclusion'. Murray observes that 'identity politics' 'atomizes society into different interest groups according to sex (or gender), race, sexual preference and more. It presumes that such characteristics are the main, or only, relevant attributes of their holders'.[149]

However, people are more complex than this sort of approach allows. As well as traditional differences such as race, sex and religion, people have different personalities, experiences, ethic and cultural backgrounds, functional backgrounds and cognitive frames.[150] The significance of particular characteristics to an individual vary and they may also vary over time. Similarly, the life experiences that a person with a particular characteristic will vary considerably. As Pelled, Ladford Jr and Mohramn observe:

> For example, the attribute *race* tends to capture a broad set of experiences, such as the traditions a person has developed, the treatment a person has received from teachers and friends, and the clubs or interest groups a person has joined. It may also capture a person's experiences at work, but those experiences are only a fraction of the total set of experiences it captures.[151]

---

149   Douglas Murray (n 68) 3.
150   Prasad (n 97) 64
151   Pelled, Ladford Jr and Mohrman (n 79) 1019.

In a particular workforce, for example, a group of people may identify with a particular religious tradition as broadly understood, leading to the view that a particular religious position is a majority position in that group. However, there is a vast difference between the implications of that membership to a person who is a sometime preacher who feels called to evangelise but is able to focus that activity outside work in his or her personal time on personal social media platforms and a nominal Christian who has no interest in Christian morality but enjoys Christmas cards and the retelling of the passion of Christ and who attends a Good Friday service once a year. As noted in part 1 above in relation to the Catholic faith, commitment and consistency with the official teachings of a religious tradition can vary markedly even within people who identify with that tradition. A committed Catholic who seeks to live his or her life in accordance with the official teaching of that Church may be in a minority even in a workforce which has a majority Catholic or majority Christian orientation by background. Diversity in this context needs to be measured not just in terms of the religious traditions within which employees might have grown up but also their commitment to their religious faith. Without this understanding, businesses may publicly support such causes as the gay and lesbian mardi gras, same sex marriage or gender neutral bathrooms and encourage the display of rainbow flags or the celebration of rainbow days in the workplace, for example, through a commitment to what they understand to be inclusion. Iain Benson has made this observation in relation to the State siding with a particular morally contested position over others, but his point applies at least equally to employers:

> [W]e need to be wary of claims that a particular position represents 'the state interest'. More often than not when what is at issue is a contestable viewpoint the state interest is multiple not singular. The state simply put should not have only 'one' view on controversial matters. These are questions that the state should keep as open as far

as possible.[152]

Here, when the State or an employer adopts a moral position on a contested moral and ethical question which is at odds with the position adopted as doctrine within a religious tradition, it sends a signal to staff members who continue to maintain their religious perspective on the topic. The message which they receive is that their religiously informed view is not respected and that they are less valued if they do not participate in supporting activities which they consider to be sinful or wrong. In doing so, as well as sending the intended message of inclusion to those who support their position on such issues, such employers may be sending a message of intolerance and exclusivity to others in the community – including potential or actual customers and employees – who have a moral view informed by a religious tradition. In pursuing policies of inclusion in this way, rather than achieving the building of acceptance, tolerance and respect, employers may instead highlight particular divisive issues and exacerbate latent but existing tensions and divisions. For religious believers who seek to continue to live by the exclusive doctrines of their religious tradition, such policies of inclusion may be impossible to follow for reasons including those identified by Laycock and Berg and by Murray in part 1 above.

A Concluding Case for True Inclusion in the workforce and society

Forcing people to act in ways which they cannot and punishing them if they do not is not inclusive. Preventing people from doing what they must is not inclusive. Inclusiveness which operates in these ways – contemporary inclusion – is not the way to build a harmonious and productive workplace or by extension a harmonious and productive society. To do so requires real respect for the many differences which exist between individuals. It requires true inclusion.

152   Iain Benson, 'The politics of drift' (2017) 33(2) *Policy* 45.

When applied to a society, true inclusion means recognising that everyone is different and not seeking to enforce conformity. Rather than creating a truly inclusive society, the contemporary approach to inclusion preferences those with certain characteristics and preferred behaviours over others. As Mascareno and Carvajal observe:

> [A]ny measure, whether public or private, must be taken with aware-
> ness of its potentially exclusionary outcomes … There can be no
> decision without consequences, especially when it comes to public
> organisations and institutions: it is not possible to precisely calculate
> the number of possible [sic] affected.[153]

An approach to inclusion which entirely ignores the exclusivity demands of religions is inimical to religious freedom and creates rather than reduces conflict. In practice, this form of inclusion is not in fact really inclusive as it makes those who have different views – be they religious or otherwise – feel at least excluded and at worst subject to termination of employment, fines and other punishment. This form of inclusion can operate to actively exclude such people including directly by the termination of employment in response to an expression of religious belief. As a consequence, there is a need to re-examine inclusion and to adopt a truer form of inclusion in which the dignity of each human person as an individual is respected through the recognition of the differences between the characteristics and behaviours of all people.

Bibilography

Albrechtsen, Janet, 'Woke hypocrites humiliated as Folaus bask in apology', *The Australian* (online, 6 December 2019) <https://www.theaustralian.com.au/inquirer/woke-hypocrites-humiliated-as-folaus-bask-in-apology/news-story/400a6e9c1d433eafff7ec01f7856b3f3>.

Alcorta, Candace S and Richard Sosis, 'Ritual, Emotion and Sacred Symbols: The Evolution of Religion as an Adaptive Complex' (2005) 16(4) *Human Nature* 323.

Allman, Dan, 'The Sociology of Social Inclusion' (2013) 3(1) *SAGE Open* 1.

---

153   Mascareño and Carvajal (n 69) 134.

Anon, 'The Growth of the Latin Mass', *The Saint's Pub* (Web Page, 7 November 2016) <https://thesaintspub.wordpress.com/2016/11/07/the-growth-of-the-latin-mass/>.

AP, 'The current situation for the TLM in Italy' (Blog Post, 23 February 2010) <https://rorate-caeli.blogspot.com/2010/02/current-situation-for-tlm-in-italy.html>.

Australian Bureau of Statistics, '2016 Census data reveals "no religion" is rising fast', *2016 Census: Religion* (Web Page, 27 June 2017) <https://www.abs.gov.au/AUSSTATS/abs@.nsf/mediareleasesbyReleaseDate/7E65A144540551D-7CA258148000E2B85>.

Baker, Joseph O, 'Social Sources of the Spirit: Connecting Rational Choice and Interactive Ritual Theories in the Study of Religion' (2010) 71(4) *Sociology of Religion* 432.

Benson, Iain, 'The politics of drift' (2017) 33(2) *Policy* 45.

Bond, Meg A and Michelle C Haynes, 'Workplace Diversity: A Social-Ecological Framework and Policy Implications' (2014) 8(1) *Social Issues and Policy Review* 167.

Catechism of the Catholic Church (St. Pauls, 1994).

Carlson, Allan, 'Family and Society the End of Liberalism', *News Weekly* (Web Page, 23 February 2019) <http://www.newsweekly.com.au/article.php?id=58435&s=d-dUIaM>.

Center for Applied Research in the Apostolate, 'Global Catholicism: Trends & Forecasts' (Report, 4 June 2015) 41 <https://cara.georgetown.edu/staff/web-pages/global%20catholicism%20release.pdf>.

Church of the New Faith v Commissioner of Pay-Roll Tax (Vic) (1983) 154 CLR 120.

Coade, Melissa, 'BigLaw and LGBTQI rights: A law firm partner reflects', *Lawyers Weekly* (online, 22 May 2018) <https://www.lawyersweekly.com.au/biglaw/23284-biglaw-and-lgbtqi-rights-a-law-firm-partner-reflects>.

Cockfield, Arthur J, 'Limiting Lawyer Liberty: How the Statement of Principles Coerces Speech' (Research Paper No 2018-100, Queens Law Research Paper Series, 15 March 2018) 23 <https://papers.ssrn.com/sol3/papers.cfm?abstract_id=3141561>.

Doherty, Bernard and James T Richardson, 'Litigation, liberty, and legitimation: The experience of the Church of Scientology in Australian law' [2019] (March) (247) *St Mark's Review* 61.

Flatt, Kevin N, D Millard Haskell and Stephanie Burgoyne, 'Secularization and

Attribution: How Mainline Protestant Clergy and Congregants Explain Church Growth and Decline> (2018) 79(1) *Sociology of Religion* 78.

Fontana, Francesca, 'Have faith in your workforce', *Weekend Professional, Weekend Australian* (Sydney, August 2017).

Grzymala-Busse, Anna, 'Good Clubs and Community Support: Explaining the Growth of Strict Religions' (2014) 56(2) *Journal of Church and State* 269.

Grim, Brian J, Greg Clark and Robert Edward Snyder, 'Is Religious Freedom Good for Business?: A Conceptual and Empirical Analysis' (2014) 10 *Interdisciplinary Journal of Research on Religion* 1.

Grim, Brian J and Melissa E Grim, 'The Socio-Economic Contribution of Religion to American Society: An Empirical Analysis' (2016) 12 *Interdisciplinary Journal of Research on Religion* 1.

Hughes Philip, 'The Multi-Dimensional Issue of Culture and Christian Ministry' (2015) (1) *Journal of Contemporary Ministry* 6.

Human Rights Law Alliance, '"Jamie" - Protecting the Religious Beliefs of our Teachers', *Our Cases* (Web Page, 20 April 2017) <https://www.hrla.org.au/jamie>.

Human Rights Law Alliance, '"Ryan" - Workplace Discrimination', *Our Cases* (Web Page, 10 June 2017) <https://www.hrla.org.au/ryan>.

Iannaccone, Laurence R, 'Why Strict Churches Are Strong' (1994) 99(5) *American Journal of Sociology* 1180.

Indermaur, David, 'Contemporary Attitudes to the Death Penalty: An Australian Perspective' (2006) 17(3) *Current Issues in Criminal Justice* 444.

International Covenant on Civil and Political Rights, G.A. Res 2200A (XXI), U.N. GAOR, 21st Sess., Supp.No.16 U.N. Doc.A/6316 (16 December 1966, entered into force on 23 March 1976).

Jamieson, David and Julie O'Mara, *Managing workforce 2000: gaining the diversity advantage* (Jossey-Bass, 1991).

Jannsens, Maddy and Patrizia Zanoni, 'What Makes an Organization Inclusive? Organizational Practices Favoring the Relational Inclusion of Ethnic Minorities in Operative Jobs' (Conference Paper, International Association for Conflict Management, 9 November 2008) 2.

Kloster, Donald, 'Traditional Latin Mass National Survey', *Liturgy Guy* (Web Page, 24 February 2019) <https://liturgyguy.com/2019/02/24/national-survey-results-what-we-learned-about-latin-mass-attendees/?fbclid=IwAR3u9tQDjUt-p4zYZnv9GKE4Bmsa5Bdb-fZ8_INYlxj2b346_QdvSOM_2iBc>.

Laycock, Douglas and Thomas Berg, 'Same-Sex Marriage and Religious Liberty' (2013) 99(1) *Virginia Law Review* 1.

Mascareño, Aldo and Fabiola Carvajal, 'The Different Faces of Inclusion and Exclusion' (2015) 116 *CEPAL Review* 127.

McClymont, Kate and Julie Power, 'Folau's group far from mainstream Christianity, leaders say', *Sydney Morning Herald* (online, 20 July 2019) <https://www.smh.com.au/national/nsw/folau-s-group-s-far-from-mainstream-christianity-leaders-say-20190720-p5292n.html>.

McDowell, Josh and Don Stewart, *Answers to tough questions about the Christian faith* (Authentic Media, 2006).

Mor-Barak, Michal E, and David A Cherin, 'A Tool to Expand Organizational Understanding of Workforce Diversity' (1998) 22(1) *Administration in Social Work* 47.

Murray, Douglas, *The Madness of Crowds* (Bloomsbury Continuum, 2019).

New Jerusalem Bible (Darton, Longman & Todd, 1994).

O'Hara, KB, TA Beehr and SM Colarelli, 'Organizational centrality: a third dimension of intraorganizational career movement' (1994) 30(2) *Journal of Applied Behavioural Science* 198.

Parkinson, Patrick, 'Protecting Religious Freedom in An Age of Militant secularism' in Robert Forsyth and Peter Kurti (eds) *Forgotten Freedom No More* (Connor Court, 2020) 99.

Payten, Ian, 'Ugly Folau saga finally ends after sacked star settles with Rugby Australia and NSW Rugby', *News* (Web Page, 4 December 2019) <https://www.rugby.com.au/news/2019/12/04/israel-folau-mediation>.

Pelled, LH, GE Ladford Jr and SA Mohrman, 'Demographic dissimilarity and workplace inclusion' (1999) 36(7) *Journal of Management Studies* 1013.

Percy, Anthony, *The Theology of the Body made Simple* (Connor Court, 2005).

Prasad, Anshuman, 'Understanding Workplace Empowerment as Inclusion: A Historical Investigation of the Discourse of Difference in the United States' (2001) 37(1) *The Journal of Applied Behavioural Science* 51.

Quinlan, Michael, 'Born (Again) This way: Why The Inherent Nature of Religiosity requires A New Approach to Australia's Discrimination laws' in Augusto Zimmermann (ed), *A Commitment to Excellence* (Connor Court, 2018) 96.

Ramus, Daniel, 'Israel Folau case exposes contradiction in ARU's inclusion policy', *Sporting News (online,* 10 May 2018) <https://www.sportingnews.com/au/

rugby/news/israel-folau-australia-rugby-union-inclusion-policy-saga-contradiction/1dc26kdcq68zp1qt432hyx7ufa>.

Ravula, Jioji, 'Pacific Communities in Australia' (Research Paper, University of Western Sydney, 2015) <https://www.uws.edu.au/__data/assets/pdf_file/0006/923361/SSP5680_Pacific_Communities_in_Aust_FA_LR.pdf>.

Religious Freedom and Business Foundation, 'Business Case For Workplace Religious Diversity & Inclusion' (Web Page) <https://religiousfreedomandbusiness.org/business-case-for-workplace-religious-diversity-and-inclusion>.

Religious Freedom and Business Foundation, 'Measuring the Fortune 100's Commitment to Religious Inclusion' (Report, 2020) 5 <https://religiousfreedomandbusiness.org/wp-content/uploads/2020/02/REDI-Index-2020-FINAL.pdf>.

Religious Freedom and Business Foundation, 'Religious Freedom Helps Businesses & Economies Grow' (Web Page, 6 May 2019) <https://religiousfreedomandbusiness.org/religious-freedom-helps-businesses-economies-grow>.

Religious Freedom and Business Foundation, 'Religious Freedom Linked to Economic Growth, Finds Global Study' (Web Page) <https://religiousfreedomandbusiness.org/religious-freedom-business>.

Religious Freedom and Business Foundation, 'Workplace Religious Discrimination Encountered by 1-in-3' (Web Page, 11 August 2014) <https://religiousfreedomandbusiness.org/business-case-for-workplace-religious-diversity-and-inclusion>.

Robbins, Joel , 'Pentecostal Networks and the Spirit of Globalization: On the Social Productivity of Ritual Forms' (2009) 53(1) *Social Analysis: The International Journal of Social and Cultural Practice* 55.

Robertson, Quinetta M, 'Disentangling the Meanings of Diversity and Inclusion in Organization' (2006) 31(2) *Group & Organization Management* 212.

Schirmer, Werner and Dimitris Michailakis, 'The Luhmannian Approach to exclusion/inclusion and its Relevance to Social Work' (2015) 15(1) *Journal of Social Work* 45.

Somek, Alexander, 'From Workers to Migrants, from Distributive Justice to Inclusion: Exploring the Changing Social-Democratic Imagination' (Research Paper, University of Iowa College of Law, December 2012) 18 <http://ssm.com/abstract=2172475>.

Sturm, Susan P, 'The Architecture of Inclusion: Advancing Workplace Equity in Higher Education' (Research Paper No 06-114, Columbia Law School, 2006).

Tanenbaum Center for Interreligious Understanding, 'What American Workers Really Think About Religion: Tanenbaum's 2013 Survey of American Workers and Religion' (Report, 2013) 4 <https://tanenbaum.org/wp-content/uploads/2014/02/Tanenbaums-2013-Survey-of-American-Workers-and-Religion.pdf>.

Tait, John, 'Did Israel Folau actually misquote the Bible? Hell, yes', *Sydney Morning Herald* (online, 17 July 2019) <https://www.smh.com.au/national/did-israel-folau-actually-misquote-the-bible-hell-yes-20190717-p5281z.html>.

The Law Society of New South Wales, 'The Flip Report 2017' (Report, 2017) 89 <https://www.lawsociety.com.au/sites/default/files/2018-03/1272952.pdf>.

The Pocket Macquarie Dictionary.

Thomas, Jeremy N and Daniel V A Olson, 'Testing the Strictness Thesis and Competing Theories of Congregational Growth' (2010) 49(4) *Journal for the Scientific Study of Religion* 619.

Truu, Maani, 'Academics sign open letter after law dean compares trans students to teens with eating disorders', *SBS News* (online, 19 September 2019) <https://www.sbs.com.au/news/academics-sign-open-letter-after-law-dean-compares-trans-students-to-teens-with-eating-disorders>.

Vardy, Peter, *Good & Bad Religion* (SCM Press, 2010).

Weidler, Danny, 'Broncos put the feelers out for Folau', *The Sun-Herald* (Sydney, 8 December 2019).

Zauzmer, Julie, 'The public will be allowed to visit the Mormon temple on the Beltway for the first time in 46 years', *The Washington Post* (online, 16 August 2017) <https://www.washingtonpost.com/news/acts-of-faith/wp/2017/08/16/the-public-will-be-allowed-to-visit-the-mormon-temple-on-the-beltway-for-the-first-time-in-46-years/>.

5

SECTION 17 OF THE 'ANTI-DISCRIMINATION ACT 1998 (TAS)' AND THE DECLINE OF CONSCIENCE AS A MEANS OF SOCIAL CONTROL.

Michael Stokes

Abstract

Section 17 of the *Anti-Discrimination Act 1998* (Tas) outlaws conduct which offends another person on the basis of (among other attributes) sexual orientation. The paper argues that the provision is aimed at preventing the bullying of an individual, not the targeting of a class. The paper then considers whether a provision extending to targeting a class is justified. It concludes that there is no justification for a provision banning insulting a class because insults do not cause sufficient harm and are not sufficiently immoral to justify a ban. Support for the provision is in part the result of a growth in secularism and moral relativism and a corresponding decline in the reliance on conscience to control behaviour. The decline of conscience has led to other means of social control, especially public shaming for breaches of accepted standards. The paper argues that the state, through provisions such as s 17, is of necessity playing a more important role in maintaining shared standards by shaming those who do not accept such standards. The growth of secularism and of shaming as a mean social control is likely to lead to less respect for freedom of religion and conscience.

Introduction

Section 17 of the *Anti-Discrimination Act 1998* (Tas) has given rise to much controversy and has been regarded as a major threat to freedom of speech, especially freedom to express religious beliefs, in public. It reads:

> A person must not engage in any conduct which offends, humiliates, intimidates, insults or ridicules another person on the basis of [among other attributes] sexual orientation, if a reasonable person, having regard to all the circumstances, would have anticipated that the other person would have been offended, humiliated, intimidated, insulted or ridiculed.

The controversy arose from three complaints to the Anti-Discrimination Commissioner under s 17. The first was brought against the Catholic Archbishop of Hobart, Archbishop Porteous. The other two were brought against a minister, the Rev Markham, and an evangelist and street preacher, Dr Gee, of the Cornerstone Presbyterian Church, Hobart. All three complaints alleged that the Christian teachings of the three men caused offence or could reasonably be anticipated to cause offence to members of the group of people who shared the attribute of being same sex attracted.

The complaint against Archbishop Porteous arose from his distribution through Catholic schools of a booklet, *Don't Mess With Marriage*, prepared by the Australian Catholic Bishops Conference setting out his church's teachings on marriage, including same sex marriage. Martine Delaney complained to the Anti-Discrimination Commission that the pamphlet insulted and offended her as a transgender person. The pamphlet was designed to influence the debate on the legalisation of same sex marriage in the lead up to the 2018 plebiscite. The complaint may have been designed to silence an influential voice in that debate, the leader of the Catholic Church in Tasmania. Hence the complaint had repercussions not only for the freedom to express religious beliefs but for the right to participate in political debates.

The complaints against Rev Markham and Dr Gee were brought with respect to their teachings in a blog and in street meetings respectively. The complainant, Samuel Mazur, made it clear to the Commissioner and online that he was not a member of the LGBTI community but brought the complaints as an ally of LGBTI people, whom he anticipated may have been offended and because he found the remarks offensive. [1] Rev Markham was most scathing of this aspect of the case, arguing that allowing third party complaints

> ... is manifestly preposterous and destructive of Australian freedom: if in our nation Person A is permitted to initiate legal proceedings against Person B on the grounds that Person C may derive feelings of humiliation or insult from something Person B has communicated, then the Australian citizen's freedom to discuss, to argue, to defend, to critique, and to express what is on their minds, is going to be very much chilled, and ultimately quenched altogether.[2]

The three cases provoked a response from both the Tasmanian and Commonwealth Parliaments. The Tasmanian Parliament considered but did not ultimately pass an amendment to s 55 of the Anti-Discrimination Act extending the exemptions granted by that section to public acts done in good faith for academic, artistic, scientific or research purposes to religious purposes.[3]

---

1   'Complaint Withdrawn, but the Emperor is Still Naked' *Tasmanian Times* July 2, 2018. < https://tasmaniantimes.com/2018/07/complaint-withdrawn-but-the-emperor-is-still-naked/> The post indicates why Mazur brought the complaint and why he ultimately withdrew it.

2   Submission 405 to the Joint Standing Committee on Defence, Foreign Affairs and Trade, Inquiry into status of the the human right to freedom of religion or belief, dot point 2; <https://www.aph.gov.au/Parliamentary_Business/Committees/Joint/Foreign_Affairs_Defence_and_Trade/Freedomofreligion/Submissions>.

3   The proposed amendment was subject to strong criticism; Forrester, Zimmermann and Finlay, 'An Opportunity Missed? A Constitutional Analysis of Proposed Reforms to Tasmania's "Hate Speech" Laws' (2016) 7 *Western*

The three cases were discussed in the Second Interim Report of the Joint Standing Committee on Defence, Foreign Affairs and Trade Inquiry into the status of the human right to freedom of religion or belief, but the report did not make any recommendations with respect to it.[4] However, the government's Religious Discrimination Bill, introduced in the last parliament, dealt with the matter in clause 42, which was intended to amend s 17 of the Tasmanian Act, by laying down that a statement of belief, including religious belief, did not contravene the section unless it was malicious or likely to harass, threaten, seriously intimidate or vilify another person or group of persons.

The paper first considers what s 17 actually does. Since Martine Delaney's complaint against Archbishop Porteous it has been assumed that s 17 is very broad, allowing complaints against public comment with respect to a class of persons who share a particular attribute which a member of the class is likely to find offensive. This paper argues that s 17, properly interpreted, does not extend to complaints such as those of Martine Delaney and Samuel Mazur. It then argues that if it does extend to such cases, it is too broad and cannot be justified.

The interpretation of s 17(1)

In my opinion, s 17 cannot be used as the basis for an action in which a member of a class of persons, in Ms Delaney's case, the class of transgender persons, complains that a general statement about the class is offensive or insulting. If that is the case, it certainly does not permit a person who is sympathetic to the class to lodge such a complaint on behalf of that class.

Australian Jurist 214, 264-275.

4   *Second interim Report: freedom of religion and belief, the Australian experience* Ch 3 'The Domestic Experience of Freedom of Religion and Belief' 3.37-45; < https:// www.aph.gov.au/Parliamentary_Business/Committees/Joint/Foreign_Affairs_ Defence_and_Trade/Freedomofreligion/Second_Interim_Report>.

Instead, the better interpretation of s 17 is that it protects an individual who is the target of offensive, insulting, humiliating or intimidating behaviour because of a personal attribute such as sexual orientation. In other words, it is aimed against the bullying of an individual on these grounds, not against general statements which may be offensive to a class of persons.

Section 19 of the Act does provide some protection to a class of people from statements with respect to attributes which they share. Section 19 prohibits hate speech, banning the incitement of hatred towards, serious contempt for or severe ridicule of a person or group of persons on the grounds of attributes such as religion or sexual orientation.

Ms Delaney and Mr Mazur had good reasons for bringing their complaints under s 17 rather than s 19. It is far easier to demonstrate that a statement, blog or pamphlet is insulting or offensive than that it incites hatred or contempt. Archbishop Porteous's pamphlet did not incite hatred or contempt for gays or lesbians, so that a complaint brought under s 19 would have failed. It is probable that complaints under s 19 against Rev Markham and Dr Gee would also have failed.

However, s 17 cannot be used in cases such as these, because the pamphlet, blog and statements did not target any particular individual. In particular, they did not target Ms Delaney and Mr Mazur respectively.

There are good reasons why s 17 should be interpreted as limited to cases in which an individual has been targeted by offensive, insulting or intimidating behaviour. Firstly s 17 contains two prohibitions. The first is the prohibition of offensive, insulting, intimidating and humiliating conduct. The second is a prohibition of sexual harassment.

The sexual harassment provision prevents the targeting of an individual by means of unwelcome sexual action or comments. Placing the provision prohibiting offensive, insulting and intimidating conduct in the same section as the prohibition of sexual harassment suggests that it too prohibits the targeting of an individual.

The language of the two prohibitions also supports the conclusion that both are limited to cases in which the behaviour targets an individual. Unlike s 19 of the Act, which bans hate speech, or s 18C of the *Racial Discrimination Act 1975* (Cth), which bans acts which are reasonably likely, in all the circumstances, to offend, insult, humiliate or intimidate on grounds of race, colour or national or ethnic origin, both ss 17(1) and (2) only apply to 'a person', not to 'a person or group of persons'. This difference in wording suggests that s 17 only bans conduct targeting an individual rather than conduct with reference to a group.

Besides, if s 17 applies to general statements, it creates an uneven playing field in public debate. Section 17 does not apply to all insulting, offensive or humiliating statements. For example, it protects against such statements with respect to sexual orientation, but not with respect to religion. So in the debate over same sex marriage, supporters of same sex marriage could attack their religious opponents with relative impunity, only being liable if their statements were so offensive that they amounted to hate speech, while, as Archbishop Porteous's problems show, even polite and restrained public statements with respect to sexual orientation may cause offence. An interpretation which limits s 17 to conduct targeting a particular individual avoids such unfairness and is to be preferred.

Section 55 of the Act does provide some support for the view that s 17(1) extends to general statements aimed at a class of individuals. It reads:

> The provisions of section 17(1) and section 19 do not apply if the person's conduct is –
>
> (a) a fair report of a public act; or
>
> (b) a communication or dissemination of a matter that is subject to a defence of absolute privilege in proceedings for defamation; or
>
> (c) a public act done in good faith for –

(i) academic, artistic, scientific or research purposes; or

(ii) any purpose in the public interest.

If s 17(1) only extends to conduct targeting an individual, it is arguable that there is little point in extending sub-clause (c) to it as it is unlikely that conduct or a statement targeting an individual will amount to a public act done in good faith for any of the listed purposes. It is more likely to be a private act and will not be in the public interest.

However, in my opinion, this argument does not outweigh the arguments derived from the express words of s 17(1). The words of s 17(1) are clear on their face and should not be modified to make more sense of s 55. Hence the better interpretation is that s 17 is limited to acts and statements targeting a specific person and does not extend to acts or statements about a class of people. So it extends to statements targeting an individual because he is gay, but not to a statement attacking gays as a group. If this interpretation is correct, it means publications such as Archbishop Porteous's pamphlet and Rev Markham's blogs cannot be in breach of s 17 because they are general statements not targeting any individual. As a result, the Anti-Discrimination Commissioner has no jurisdiction to hear complaints such as that of Martine Delaney and Samuel Mazur.

If s 17 does extend to statements targeting a group rather than an individual, it is arguable that it is unconstitutional as a breach of the implied guarantee of freedom of political communication.[5] It is much less likely to breach the implied guarantee if it is limited to conduct targeting a specific individual not a group. As a rule, the courts favour a narrow interpretation of provisions limiting free speech to ensure consistency with the implied

---

5   *Sunol v Collier (no 2)* (2012) 289 ALR 128, [2012] NSWCA 44, [59]-[74] (Allsop P); Aroney, Nicholas 'The Constitutional (In)validity of Religious Vilification Laws: Implications for their Interpretation' (2006) 34(2) *Federal Law Review* 287; Forrester, Zimmerman and Finlay, above n3, 219-264.

guarantee.[6]

It is likely for these reasons that the courts will limit s 17 to the prohibition of conduct targeting an individual rather than a group. If there is any doubt about the scope of s 17, it should be amended to make it clear that it is limited to the targeting and bullying of individuals. That could be done by adding a subsection making it clear that it does not apply to broad statements which do not target particular individuals but are critical of a group. Its scope should also be extended so that it prevents targeting individuals on other grounds, such as religion. In the current climate, it is easy to imagine that some Muslims have been targets of harassment, ridicule and offensive comments because of their religion. They are as worthy of protection as are members of groups who share protected attributes, such as gays and lesbians.

When are we entitled to use the law to regulate or prohibit behaviour or speech which offends, insults, humiliates or ridicules another?

The argument about the interpretation of s 17 of the *Anti-Discrimination Act* raises the question of when society is entitled to use the law to regulate speech or conduct which offends another. If s 17 extends to general comments, it may impose significant limitations on freedom of speech, preventing a person making general statements which another is likely to find offensive, humiliating or insulting. This may silence some arguments on important social issues.

As discussed above, s 17 prohibits conduct which offends, humiliates, intimidates, insults or ridicules another on the basis of specified attributes, in circumstances where a reasonable person would have anticipated that the other person would be offended, humiliated, intimidated, insulted or ridi-

---

6   *Sunol v Collier (no 2)* (2012) 289 ALR 128, [2012] NSWCA 44, [59] (Allsop P.)

culed. The specified attributes include race, age, gender, sexual orientation, marital and relationship status, parental status, breastfeeding and disability, but significantly not political or religious affiliation and activity. Similarly, s 18 of the *Racial Discrimination Act 1975* (Cth) bans behaviour, including speech, which is reasonably likely, in all the circumstances, to offend, insult, humiliate or intimidate on grounds of race, colour or national or ethnic origin.

These provisions differ from provisions such as s 19 of the *Anti-Discrimination Act* (Tas) which bans the incitement of hatred, contempt or severe ridicule of persons on the basis of one of the specified attributes. Section 19 focuses on the impact of the conduct on others. It does not outlaw the mere expression of hatred or contempt, but bans behaviour which urges or encourages others to change their attitudes and behaviour towards the target person or group.[7] On the other hand, s 17 focuses on the impact of the behaviour on the target person or group. It is easier to justify the banning of the former rather than the latter because if conduct or a statement succeeds in changing peoples' attitudes towards the target group in a negative way, members of that group may suffer more discrimination and abuse in the future. Hence, the conduct may have a serious, negative impact on their lives.

Banning behaviour because it insults, offends or ridicules a person or a group of persons is more problematic because the behaviour in question may have no impact on the way others treat the target individual or group. Its impact on the lives of the target group is more limited, depending on their reaction to it, rather than the reaction of other members of the community. Hence conduct may be banned even though it did not lead to anyone other than the perpetrator treating the target individual or group badly.

---

7   *Sunol v Collier (No 2)* [2012] NSWCA 44, [26]-[28]. (Bathurst CJ); *Catch the Fire Ministries Inc & Ors v Islamic Council of Victoria Inc* [2006] VSCA 284 [14] (Nettle JA). The behaviour does not have to be intended to change the behaviour of others or to succeed in doing so; *Sunol v Collier (no 2)* [30-31] and [29] respectively.

Section 17 has been understood as allowing complaints against conduct which targets a group which has one of the specified attributes as well as against an individual who has that attribute. It is more difficult to justify a section which bans behaviour which targets a group rather than a single individual. There are good reasons for prohibiting behaviour targeting an individual, especially if it is persistent and/or if the perpetrator has a degree of power over the target, because in these circumstances, such behaviour is likely to amount to bullying. However, statements targeting a group rather than an individual can rarely if ever be regarded as bullying because it is hard for an individual to bully a group, many of whom he or she may not even know. Hence if s 17 does prohibit statements attacking a group for no other reason than that they are likely to be offensive to some or all members of that group, it would be more difficult to justify; the fact that conduct or statements are offensive, even grossly offensive, may not by itself justify legal prohibition.

Prohibitions must be enforced to be effective, typically by punishing those who breach the prohibition. Punishment causes suffering. Therefore, people should not be punished except for good reason, for example to prevent them harming others or for serious breaches of moral standards. Prohibiting conduct or punishing actions solely on the ground that they deeply offend others comes close to punishing statements and behaviour simply because many people strongly disagree with them. It is hard to justify punishing or disciplining people for no other reason than that many people strongly disagree with their behaviour. The fact that others disapprove of their conduct does not demonstrate that the behaviour in question harms individuals or society or that it is wrong. We should not punish people for refusing to comply with prevailing social standards whether or not those standards are right or wrong.

Defenders of s 17 may argue that the section is needed to impose proper standards of civility and respect on speech and conduct. For example, Mazur defended his complaints against Gee by arguing that:

> It was not my intention to shut down free speech or public debate.

> What I hoped for was that we would find some common ground that allowed David Gee and Cornerstone Church to express their views without causing harm to the LGBTI community.

> This kind of language has an obvious impact on LGBTQI people, in particular the staff working at shops near Speakers Corner who are quite literally forced to endure this kind of language, and many younger people on their way home from school, often caught off guard by the degrading way their sexuality is described at such volume.

> Shoppers are also subjected to this kind of language, as the volume carries directly into local stores disrupting their business.

> Members of the general public are expected to behave more respectfully than those expressing these insulting views....

> Apparently this does not extend to street preaching, which quite literally forces staff and customers to hear hateful religious rhetoric against their will.

If s 17 is to be justified as necessary to ensure proper standards of civility and respect in public debate, the section should specify the content of those standards rather than prohibiting conduct which is likely to cause offence. However, even if the section did lay down clear standards of civility, it is doubtful that it could be justified. People ought to be able to express their opinions and to do so in robust language, even if it shocks others. Mill argued that to silence an opinion, even if held by only one person, was unjustified because it robbed people of something of value, that opinion, whether it was right or wrong. We are not infallible and hence opinions, even when held by most people, are not necessarily correct. To silence an opinion robs us of the opportunity, if the opinion is correct, to have our error corrected, and if it is wrong, to refute the error and thus gain greater understanding of why our opinion is right:

If all mankind minus one, were of one opinion, and only one person were of the contrary opinion, mankind would be no more justified in silencing that one person, than he, if he had the power, would be justified in silencing mankind. Were an opinion a personal possession of no value except to the owner; if to be obstructed in the enjoyment of it were simply a private injury, it would make some difference whether the injury was inflicted only on a few persons or on many. But the peculiar evil of silencing the expression of an opinion is, that it is robbing the human race; posterity as well as the existing generation; those who dissent from the opinion, still more than those who hold it. If the opinion is right, they are deprived of the opportunity of exchanging error for truth: if wrong, they lose, what is almost as great a benefit, the clearer perception and livelier impression of truth, produced by its collision with error.[8]

In other areas, Mill concedes that we, and society as a whole, are justified in acting on our best judgment although, as we are fallible, that judgment may be incorrect. If we could not act on our best judgment, although we might be wrong, we could not act at all.[9] However, Mill denies that we are entitled to act on our best judgment to suppress opinions which we have concluded are incorrect, not because we may be wrong but because, if we suppress an opinion, we are denying ourselves the opportunity to hear the arguments against our opinion and to have our errors corrected.

We are entitled to make decisions in many areas of our lives, although those decisions may be wrong. But we must be prepared to defend those decisions if they are criticised. Defending our decisions against criticism helps us determine if our actions are justified. But people can only criticise and question if they are allowed to express their opinions freely. Hence it is wrong to suppress opinions which we are convinced are wrong or which we find offensive.[10]

---

8   John Stuart Mill *On Liberty* (Gutenberg,org) <http://www.gutenberg.org/files/34901/34901-h/34901-h.htm> Ch 2, 30-31.

9   Ibid 33

10   Ibid 34-40.

Mill conceded that statements could be suppressed where they harmed others, by for example, inciting violence against them or libelling them.[11] Supporters of provisions such as s 17 of the *Anti-Discrimination Act* have attempted to justify them on the grounds that the behaviour which the provisions target may cause serious harm unless controlled. They argue that provisions such as s 17 are justifiable because they aim to prevent conduct and statements which are offensive to groups traditionally discriminated against in order to protect them from the distress and trauma such conduct may cause. That this may be s 17's purpose is apparent when we examine the whole of the provision, which prohibits not only conduct which offends but also conduct which humiliates, intimidates, insults or ridicules. Is this a sufficient reason for the state's intervening to prevent such offensive statements given the strength of Mill's arguments against banning speech and opinions?

There is an objection to this defence of the provision. Some of the defined attributes are very broad, such as race, age, gender, marital and relationship status, so that every member of the population shares some of these attributes. Therefore, the section may appear to protect almost every person from some types of offence and ridicule, not just members of vulnerable minorities.

Although most people have at least one or more of the defined attributes, the section can still be seen as protecting vulnerable groups. Statements with respect to the race, gender or marital status of dominant or majority groups are much less likely to cause offence than statements with respect to minority or vulnerable groups. Therefore, although dominant and majority groups are protected, they will be able to avail themselves of that protection much less frequently than minority groups.

It is arguable that members of majority and dominant groups should have

---

11   This was particularly the case where the incitement was acted upon; see Mill's discussion of tyrannicide, above, (n 8), Ch 2, 102, fn 6.

no protection from statements which offend and members of vulnerable groups should not be completely immune from statements which shock and offend. Artists and others often engage in outrageous conduct which is designed to offend. They do so in order to challenge existing assumptions and attitudes. As reasonable people they not only anticipate but intend that their conduct will cause offence. Their conduct may be prohibited under s 17 if it targets people with one of the attributes which that section lists, even if those people belonged to a majority or dominant group.

Besides, it may not be possible to express deeply held convictions on controversial matters of religion and politics without offending some people. For example, the supporter of same sex marriage and same sex equality may find the mere expression of opposition to same sex marriage or of the view that same sex sex is wrong deeply offensive.[12]

Section 55 of the Act recognises that sometimes we are justified in shocking and offending. As noted above, it exempts public acts done in good faith for academic, artistic, scientific or research purposes, or for any purpose in the public interest from the scope of s 17(1). The scope of this section was not clarified in the Porteous, Markham and Gee cases. Much will depend upon how the terms 'good faith' and 'in the public interest' are defined. If defined broadly, they could greatly reduce the impact of s 17 on free speech, allowing considerable scope for statements and conduct designed to shock and offend.

Courts and Tribunals have differed in their interpretation of good faith requirements in this and other legislation. In *Delaney v Liberal Party of Australia (Tas)*,[13] the Tasmanian Anti-Discrimination Tribunal defined good faith

---

12   Kurti 'The Forgotten freedom: Threats to religious freedom in Australia' CIS Policy monograph 139,< https://www.cis.org.au/publications/policy-monographs/the-forgotten-freedom-threats-to-religious-liberty-in-australia/>, 17-18.

13   [2008] TASADT 2

broadly, holding that a statement was made in good faith if made without spite, ill will or other improper motive. Similarly, Nettle JA of the Victorian Supreme Court of Appeal held in *Catch the Fire Ministries Inc & Ors v Islamic Council of Victoria Inc* that a statement was made in good faith for a religious purpose if made with the subjectively honest belief that it was necessary or desirable to achieve that purpose.[14] His interpretation was adopted by Bathurst CJ of the NSW CA in *Sunol v Collier (no 2)*.[15] In that case, Allsop P also adopted a broad interpretation, stating that good faith statements could be trenchant, robust, passionate, indecorous, even rancorous.[16]

If these interpretations were adopted, the good faith requirement would not impose major limitations on the protection which s 55 gives to public speech and conduct. However, in *Bropho v Human Rights and Equal Opportunity Commission*,[17] French and Lee JJ adopted a narrower interpretation of the good faith requirement in s 18D of the *Racial Discrimination Act* (Cth), a provision which is similar to s 55 of the Tasmanian Act. They held that a person acts in good faith for the purposes of s 18D if they are honest and 'has taken a conscientious approach to advancing the exercising of that freedom [freedom of speech and expression which s 18D protects] in a way that is designed to minimise the offence or insult, humiliation or intimidation suffered by people affected by it.'[18]

The approach of French and Lee JJ, imposing a good faith requirement to minimise the offence, insult or humiliation caused by an exercise of free speech, greatly limits the right to offend or shock. They justified their approach by arguing that the seriousness of the harm which s 18D of the *Racial Discrimination Act* (Cth) and, by parity of reasoning, s 17 of the *An-*

---

14   [2006] VSCA 284 [92]; (2006) 15 VR 207, 240.
15   (2012) 289 ALR 128, 137; [2012] NSWCA 44, [36-41].
16   Ibid [71].
17   (2004) 135 FCR 105; [2004] FCAFC 16.
18   Ibid, [102] per French J; see also [144] per Lee J.

ti-Discrimination Act (Tas) are designed to prevent, warrants interpreting good faith as requiring the speaker to minimise the harm their statements may cause, rather than mere honesty.[19]

Even if we concede that statements which offend can cause harm, there are strong arguments suggesting that normally the harm caused is insufficient to warrant prohibition. Intimidation and perhaps humiliation are different in that the state ought to protect people from intimidating and humiliating conduct. Such conduct causes fear and people have a genuine interest in not being subject to threats and other intimidating behaviour which puts them in fear of violence or other harm.

Behaviour harms another when it interferes with that person's personal, family, property, reputation and other important interests. In considering whether behaviour which offends, ridicules, humiliates or insults interferes with genuine interests which the law ought to protect, we need to distinguish between conduct offending, ridiculing, humiliating or insulting an individual and similar conduct aimed at a class of people. It may, for reasons given above, be that prohibition of such conduct aimed at an individual is justified on the grounds that it prevents bullying, especially where there is an imbalance of power in favour of the person engaged in the conduct in question. However, the prohibition of behaviour and speech offensive to a class cannot be justified on the grounds that it is necessary to prevent bullying because it is difficult if not impossible to bully a class.

Where the target of the conduct in question is a class of people, the conduct is likely to be public conduct. For example, Archbishop Porteous published the pamphlet which caused offence to Ms Delaney. If the conduct is public, it may be designed to influence the public at large as much as the group which it targets. Hence, it could be seen as shading into conduct of the type which is prohibited under s 19, conduct inciting hatred or con-

---

19   Ibid [94-102] (French J) and [138] (Lee J).

tempt for a group or severely ridiculing that group. As pointed out above, people have an interest in being protected from conduct which is calculated to influence the public to treat them badly, because that conduct may lead to members of the public discriminating against them. Lee J adopted such a justification for a broad interpretation of the good faith requirement in *Bropho*, where he stated:

> Humiliation or intimidation involves more than destruction of self-perception or self-esteem of a person. It affects others in the community by lowering their regard for, and demeaning the worthiness of, the person, or persons, subjected to that conduct. It stimulates contempt or hostility between groups of people within the community and it is the intent of the Act that such socially corrosive conduct be controlled.[20]

In my opinion, it is hard to justify section 17 on this ground for a number of reasons. Firstly, if section 17 is aimed at preventing conduct similar to that prohibited by section 19, that is conduct designed to influence the attitudes of the public at large, it makes section 19 redundant. Section 17 is broader than section 19 but would cover the same ground in that conduct inciting hatred and contempt is likely to offend, insult, ridicule, and humiliate.

More importantly, section 19 strikes the right balance between freedom of speech and the right of groups not to be subjected to vilification. The expression of hatred and contempt does not by itself fall within the prohibition imposed by sections such as section 19.[21] These provisions prohibit urging or encouraging others to hate because if successful, urging others to hate will have a serious, detrimental impact on the lives of the target group. Merely holding people up to ridicule or humiliating them without inciting hatred or contempt does not have the same consequences. Ridiculing and humiliating people can be an effective way of inciting hatred and contempt.

---

20   Ibid [138]

21   *Sunol v Collier (No 2)* n 7, [26]-[28]. (Bathurst CJ); *Catch the Fire Ministries Inc & Ors v Islamic Council of Victoria Inc* n 7, [14] (Nettle JA).

Where that is the case, the ridiculing and humiliating conduct is a breach of section 19 as well as section 17.

Besides, private as well as public behaviour may humiliate and intimidate. Although conduct designed to offend or humiliate a group or class is often public, when it targets an individual it may be private so that no one but the person it targets may be aware of it. And it may be easy to humiliate or intimidate a group through social media and in other ways so that no one outside the group is aware of what has happened.

Section 17 appears to have a different rationale. It appears to prohibit behaviour because of its likely effect on the target group, not because of its effect on the public at large. Hence, behaviour which offends, insults, ridicules and humiliates is prohibited regardless of its impact on the general public. Does it cause sufficient harm to the interests of the target group to justify its prohibition?

When we offend, we cause another or others to feel annoyed, distressed, upset, or resentful. These feelings are the result of the other person's reaction to our conduct. Should the state intervene because this reaction is predictable? Especially where the target group is a vulnerable minority who have in the past been subject to discrimination and mistreatment?

In *On Liberty*, John Stuart Mill argued that we were not justified in using the law to enforce prevailing standards or even to make people better. Instead, he argued that we were only entitled to use the law to prevent people causing harm to others.[22] Because we live in a society, many of our actions can harm others. For example, if we make offensive comments, they may distress others. That distress is a real harm as it reduces their happiness and wellbeing. But Mill argued that it is not enough that our actions may harm others; the harm has to be 'direct' before the law may intervene. The basic meaning of 'direct' contrasts behaviour which has a direct impact on others

---

22   Mill (n 8), 17-18.

such as an attack on their person or property with behaviour which has an indirect effect on them by means of its impact on the actor or on others. So drunkenness may have an indirect impact on others by means of its impact on the drunkard.[23]

Mill limited cases in which the law could justifiably intervene to cases of direct harm because he valued personal autonomy and wanted to maximise individual liberty and minimise social and state-imposed limits on people's freedom.[24] He feared that if the law could be used to prevent behaviour which indirectly harmed others, it could be used to enslave people. For example, if I am always drunk, my drunkenness may harm the rest of society by making me unproductive and dependent. But this harm is indirect and should fall outside the control of the law because the only effective remedy, stopping my getting drunk, requires that society controls my life.[25]

Mill did not define 'direct harm', but developed the idea by examples. Hence it is not completely clear what he meant. But it is clear that the harm caused by offending others is not direct harm unless we target others and deliberately set out to offend them. Mill would not have denied that offending others causes harm because those offended may suffer real distress. He would have denied that the harm was direct unless intended because it was as much the result of the offended person's reaction to the offensive conduct as it was the result of the offensive conduct itself.[26] Some offended people may be merely annoyed, others may be greatly distressed and even traumatised. If we are legally responsible for the reactions of others, especially members of the public whom we do not know, to our statements and conduct, we are likely to be very careful in what we do and say. In particular, we are less likely to depart from accepted standards of behaviour if members of the public can hold us legally accountable for the offence our behaviour may cause

---

23   Ibid 21-2.
24   Ibid Ch 3, 'On Individuality as one of the Elements of Well-Being'.
25   Ibid 168-70
26   Ibid 158-63.

them. Holding people legally accountable to strangers for the offence they cause is a way of implementing the conformity which Mill feared.

Section 17 attempts to meet some of these objections by introducing a degree of objectivity into the test. Under the section, a person is not liable for offending an unknown other whose reactions they could not predict, but is only liable if 'a reasonable person, having regard to all the circumstances, would have anticipated that the other person would be offended, humiliated, intimidated, insulted or ridiculed'. Introducing the reasonable person test is not sufficient in my opinion to bring the harm within the category of direct harm. It limits the scope of the section to cases in which offence is predictable but not to cases in which the offence causes real harm such as great distress or trauma rather than minimal harm or mere annoyance. That is not sufficient to change the nature of offence so that it falls within the category of direct harm.

To limit s 17 to cases of direct harm, the behaviour from which the section provides protection needs to more be clearly defined so as to provide the protection which the vulnerable need and no more. For example, it could be limited to conduct and speech likely to cause emotional and/or psychological trauma to members of the vulnerable groups in question. That would both reduce its impact on freedom of speech and expression and make it clear that it is designed to protect the vulnerable rather than impose a wide ranging limitation on freedom of expression.

The problems in identifying the harm which s 17 prevents by prohibiting the giving of offence are so great that they lead to the conclusion that it cannot be justified as a provision designed to protect defined classes of people from certain types of harm. Other justifications suggest themselves. The first is that it is designed to impose state sanctioned standards of politeness and civility, not because departing from these standards causes identifiable harm but because the standards are right. In other words, the provision is a state sanctioned attempt to raise standards of behaviour and to make people better.

Many liberal political philosophers object in principle to state sanctioned attempts to make people better. Like Mill, they argue that the role of the state is to prevent people harming each other, or like Rawls, they argue that the state's sole concern should be justice and that standards of good and bad, and right and wrong are matters of private choice.[27] Such liberals favour personal autonomy and individual liberty over state sanctioned attempts to make people better, no matter how enlightened.

Leaving aside issues of individual freedom and personal autonomy, the state could only be justified in imposing standards of politeness and civility if it is morally wrong to engage in conduct which offends others. In my opinion, this cannot be accepted as a general proposition. Sometimes it is right to point out to others that what they are proposing to do is wrong or that their beliefs are incorrect, even if in doing so we cause offence. So we need to qualify the proposition to become it is wrong to engage in conduct which offends others without good reason.

It is arguable that s 55 limits s 17 to cases in which a person gives offence without any good reason. Section 55, as noted above, exempts public acts done in good faith for academic, artistic, scientific or research purposes or for any purpose in the public interest, from the scope of s 17(1). Much depends on how broadly the terms 'good faith'[28] and 'purpose in the public interest' are interpreted. If they are interpreted so as to permit, among other things, informing the public of our views whether those views are correct or popular or encouraging the public to adopt standards which may not be popular, they may limit the scope of s 17(1) to giving offence without good

---

27   John Rawls *A Theory of Justice Revised Edition* (Harvard University Press Cambridge Mass 1999) 27-8, 394-5.

28   The interpretation of 'good faith' was discussed above, text accompanying fn 12-18.

reason. If they are interpreted in this way, they would exclude the cases of Archbishop Porteous, Rev Markham and Dr Gee from the scope of s 17 because those were cases of informing the public of the views of their churches and or encouraging people to change their lives and live in accord with those standards.

Even if s 55 does limit s 17 to cases in which a person offends without good reason, section 17 remains difficult to justify. We may agree that to offend without good reason is wrong, in that it is rude and disrespectful. However, that is not sufficient to justify state intervention. If the state is justified in acting as a censor of good manners, with a brief to outlaw rude and disrespectful behaviour, there will be few aspects of our lives outside its control.

Rude, insulting and offensive behaviour may annoy but often does not cause any serious harm. It has long been recognised as a normal part of public debate. Attempts to prohibit it on grounds of public interest in order to implement standards of civility may fall foul of the constitutional guarantee of political communication.[29] Unless it causes serious harm, it is not a serious enough wrong to warrant prohibition and punishment. Hence, the argument that the state is justified in prohibiting conduct causing offence to groups who may be vulnerable because it is wrong to do so does not justify s 17.

To sum up, there is no coherent justification for s 17 if it prohibits conduct targeting groups rather than individuals. It imposes major restrictions on personal autonomy and individual liberty, especially on freedom of speech and expression. Given the strength of Mill's arguments for allowing freedom of speech and expression it requires a strong justification. But the suggested justifications are flawed and unacceptable. It is not justified as

---

29   *Coleman v Power* (2004) 220 CLR 1; 209 ALR 182; [2004] HCA 39, [102]-[105] (McHugh J); [197-9] (Gummow and Hayne JJ): [237]-[239] (Kirby J).

an attempt by the state to impose morally acceptable standards of politeness and civility in public debate because it is not always morally wrong to offend others and because even gratuitous insults should be permitted unless they cause harm. Nor is it justified as protecting vulnerable groups from the harm caused by offensive and insulting language and conduct much of which may only annoy but does not cause serious harm. Causing offence is too low a threshold for intervention and the section should be limited to causing deep distress or psychological trauma.

Why is the state intervening now?

Given that s 17 is difficult to justify, why is there such support for it? Firstly, Mill's defence of liberty seems to have fallen out of favour. It was based on an optimistic view of human nature and a belief in progress which are no longer fashionable. Secondly, we seem to have forgotten the important insight that behaviour is not wrong because it offends but may offend because it is wrong.

But there are two more profound social changes which have opened the door to legislation such as s 17. The first is the growth in moral relativism, especially with respect to sex and sexual behaviour. The second, which is related, is a decline in reliance on conscience as a way of controlling social behaviour.

Moral relativism with respect to sex and sexuality played a relatively minor role in the 20th century debates about the legalisation of homosexual sex between consenting adults. Instead, those who argued for law reform argued that crime had to be distinguished from immorality or sin. It was not the role of the state to stop people from immoral or sinful acts or to force them to be good. The role of the state was to protect others from violent, fraudulent and dishonest behaviour – crimes which caused harm to a person or to their property – rather than to make people good. Hence, it was consistent to argue that same sex sex was morally wrong but should not be a crime because it did not harm others sufficiently.[30]

Moral relativism

Today, there is growing moral relativism in general and especially in relation to sex and sexuality. According to the moral relativist, behaviour, especially sexual behaviour, is neither right nor wrong. As there is no right or wrong, people are free to do as they choose, at least if there is no fraud or violence and everyone is consenting. It follows that there is no moral basis for criticising anyone's choice. Nor is there any basis for discriminating or marginalising people because their sexual or other choices are seen as wrong:

> the mark of a good citizen of the liberal state is no longer the display of personal conviction but, rather, the deliberate and even ostentatious display of what might pass for open-mindedness—one that is, in reality, a form of moralistic relativism concerned with elevating the rights and interests of any who are perceived to be victims of discriminatory or marginalising behaviour.[31]

Moral relativism and conscience

The growth of moral relativism has led to less reliance on conscience as means of social control. Conscience, acting on moral principle, assumes the possibility of moral argument about what is right and wrong. Appeals to conscience, which play an important role in societies where conscience is relied on as a means of social control, are a way of persuading people to change their mind and to act in accordance with moral principles. But appeals to conscience assume a degree of moral objectivity. They cannot

---

30   HLA Hart *Law Liberty and Morality* (OUP 1963). The whole book is an elaboration of this distinction. Wollheim 'Crime, Sin and Mr Justice Devlin' *Encounter* 1959, 34-40 <https://nakulkrishna.files.wordpress.com/2018/10/richard-wollheim-crime-justice-and-mr-devlin.pdf>.

31   Kurti (n 12), 3-4.

work in a society which assumes moral relativism, because in such a society it is agreed that there are no standards of right and wrong to which one can appeal.

Conscience as a means of social control has a price. Conscience, acting on moral principle, may lead people to do things we disagree with, or to claim exemption from social obligations - eg Quakers and military service. Because we do not all agree on every question of moral principle, using conscience as a means of social control requires permitting a degree of autonomy to the individual conscience and tolerating decisions with which we disagree. If we do not permit a degree of autonomy to the individual conscience and do not tolerate decisions based on moral principles with which we disagree, we cannot expect people to use their consciences or to act on moral principle to control their behaviour.

For the moral relativist, the person who acts on conscience is not acting on moral principle but simply asserting their preferences based more on emotion than reason. So the person who as a matter of moral principle condemns same sex acts or opposes same sex marriage is simply homophobic; they have no argument and are acting on feelings of distaste and dislike or learned prejudices.

The moral relativist sees no good reason for using conscience as means of social control. As there are no objective moral principles, the conscientious objector's appeal to moral principle has no rational foundation. Hence, the growth of relativism has led to a decline in reliance on conscience as means of social control. As a result, there is a growing tendency to reject claims of conscience with which we disagree. For example, some of the new Abortion Acts give little recognition to the claims of conscience on doctors with a conscientious objection to abortion. These Acts only recognise claims of conscience to the extent that they do not force doctors with a conscientious objection to abortion to perform abortions. However, that recognition is limited in that some of the Acts impose a duty on the doctor who is a conscientious objector to be a party to abortion by requiring them to provide information which will enable the patient to find a doctor who has no such objection, or to refer the patient to such a doctor or to transfer the patient's care to such a doctor.[32]

The decline in reliance on conscience as a means of social control requires the adoption of other means of social control. Hence, there is a growing reliance on shaming and publicly humiliating those who disagree with the prevailing relativism to force them to comply. Societies which rely on conscience as a means of social control appeal to moral arguments to persuade people to act in accordance with the demands of conscience. As we move away from conscience, we rely less on argument and more on abusive terms to shame and humiliate persons who take a stand on conscience against the prevailing relativism. Hence there is typically no attempt to persuade people who believe that homosexual behaviour is immoral that they are wrong. Instead they are abused and shamed as homophobic whether that is true or not.

Relativism and inclusion

The current emphasis on inclusion is a result of the growth of moral relativism. According to the relativist, our moral views are merely preferences.

---

32   The Acts vary in their approach, some imposing a duty to refer, others a duty to provide information and others a duty to transfer the patient to another doctor. The NSW Act imposes a duty to provide information or to transfer care of the patient to another doctor; *Abortion Law Reform Act 2019* s 9(3). In Victoria and the Northern Territory, the Act imposes a duty to refer to a doctor who does not have a conscientious objection to abortion; *Abortion Law Reform Act 2008*, s 8(1) and the *Termination of Pregnancy Law Reform Act 2017*, s 11(2)(b) respectively. The Queensland Act imposes a duty to refer the patient to a doctor who does not have a conscientious objection to abortion or to transfer care of the patient to such a doctor; *Termination of Pregnancy Act 2018*, s 8. The Tasmanian Act goes further than the others in recognising the claims of conscience, requiring the doctor with a conscientious objection 'to provide the woman with a list of prescribed health services from which the woman may seek advice, information or counselling on the full range of pregnancy options'; *Reproductive Health (Access to Terminations) Act 2017*, s 7.

We need to recognise that and stop relying on them to condemn others whose preferences differ. Once we realise that we have no reason for condemning others whose behaviour and values differ from ours, we are able to see that we have no reason for excluding them. Social peace and harmony, and perhaps justice, requires inclusion.

Some religious people, such as Israel Folau, no doubt believe that they have been excluded and punished in the name of inclusion for expressing their beliefs that some sexual or other behaviour is wrong. Such people may conclude that the new inclusiveness is in fact discriminatory, including those who adopt the new relativism and excluding those who do not for no reason other than dislike.

Although there is some truth in this conclusion, it is not the whole truth. There is some logic behind the tendency of the new inclusiveness to exclude those, such as religious people, with strong moral views especially in the area of sexuality and the body. Inclusion tends to exclude those with strong views of right and wrong because they are seen as wrong and as in the wrong in that they fail to understand that their moral views are merely preferences. Hence, if they are critical of the behaviour of others, they are acting on the basis of personal dislike. If they encourage others to change their behaviour, or, if, like Israel Folau, they warn them of the coming judgment of God, they are accused of wanting to impose their preferences on others.

From the perspective of the new inclusiveness and the moral relativism which drives it, the behaviour of those who voice strong moral views about the behaviour of others is intolerant, disrespectful, and unjustifiable:

> Intolerance .... must be understood to be any questioning or contradicting the view that all opinions are equal in value, that all worldviews have equal worth, that all stances are equally valid. To question such postmodern axioms is by definition intolerant. For such questioning there is no tolerance whatsoever, for it is classed as intolerance and

must therefore be condemned. It has become the supreme vice.[33]

By criticising others without any justification, we show a lack of respect for them and their choices. That lack of respect can lead to arguments and threaten social peace. If the critics refuse to remain silent, they may need to be coerced.

Public shaming as a means of social control

The growth of relativism and the corresponding decline in reliance on conscience as a means of social control have necessitated the development of other means of social control. Without new means of social control, the growing relativism may lead to an increase in anti-social behaviour. In a relativist social world, people cannot be relied on to act in accordance with conscience. If, as relativism claims, actions are neither right nor wrong, people have no good reason for not pursuing their own desires and self interest, even at the expense of others and of social harmony. Hence, people are less likely to restrain themselves.

Society may fall into chaos if people accept no standards of behaviour, no limits on their actions. The relativist is committed to the view that no action is inherently right or wrong, but, to prevent chaos, has to settle on some standards of acceptable behaviour. Hence, he or she tends to fall back on consensus. In a relativist social world, consensus about what is acceptable rather than moral rightness becomes the test by which behaviour is evaluated.

Because people are less likely to restrain themselves in a relativist social world, the coercive role of society and of the state necessarily grows. As conscience can no longer be relied on to motivate people to do what is right, they must be shamed into acting in socially acceptable ways. In this context,

33   Donald Carson, The Intolerance of Tolerance (William B Eedermans Publishing, Grand Rapids, Michigan/Cambridge UK, 2012) 12.

shame may be defined as the emotion a person feels when publicly named and disgraced for breaching important social norms. Families may also feel shame when a family member is named and disgraced for such breaches.

As conscience has become less important as a means of social control, the public shaming of people for breaching acceptable standards has become more important as a means of emphasising the importance of those standards and as a means of social control. Public confessions and apologies by prominent people who have been caught breaking agreed social norms have become an established method of reinforcing accepted standards of behaviour and an accepted means of social control.[34] Where there has been no confession, often because the person concerned feels no need to apologise, publicly accepted standards have been enforced by publicly outing and naming the person, for example as a homophobe.

The government is playing an important role in the public shaming of people who do not comply with accepted standards of behaviour through institutions such as Anti-Discrimination Tribunals. These Tribunals have amongst other powers, the power to order a party to retract their statements or behaviour and to apologise.[35] This is an attempt to use the coercive

---

34   Outstanding recent examples include the public apologies of disgraced Australian cricket captain and vice-captain, Steven Smith and David Warner, for ball tampering; 'Tearful Steve Smith apologises for ball-tampering scandal' (ITV News YouTube Mar 29, 2018) <https://www.youtube.com/watch?v=vWiSdIS-JsuA> and 'David Warner's tearful apology' (ESPNcricinfo YouTube March 31, 2018) <https://www.youtube.com/watch?v=lT0BUkpt4as> respectively. There are striking parallels between these confessions and apologies and those of disgraced Communist party officials during the Cultural Revolution in China, when public shaming was used as a means of reinforcing accepted standards and of maintaining social control. Similar parallels may be drawn between attempts to name and shame people as homophobic and the name calling which accompanied the public shaming of disgraced officials during the Cultural Revolution. I point to the parallels not to suggest that we currently face anything as orchestrated as the Cultural Revolution but merely to point out that these types of behaviour tend to accompany the use of shaming as a means of social control.

35   *Anti-Discrimination Act 1977* (NSW) s 108(2)(d); *Anti-Discrimination Act 1991* (QLD) s 209(1)(d) and (e); Anti-*Discrimination Act 1998* (Tas) s 92; *Anti-Discrimination Act 1992* (NT) s 89. Refusal to apologise and retract can lead to a fine,

powers of the state to force those who do not accept the new relativism to publicly admit the error of their ways and to apologise for their behaviour.

Relativism and freedom of religion and conscience

I am not optimistic about continued social recognition of freedom of religion and conscience. The two are closely related, in that historically the two developed in tandem, people claiming the right to worship God as their consciences dictated. It is likely that as conscience declines as a means of social control with growing relativism, the perceived importance of freedom of religion will decline also.

That decline will accelerate as society becomes more secular. When most people were committed to one religion or another, most people valued freedom of religion. They understood that if freedom of religion were lost, they might lose the right to worship God as they saw fit. Now that religious commitment is declining, most people will lose nothing of personal significance if freedom of religion is lost. Although they may support freedom of religion in principle, they are less likely to see it as something worth fighting for than in the past.

At the same time, opposition to freedom of religion and freedom of conscience is growing. Its opponents characterise it as freedom to discriminate and to persecute minority groups, especially in the area of provision of services. The provider of a service may have a religious or moral objection to providing a particular service or to providing it to members of a particular group. For example, a medical practitioner may have a conscientious objection to participating in abortion or a baker may have a conscientious objection to the provision of a wedding cake for a same sex marriage. It is easy to portray a conscientious refusal to provide the service as unreason-

---

and in NSW to an order for compensation, s 108(7).

able discrimination.[36]

It is beyond the scope of this paper to analyse all the issues surrounding freedom of religion and conscience and discrimination. The issues are complex and as the submissions on the federal government's religious freedom bill show, there are no easy answers. However, it is necessary to reiterate that the price of using conscience as a means of social control is that we need to tolerate decisions with which we profoundly disagree. People disagree on moral and religious issues so that if we give weight to conscience we must be prepared to respect decisions and conduct which we think are wrong.

Conclusion

Although it is not costless, we need to defend freedom of conscience because it undermines the dignity of the individual to deny it and to enforce conformity. Otherwise we risk forcing people to be complicit in actions which they believe to be profoundly immoral. Some of the areas where there is a tendency to deny claims of conscience, such as abortion and gender realignment, raise complex moral issues about the sanctity of human life and the limits of personal autonomy. We would be arrogant and foolish to act as if we were certain that we had the right answer on these issues.

Allowing freedom of conscience and of religion encourage free thinking and the criticism of current attitudes and behaviour. We need to encourage criticism of current attitudes and behaviour, no matter how unpalatable. Without it, society will become stagnant and self satisfied. If s 17 of the *Anti-Discrimination Act* (Tas) extends beyond targeting individuals to prohib-

---

36   See for example Van Badham 'The freedom of religion bill has nothing to do with religion – it excludes and it traumatises' *The Guardian Australia Edition* Wed 12 Feb 2020. For a detailed analysis of the ways in which expanding the protection of freedom of religion and freedom of conscience may permit discrimination in the name of religion, see the submission of the Australian Human Rights Commission on the Religious Freedom Bills, 27 September 2019 <human rights.gov.au>.

it general comment which some people find offensive, it imposes unacceptable constraints on public comment and criticism and should be amended to limit it to conduct causing real harm or repealed.

Bibliography

Abortion Law Reform Act 2019 (NSW).

Abortion Law Reform Act 2008, (Vic).

Anti-Discrimination Act 1977 (NSW).

Anti-Discrimination Act 1992 (NT).

Anti-Discrimination Act 1991 (Qld).

Anti-Discrimination Act 1998 (Tas).

Aroney, Nicholas 'The Constitutional (In)validity of Religious Vilification Laws: Implications for their Interpretation' (2006) 34(2) *Federal Law Review* 287.

Bropho v Human Rights and Equal Opportunity Commission (2004) 135 FCR 105; [2004] FCAFC 16.

Carson, Donald, *The Intolerance of Tolerance* (William B Eedermans Publishing, Grand Rapids, Michigan/Cambridge UK, 2012).

Catch the Fire Ministries Inc & Ors v Islamic Council of Victoria Inc (2006) 15 VR 207, [2006] VSCA 284.

Coleman v Power (2004) 220 CLR 1; 209 ALR 182; [2004] HCA 39.

'Complaint Withdrawn but the Emperor is Still Naked' *Tasmanian Times* posted July 2 2018 <https://tasmaniantimes.com/2018/07/complaint-withdrawn-but-the-emperor-is-still-naked/>.

'David Warner's tearful apology' (ESPNcricinfo YouTube March 31, 2018) <https://www.youtube.com/watch?v=lT0BUkpt4as>.

Delaney v Liberal Party of Australia (Tas) [2008] TASADT 2.

Forrester, Zimmerman and Finlay, 'An Opportunity Missed? A Constitutional Analysis of Proposed Reforms to Tasmania's "Hate Speech" Laws' (2016) 7 *Western Australian Jurist* 214, 264-275.

Hart, HLA, *Law Liberty and Morality* (OUP 1963).

Kurti, Peter, 'The Forgotten freedom: Threats to religious freedom in Australia'

CIS Policy monograph 139, < https://www.cis.org.au/publications/policy-monographs/the-forgotten-freedom-threats-to-religious-liberty-in-australia/>.

Mill, John Stuart, *On Liberty* (Gutenberg,org) < http://www.gutenberg.org/files/34901/34901-h/34901-h.htm>.

Rawls, John, *A Theory of Justice Revised Edition* (Harvard University Press Cambridge Mass 1999).

Reproductive Health (Access to Terminations) Act 2017 (Tas).

Second interim Report: freedom of religion and belief, the Australian experience Ch 3 'The Domestic Experience of Freedom of Religion and Belief' 3.37-45; <https://www.aph.gov.au/Parliamentary_Business/Committees/Joint/Foreign_Affairs_Defence_and_Trade/Freedomofreligion/Second_Interim_Report>.

Submission 405 to the Joint Standing Committee on Defence, Foreign Affairs and Trade, Inquiry into status of the the human right to freedom of religion or belief, dot point 2, <https://www.aph.gov.au/DocumentStore.ashx?id=0aa782a1-08f9-4156-8807-e67e65a5a17c&subId=612045>.

Submission of the Australian Human Rights Commission on the Religious Freedom Bills, 27 September 2019 < https://humanrights.gov.au/our-work/legal/submission/religious-freedom-bills>.

Sunol v Collier (no 2) (2012) 289 ALR 128, [2012] NSWCA 44.

'Tearful Steve Smith apologises for ball-tampering scandal' (ITV News YouTube Mar 29, 2018) < https://www.youtube.com/watch?v=vWiSdISJsuA>.

Termination of Pregnancy Act 2018 (Qld).

Termination of Pregnancy Law Reform Act 2017, (NT).

Van Badham 'The freedom of religion bill has nothing to do with religion - it excludes and it traumatises' *The Guardian Australia Edition* Wed 12 Feb 2020, <https://www.theguardian.com/commentisfree/2020/feb/12/the-religious-freedom-bill-has-nothing-to-do-with-religion-it-excludes-and-it-traumatises>.

Wollheim 'Crime, Sin and Mr Justice Devlin' *Encounter* 1959, 34-40; < https://nakulkrishna.files.wordpress.com/2018/10/richard-wollheim-crime-justice-and-mr-devlin.pdf>.

6

WHAT ON EARTH DOES AUSTRALIA THINK OF RELIGIOUS FREEDOM? NOT VERY INCLUSIVE

Paul Taylor

Abstract

In some societies, religion is criticised as fractional or non-inclusive. The *International Covenant on Civil and Political Rights* (*ICCPR*) demands protection for freedom of religion (whether the religion in question is popular or not) among a suite of provisions which promote individual and collective self-identity, self-autonomy, and self-expression, and protect against attribute-based discrimination. It assumes and supports difference. When protection is claimed for freedom of religion in Australia to the standards of the *ICCPR*, concerns are sometimes expressed that this is a quest to privilege that freedom, or to position it so that it trumps other rights. This paper briefly explores these issues by reference to: the fundamental dignity of the human person and importance of equality; the parity of rights; the scope and limits of rights; and certain aspects of domestic implementation. The *ICCPR* provides an integrated scheme of protection for fundamental rights, to be enjoyed concurrently. Religious liberty, like other rights, supports personal and collective autonomy without undue interference. Yet some forms of contemporary opposition to freedom of religion reflect a view that is not inclusive, and fail to give recognition to the co-existence of rights that is intended under the *ICCPR* and related UN instruments.

Introduction

In the debate which has attended successive inquiries and legislative proposals on freedom of religion, those who urge greater protection for religious freedom are represented as non-inclusive. This is driven in part by the framework of Australian anti-discrimination legislation, which addresses serious ills, in a remedial way, and raises the expectation that exceptions such as those based on freedom of religion should not be tolerated. It has also frequently been asserted (quite rightly) that no single human right occupies a position of superiority over others, and (wrongly) that those who advocate freedom of religion to the standards of the *International Covenant on Civil and Political Rights* (*ICCPR*) are unjustifiably urging that freedom of religion should trump other rights. This article aims to explain why it is hard to make the case for improved protection of freedom of religion in Australia to Article 18 standards but why that case nevertheless needs to be put. It commends the *ICCPR* as a model for greater inclusiveness through the comprehensive enjoyment by everyone of all human rights. This may be achieved partly by better domestic implementation of *ICCPR* obligations, and broader public acceptance that this does not entail subtraction from other rights.

1 The fundamental dignity of the human person and the importance of equality

It is important to redress any mistaken belief that principles of equality and anti-discrimination are the enemies of religious freedom.

It is worth reflecting for a moment on the profound changes inaugurated by the *Universal Declaration* in 1948, and in binding form by the *ICCPR* in 1966 when establishing principles of equality and non-discrimination. Until then human rights systems were distinctive in creating different classes of rights holder, and defining rights or lack of them according to that style of classification. The Persians may have been the first to attempt a human rights code under Cyrus the Great, marking the end of the Babylonian exile by settling the terms which allowed Jewish captives to return home (a combination of freedom of religion and freedom of movement). Differentiation between categories of rights holders was characteristic of codes and charters that followed, including the *ius civis* in Roman law which defined the rights of Roman citizenry depending on whether they were free or servile. Even France's *Declaration of the Rights of Man and Citizen* recognised political rights only for men who paid taxes over a given amount. Slavery continued in the US unaffected by the *Declaration of Independence* in spite of proclaiming that "all men are created equal," and the enfranchisement of women was not achieved until almost the dawn of the UN era. The recasting of rights on the foundational principles of equality and non-discrimination represents a landmark established by the *Universal Declaration* and built upon by the *ICCPR*, which should not be underestimated. The *ICCPR* establishes in binding form the guarantees which each Contracting State is, according to Article 2(1), to "respect and to ensure to *all individuals*... within its territory and subject to its jurisdiction...without distinction of any kind, such as race, colour, sex, language, religion, political or other opinion, national or social origin, property, birth or other status". Article 2(1) only secures protection against status-based discrimination in the enjoyment of the rights set out in the *ICCPR*. Article 26, however, is autonomous and concerns distinctions which relate either to equality before the law, or the equal protection of the law, where the subject of that protection may extend to matters not covered by the *ICCPR*. Discrimination under both Articles 2 and 26 have one feature in common, particularly well described by the Italian delegate

Francesco Capotorti during the drafting of the *ICCPR*, when explaining that "there were cases in which the law was justified in making distinctions between individuals or groups, but the purpose of the article was to prohibit discrimination, in the sense of unfavourable and odious distinctions which lacked any objective or reasonable basis."[1]

The standard test under the *ICCPR* is whether the differentiation at issue is based on reasonable and objective criteria; if it is, it does not amount to prohibited discrimination.[2] The same applies to indirect discrimination, which occurs where lack of differentiation disproportionately disadvantages those in a particular group, without reasonable and objective justification.[3] The conditions for meeting the "reasonable and objective criteria" are the same under Articles 2, 3 (gender discrimination) and 26, and have been subject of extensive commentary.[4]

The Human Rights Committee, the *ICCPR* monitoring body, routinely criticises countries (including Australia) for failure to implement the non-discrimination provisions of the *ICCPR*, for example, because prohibited grounds such as religion are missing.[5] It is all the more surprising that

---

1   Manfred Nowak, *CCPR Commentary*, 2nd revised edition, (Engel, 2005), p. 629, n. 155.

2   *Broeks v. Netherlands*, Communication No. 172/1984, CCPR/C/OP/2 at 196, 9 April 1987 [12.4]-[13], *Zwaan-de-Vries v. Netherlands*, Communication No. 182/1984, CCPR/C/OP/2 at 209, 9 April 1987 [12.4]-[13], *L.G. Danning v. Netherlands*, Communication No. 180/1984, CCPR/C/OP/2 at 205, 9 April 1987 [12.4]-[13]; *Gueye et al. v. France*, CCPR/C/35/D/196/1985, 3 April 1989 [9.5]; *Waldman v. Canada*, CCPR/C/67/D/694/1996, 3 November 1999 [10.6].

3   See e.g. *Q v. Denmark*, CCPR/C/113/D/2001/2010, 1 April 2015 [7.5].

4   See e.g. Christopher McCrudden (ed.), *Anti-Discrimination Law* (Ashgate Publishing, 2004); Sandra Fredman, *Human Rights Transformed: Positive Rights and Positive Duties* (Oxford University Press, 2008); Christopher McCrudden, *Equality and Non-Discrimination*, in David Feldman (Ed), *English Public Law* (Oxford University Press, 2nd ed, 2009), p. 499.

5   E.g. Korea A/47/40 (1992) 477; Austria CCPR/C/AUT/CO/5 (2015) 12; Poland CCPR/C/POL/CO/7 (2016) 13; Australia CCPR/C/AUS/CO/6 (2017) 17; Algeria CCPR/C/DZA/CO/4 (2018) 19; Belize CCPR/C/BLZ/CO/1/Add.1 (2018) 11.

for so long there have been, and to an extent still are,[6] gaps in Australia's discrimination laws for religion as a prohibited ground. Two factors may account for this. One is mistrust of Australian anti-discrimination and anti-vilification laws because of their potential use as weaponry by private parties against each other, particularly after the claim brought against two pastors in the *Catch the Fire* litigation under Victoria's Racial and Religious Tolerance Act 2001.[7] Also, there has been a false perception that freedom of religion and protection against discrimination (on grounds others than religion, particularly gender and sexuality) exist in some barometric relationship, where one increases at the expense of the other. Any such myth would be dispelled by recovering protection against discrimination on all grounds (including religion), and religious freedom, to *ICCPR* standards. All *ICCPR* rights should be regarded as according dignity-based protection.

2 Equal parity of rights

Over many years there has been discussion on whether there exists a hierarchy of human rights.[8] There appears to be more consensus on the principle that human rights are interdependent, interrelated and indivisible,

---

6   In New South Wales and South Australia nothing specifically prohibits discrimination on the grounds of religion. The Anti-Discrimination Act 1977 (NSW) s.4 defines "race" to include "ethno-religious origin" to bring it with the prohibition against discrimination on the basis of race; the Equal Opportunity Act 1984 (SA) ss. 85T(7), 85U and 85ZD concern the prohibition discrimination based on "religious appearance or dress".

7   For the appeal decision see *Cath the Fire Ministries Inc and Others v Islamic Council of Victoria Inc* and Another, [2006] VSCA 284.

8   For a sample see: Theodor Meron, On a Hierarchy of International Human Rights, 80 Am. J. Int'l L. 1 (1986); Tom Farer, *The Hierarchy of Human Rights*, American University International Law Review 8:1 (1992), pp. 115-119; Teraya Koji, *Emerging Hierarchy in International Human Rights and Beyond: From the Perspective of Non-derogable Rights*, European Journal of International Law 12:5 (2001), pp.917-941; John D. Montgomery, *Is there a hierarchy of human rights?*, Journal of Human Rights 1:3 (2002), pp.373-385; Fernando Suárez Müller, *The Hierarchy of Human Rights and the Transcendental System of Right*, Hum Rights Rev 20(1) (2019), pp. 47-66.

described by Asbjørn Eide as "fundamental from the very establishment of the United Nations, and ... an inherent part of the notion that the rights adopted by the United Nations are universal".[9] It describes a particular critical relationship of complementarity between the *ICCPR* and its twin, the *International Covenant on Economic, Social and Cultural Rights*, recognised in the Preambles of each instrument. The Proclamation of Teheran in 1968 emphasised shortly after they were both concluded that "the full realisation of civil and political rights without the enjoyment of economic, social and cultural rights is impossible".[10] In 1993, following the break-up of the former Soviet Union, the Vienna Declaration and Programme of Action proclaimed:

> All human rights are universal, indivisible and interdependent and interrelated. The international community must treat human rights globally in a fair and equal manner, on the same footing, and with the same emphasis. While the significance of national and regional particularities and various historical, cultural and religious backgrounds must be borne in mind, it is the duty of States, regardless of their political, economic and cultural systems, to promote and protect all human rights and fundamental freedoms.[11]

The indivisibility of human rights has now become an 'official doctrine' of the United Nations.[12]

It would of course be wrong in principle to assert a superior ordinal position for freedom of religion. Those seeking protection for religious freedom to *ICCPR* standards are often pasquinaded for wanting it to trump

---

9   Asbjørn Eide, 'Interdependence and Indivisibility of Human Rights', in Yvonne Donders and Vladimir Volodin (eds.), *Human Rights in Education, Science and Culture: Legal Developments and Challenges* (Ashgate, 2007), p. 11.

10   Proclamation of Teheran, Final Act of the International Conference on Human Rights, Teheran, 22 April-13 May 1968, A/CONF.32/41 (1968) [13]: 'Since human rights and fundamental freedoms are indivisible, the full realisation of civil and political rights without the enjoyment of economic, social and cultural rights is impossible'.

11   *Vienna Declaration and Programme of Action*, 12 July 1993, A/CONF.157/23 [5].

12   James Nickel, 'Rethinking Indivisibility: Towards a Theory Supporting Relations Between Human Rights', (2008) 30 Hum. Rts. Q, p. 984, at p. 985.

other rights, and the indivisibility principle is cited against them. It is easier to make the claim when legislative proposals are convoluted and fail to give clear recognition for freedom of religion resembling even remotely the substance of Article 18.[13] However, it is entirely misplaced in response to proposals to make good *ICCPR* deficiencies.

The maxim that "all human rights are universal, indivisible and interdependent and interrelated" is something that promoters of freedom of religion may be taken to stand by, in the sense in which it is and always was meant, when advocating protection to *ICCPR* standards.

3 The inherent scope of rights and the limitation of rights

Nevertheless, accusations still stick in the public mind that protection for religious freedom will privilege religion, particularly by violating principles of equality. The reason lies partly in the way anti-discrimination legislation is drafted in Australia (at Commonwealth as well as state and territory levels), to render unlawful discrimination on prohibited grounds, but for particular exceptions. In Australia we are habituated to the belief that all forms of distinction should carry the stigma of prohibited discrimination, and so any exception or exemption is perceived as concessionary, to authorise what Caportorti described as odious. The public inevitably then asks, and not unreasonably, "why it is that religious schools and other bodies should be given what seems to be a 'right' or 'privilege' to discriminate"? Of course under the *ICCPR*, differentiation only constitutes discrimination at the threshold

---

13   See e.g. *Religious discrimination bill may breach constitution by allowing doctors to refuse treatment* https://www.theguardian.com/world/2019/sep/30/religious-discrimination-bill-may-breach-constitution-by-allowing-doctors-to-refuse-treatment; Law Council of Australia submission, Religious Freedom Bills, 3 October 2019, in response to the Australian Government's proposed package of legislative reforms on religious freedom in the:Religious Discrimination Bill 2019, Religious Discrimination (Consequential Amendments) Bill 2019, and Human Rights Legislation Amendment (Freedom of Religion) Bill 2019.

already mentioned, where it is not based on reasonable and objective criteria – the same threshold that applies also under the *European Convention* and
the *ILO employment and occupation convention*.[14] When exemptions for religious
bodies and schools are found at Commonwealth level, in sections 37 and 38
of the *Sex Discrimination Act 1984*, which protects against gender and sexuality-based discrimination, it only cements a thoroughly negative impression
that it is the purpose and pleasure of religious bodies to discriminate on
grounds of sexuality above all things, and that those which do so are little
more than institutions established for the furtherance of advanced forms
of religious bigotry. Exemptions in anti-discrimination legislation which
meet the Article 2 and 26 justification should not be treated concessionary,
nor as a "licence to discriminate".

It is a difficult to expect the Australian public to understand readily that
there is no trumping, or privileging on the part of religious freedom when
merely seeking adjustment to discrimination laws to reflect international law
standards, particularly when Australian discrimination legislation is remedial, addressing serious ills (as it does), in such a way as to raise the expectation
that exceptions should not be tolerated.

So it is necessary to clarify that the basis on which religious schools intend
to operate is freedom of religion, in its positive collective dimension, not
some skewed, negative and pointed form of gender and sexuality-based
discrimination, in spite of the regrettable impression which ss 37 and 38 of
the *Sex Discrimination Act* create. Religious bodies and schools simply seek
the ethos-based protection which is well recognised at international law,[15]
particularly in the work of the Special Rapporteur on religion and belief,[16]

---

14   International Labour Organisation, Discrimination (Employment and Occupa-
      tion) Convention, 1958 (No. 111).
15   For further discussion see Nicholas Aroney and Paul Taylor, *The politics of freedom
      of religion in Australia: Can international human rights standards point the way forward?*
16   A/69/261 (2014) [38]-[41].

the jurisprudence of the European Court of Human Rights,[17] and the long established terms of a European workplace directive on discrimination.[18] Ethos-based protection could be expressed more generally and positively than in isolated sex discrimination legislation. To do so would be much more fitting and less divisive. The approach taken in the European Convention institutional ethos cases, when examining whether any support for ethos has gone too far in impinging on an employee's right, is to balance the individual's right (most often their private and family life, or freedom of religion) on the one hand, and the right of religious organisations to autonomy, on the other. Since the State is called upon to guarantee these rights, its job is to choose adequate means to make any interference proportionate to the aim pursued.[19] Those decisions may be summarised as offering strong support for loyalty to ethos in their findings, except where the matter was seriously mishandled procedurally.[20]

The Human Rights Committee does not take a similar "balancing" approach to claims under the *ICCPR*. If in response to a discrimination claim the Committee were to find that there was no violation, in circumstances where protection available for organisational ethos supplied the appropriate reasonable and objective criteria for differentiation, the question of justified limitation of freedom of religion or association may not even arise. It is quite possible that the question of limitation of freedom of religion may not even be enlivened, where the threshold for prohibited discrimination under the *ICCPR* is not reached.

---

17   *Obst v Germany*, App.No. 425/03, Judgment of 23 September 2010; *Siebenhaar v. Germany*, App.No. 18136/02, Judgment of 3 February 2011; *Fernández Martínez v Spain*, App. No. 56030/07, [2014] ECHR 615, *Travaš v. Croatia*, App.No. 75581/13, Judgment of 4 October 2016.

18   *European Council Directive 2000/78/EC of 27 November 2000 establishing a general framework for equal treatment in employment and occupation.*

19   *Fernández Martínez v Spain*, App. No. 56030/07, [2014] ECHR 615, [122].

20   *Vallauri v Italy*, App.No 39128/05, Judgment of 20 October 2009; *Schüth v Germany* App. No. 1620/03, Judgment of 23 September 2010.

It is regrettable that the clear recognition at international law in support of institutional ethos is not well acknowledged in Australia, and that the mythology prevails that freedom of religion which supports it is being asserted in order to trump other rights. The Hon Justice Derrington commented as follows recently in a speech in the context of the Religious Discrimination Bill.

> The ALRC will be unable to propose any legislative solution that "guarantees" the rights of religious institutions to conduct their affairs in a way consistent with their religious ethos. Within the complex framework of international human rights law and its intersection with domestic anti-discrimination law, there is no justification in law, nor practical means, of "guaranteeing" that one right, let alone an institutional right rather than an individual right, will trump any other rights.[21]

She continues, "A 'Freedom of Religion Act', or equivalent, is of course one way that a more positive statement of religious rights could be enshrined. However, and without venturing into the debate about bills of rights, there is much force in the view that one right should not be seen to be privileged over any other right."[22]

Incidentally, freedom of association is not an "institutional right". The beneficiaries are individuals (emphasised by the word "everyone" in Article 22 of the *ICCPR*) in their collective pursuits. Justice Derrington also raised something which is specifically addressed by Article 5 of the *ICCPR*, when noting that "[t]he exercise of any right must not cause injury or harm to another, and the existence of any one right does not entitle anyone to engage in any activity aimed at the destruction or limitation of another right to a

---

21   The Hon Justice S C Derrington, *Of shields and swords – let the jousting begin!*, Freedom19 Conference, 4 September 2019, NSW Parliament House, Sydney. She also mentioned among the principles which guide the ALRC, that "[a]ll Australians are entitled to the protection of their fundamental human rights and no one right is subordinate to another right — rights that are invisible [sic] may lead to a diminution of the equal and inalienable rights of all people".

22   Ibid.

greater extent than is provided for at law". Article 5 states that "[n]othing in the [*ICCPR*] may be interpreted as implying for any State, group or person any right to engage in any activity or perform any act aimed at the destruction of any [*ICCPR* rights] or at their limitation to a greater extent than is provided for in the [*ICCPR*]." Article 5 is an interpretive provision which is often used by some to supplement their criticisms that freedom of religion should not trump other rights. Yet it is most relevant for its firm endorsement of the importance of limitation terms. Each *ICCPR* right is defined by reference to two things: its scope and terms of limitation. It is worth clarifying that whenever an *ICCPR* right is restricted permissibly (i.e. within its terms of limitation), including when two *ICCPR* rights are asserted concurrently, the person whose rights are thereby restricted is not normally said to suffer "injury or harm".

Arguments to confine freedom of religion often suggest that Article 18(3) allows the freedom to be subjected to broad restriction. It is important to understand the purpose which terms of limitation such as Article 18(3) serve. Article 18(3) should not be conceived as a provision which gives with one hand (when defining the scope of religious freedom) and takes away with the other (in the terms of limitation). The essence of freedom of religion lies in the protection which the terms of limitation themselves accord. Article 18(3) operates as a guarantee that the freedom will not be encroached upon, in breach of its terms, where it is not necessary to do so, measured against very strict standards. Paragraph 8 of General Comment 22 provides a neat synopsis of these:

> States parties should proceed from the need to protect the rights guaranteed under the Covenant, including the right to equality and non-discrimination on all grounds specified in Articles 2, 3 and 26. Limitations imposed must be established by law and must not be applied in a manner that would vitiate the rights guaranteed in Article 18. The Committee observes that paragraph 3 of Article 18 is to be strictly interpreted: restrictions are not allowed on grounds not speci-

fied there, even if they would be allowed as restrictions to other rights protected in the Covenant, such as national security. Limitations may be applied only for those purposes for which they were prescribed and must be directly related and proportionate to the specific need on which they are predicated. Restrictions may not be imposed for discriminatory purposes or applied in a discriminatory manner.[23]

Protection equivalent in substance to that in Article 18(3) is meant to be secured in Australian domestic law. Without it freedom of religion is not 'given effect', according to Australia's *ICCPR* promises. The Human Rights Committee is largely non-prescriptive about the means of domestic implementation. However, limitation terms are especially important, and the permissive scope of limitation should by some means be reflected in domestic law where the *ICCPR* is not directly incorporated. It has recommended revision of domestic law "in order to ensure that all the requirements of the Covenant are reflected", thereby "ensuring that the limitations imposed on the exercise of rights and freedoms under national legislation do not go beyond those permitted under the Covenant'.[24] It has scrutinised compliance with Article 18(3) to determine whether national security is wrongly permitted as a ground of limitation;[25] it has addressed other bases of limitation which are not legitimate,[26] such as 'subversive propaganda',[27] the use of religion for 'political ends',[28] and where religious practice provokes

---

23   *General Comment No. 22: Article 18 (Freedom of Thought, Conscience or Religion)*, 30 July 1993, CCPR/C/21/Rev.1/Add.4 [8].

24   Morocco CCPR/C/79/Add.44 (1994) 17. See also Hungary CCPR/C/79/ Add.22 (1993) 11; Grenada CCPR/C/GRD/CO/1 (2009) 6.

25   E.g. Bulgaria CCPR A/48/40 (1993) 739 (protection of the security of the State was not one of the criteria listed in Art. 18 of the Covenant, but that was not the case of Bulgarian legislation).

26   E.g. Kazakhstan CCPR/C/KAZ/CO/2 (2016) 48 (recommendation to revise all relevant laws and practices with a view to removing all restrictions that go beyond the narrowly construed restrictions permitted under Art. 18); Turkmenistan CCPR/C/TKM/CO/2 (2017) 39 (guarantee the effective exercise of freedom of religion and belief in practice and refrain from any action that may restrict it beyond the narrowly construed restrictions permitted under Art. 18).

27   Dominican Republic A/45/40 (1990) 375.

28   Congo A/42/40 (1987) 238.

'public indignation'.[29] It has also paid close attention to whether domestic law allows derogation from Article 18 in a state of emergency.[30] It has even noted that under the *ICCPR* permissible restrictions are "less broad-based" than under the European Convention, for those States conforming their domestic legislation only to the latter.[31]

The question of progressing social standards is an important one in this context. Justice Derrington made some useful observations about the history of advances in the anti-discrimination legislation in Australia to note that, when considering the intersection between freedom of religion and freedom of equality, "[i]t tends to reveal a reactive approach to social issues that are emerging and evolving, almost in real time, and which cannot be reconciled immediately with the generally more static questions of religious doctrines and practices which may take centuries to evolve, if at all. But we know that religious doctrines and practices do evolve." It begs the question whether those who hold to religious doctrines and practices should be required to move with the times, which also touches on the nature of freedom of religion to be guaranteed. The freedom is surely most needed precisely when there is a tendency for undue restriction to occur because minority belief systems do not fit with the doctrine of the State or popular standards. It is inimical to human rights protection, in particular under Article 18, that belief systems should be sanitised of incompatibility with prevailing social standards. The obligation of the State under the *ICCPR* is to ensure the *ICCPR* standards of protection to all individuals, in such circumstances through State impartiality. This excludes any discretion on the part of the

---

29   Sweden A/33/40 (1978) 79; Sweden A/41/40 (1986) 146.
30   E.g. Algeria, A/47/40 (1992) 299; Nepal CCPR/C/79/Add.42 (1994) 9; Armenia CCPR/C/79/Add.100 (1998) 7; Ukraine CCPR/CO/73/UKR (2001) 11; Gambia CCPR/C/GMB/CO/2 (2018) 19 (the Constitution provides for derogation of the right to freedom of thought, conscience and religion during a state of emergency).
31   Malta CCPR/C/79/Add.29 (1993) 9; Iceland CCPR/C/79/Add.26 (1993) 8; Denmark CCPR/C/79/Add.68 (1996) 11.

State to determine whether religious beliefs or the means used to express such beliefs are legitimate.[32]

The comments of the UN Special Rapporteur on religion or belief on this issue are instructive. He addressed the question of *ICCPR*-incompatibility within particular belief systems when he noted that positions of authority in many denominations are occupied exclusively by men, such as bishop, imam, preacher, priest, rabbi or reverend, in conflict with the gender equality principle of Article 3 of the *ICCPR*. He nevertheless reiterated various obligations on the State to support religious autonomy, and to promote religious pluralism even where the relevant beliefs conflict with *ICCPR* (equality) standards.

> It is a well-known fact that in many (not all) denominations, positions of religious authority, such as bishop, imam, preacher, priest, rabbi or reverend, remain reserved to males, a state of affairs that collides with the principle of equality between men and women as established in international human rights law. Unsurprisingly, this has led to numerous conflicts...It cannot be the business of the State to shape or reshape religious traditions, nor can the State claim any binding authority in the interpretation of religious sources or in the definition of the tenets of faith. Freedom of religion or belief is a right of human beings, after all, not a right of the State. As mentioned above, questions of how to institutionalize community life may significantly affect the religious self-understanding of a community. From this it follows that the State must generally respect the autonomy of religious institutions, also in policies of promoting equality between men and women...At the same time, one should bear in mind that freedom of religion or belief includes the right of internal dissidents, including women, to come up with alternative views, provide new readings of religious sources and try to exercise influence on a community's religious self-understanding, which may change over time.

---

32   *Hasan and Chaush v. Bulgaria* [GC], App.No. 30985/96, ECHR 2000-XI [78] [62], [78]. Note also that the principle of religious autonomy prevents the State from obliging a religious community to admit or exclude an individual or to entrust someone with a particular religious duty (*Svyato-Mykhaylivska Parafiya v. Ukraine*, App. No. 77703/01 (2007) [146]).

In situations in which internal dissidents or proponents of new religious understandings face coercion from within their religious communities, which sometimes happens, the State is obliged to provide protection.[33]

The scope of rights and limitation are therefore equally important in guaranteeing protection, and in order to be effectually incorporated must subsist substantively in Australian domestic law by some means. This still needs correction. Human rights charters do nothing to improve the position, only worsen it, because they describe *ICCPR* rights in a menu listing, without the terms of limitation which bestow on them the essential character as guarantees.[34] Charters simply list all *ICCPR* and in single, omnibus limitation provisions declare that they may be restricted impermissibly, by adopting terminology which departs significantly from that required.

4 Implementation and violation – differentiate

There is a crucial difference between implementation and violation. The standard for reform for freedom of religion should not be whether there is evidence of obvious and persistent violation, but whether Article 18 standards are reflected in domestic law. They are not. Australia's obligations of implementation in this respect have been fundamentally unaddressed since Australia's ratification of the *ICCPR* in 1980, requiring it to "take the necessary steps to adopt such laws and other measures as may be necessary to give effect to ICCPR rights". It is not a principled approach to reform to say there is no surfeit of examples of serious violation, when obligations of implementation are foundational to bringing rights home, domestically, and on a non-discriminatory basis.

---

33   Report to the General Assembly of the Special Rapporteur on freedom of religion or belief, Heiner Bielefeldt, A/68/290, 7 August 2013, [58-60].

34   *Charter of Human Rights and Responsibilities Act 2006* (Vic) s 7(2); *Human Rights Act 2019* (Qld) s 13(1); *Human Rights Act 2004* (ACT) s 28(1).

5. Conclusions on religious freedom and inclusivity

All *ICCPR* rights "derive from the inherent dignity of the human person", and build on the recognition given in the *Universal Declaration* of "the inherent dignity and of the equal and inalienable rights of all members of the human family". The *ICCPR* provides an integrated scheme of protection for fundamental rights, enjoyed in parallel with each other, in an interface which gives explicit recognition to the coexistence of other rights in terms of limitation, by definitional thresholds, and interpretive provisions, among other things. It is decidedly focused on the individual, not only to guard against threats to liberty and personal security, but also in support of personal and collective autonomy without undue interference. In practice these are enjoyed in variety and plurality by everyone, or should be.

The *ICCPR* recognises in its Preamble that the individual has duties to fellow individuals, and the wider community, to strive for the promotion and observance of all *ICCPR* rights, and this seems an appropriate moment to press the refresh button on that. This article commends the *ICCPR* for all its imperfections as an inclusive universal model.

Bibliography

Addresses and Reports

Heiner Bielefeldt, Report to the General Assembly of the Special Rapporteur on freedom of religion or belief, A/68/290, 7 August 2013.

Heiner Bielefeldt, Report to the General Assembly of the Special Rapporteur on freedom of religion or belief, A/69/261, 5 August 2014.

The Hon Justice S C Derrington, *Of shields and swords – let the jousting begin!*, Freedom19 Conference, 4 September 2019, NSW Parliament House, Sydney.

Books and book chapters

Asbjørn Eide, 'Interdependence and Indivisibility of Human Rights', in Yvonne Donders and Vladimir Volodin (eds.), *Human Rights in Education, Science and*

Culture: Legal Developments and Challenges (Ashgate, 2007), 11-52.

Sandra Fredman, *Human Rights Transformed: Positive Rights and Positive Duties* (Oxford University Press, 2008).

Christopher McCrudden (ed.), *Anti-Discrimination Law* (Ashgate Publishing, 2004).

Christopher McCrudden, *Equality and Non-Discrimination*, in David Feldman (Ed), *English Public Law* (Oxford University Press, 2nd ed, 2009).

Manfred Nowak, *CCPR Commentary*, 2nd revised edition, (Engel, 2005).

Journal Articles

Tom Farer, 'The Hierarchy of Human Rights', *American University International Law Review* 8:1 (1992), 115-119.

Teraya Koji, "Emerging Hierarchy in International Human Rights and Beyond: From the Perspective of Non-derogable Rights, *European Journal of International Law* 12:5 (2001) 917-941.

Theodor Meron, 'On a Hierarchy of International Human Rights', 80 *Am. J. Int'l L.* 1 (1986).

John D. Montgomery, 'Is there a hierarchy of human rights?', *Journal of Human Rights* 1:3 (2002) 373-385.

Fernando Suárez Müller, 'The Hierarchy of Human Rights and the Transcendental System of Right', *Hum Rights Rev* 20(1) (2019) 47-66.

James Nickel, 'Rethinking Indivisibility: Towards a Theory Supporting Relations Between Human Rights', (2008) 30 *Hum. Rts. Q,* 984-1001.

International instruments, declarations, directives and proclamations

European Council Directive 2000/78/EC of 27 November 2000 establishing a general framework for equal treatment in employment and occupation.

General Comment No. 22: Article 18 (Freedom of Thought, Conscience or Religion), 30 July 1993, CCPR/C/21/Rev.1/Add.4.

International Covenant on Civil and Political Rights, G.A. Res 2200A (XXI), U.N. GAOR, 21st Sess., Supp.No.16 U.N. Doc.A/6316 (16 December 1966, entered into force on 23 March 1976).

International Labour Organisation, Discrimination (Employment and Occupation)

Convention, 1958 (No. 111).

Proclamation of Teheran, Final Act of the International Conference on Human Rights, Teheran, 22 April-13 May 1968, A/CONF.32/41 (1968).

Vienna Declaration and Programme of Action, 12 July 1993, A/CONF.157/23.

7

RELIGIOUS FREEDOM HAS ALWAYS BEEN ABOUT INCLUDING MINORITIES

Keith Thompson

Abstract

The idea of religious freedom has always been about inclusion. There was a time when religious freedom was academically popular. Religious minorities were arguably the first minorities that needed to be accommodated in a society that sought peace because religious minorities could not be successfully suppressed. In this essay I argue that the history of the idea of religious freedom provides a template for inclusion generally. If we analyse how societies in the past have learned to manage religious difference and dissent, we will find that we already know how to protect the minorities we have chosen to recognise more recently. The conclusion is that we can accommodate all minorities so long as they do not physically or economically harm us by 'picking our pockets or breaking our legs'[1] as Thomas Jefferson might have taught.

---

[1]   Thomas Jefferson, *Notes on the State of Virginia* (John Stockdale, 2nd ed, 1787) 265.

Introduction

There are many differences which can divide a family, a city, a state, a country or a civilisation. Edward Gibbon suggests Rome fell because Christianity took away its virility and aggression. Others point to the survival of the Roman Empire's Eastern part, united by Orthodoxy for nearly another thousand years, and argue that Western Rome did not fall but evolved[2] and continues to this day with other more important overlapping consensuses at its core.

If Rome did not fall and what remains of the Holy Roman Empire is Western Civilisation without Christianity, then what is the social glue that continues to hold it together ? What changing residues of consensus have enabled us to return to peace after the World Wars of the twentieth century and the bases of our social agreement changing? If religion is no longer part of the agreement beneath our social compact, what is the essence of the Western social consensus now and what will it be twenty years from now? The culture wars, including the sexual revolution of the 1960s and the same-sex marriage revolution of the 'two thousand and teens', have rattled the cage of religious orthodoxy, but we do seem to be in the process of refashioning our consensus. In Australia at least, that is manifest in the return of freedom of conscience and religion to the centre of political debate in the wake of the same-sex marriage revolution.

To survive as a cohesive society, must new discrimination norms suppress all the old? Contemporary debate in Hong Kong is an example. Must those who advocate new extra norms crush bodies and shatter bones to achieve homogenised consensus as Xi Jinping recently threatened the Hong Kong

---

2   'Section 8: The Fall of Rome: Facts and Fictions', *Utah State University* (Web Page, 2019) < https://www.usu.edu/markdamen/1320Hist&Civ/chapters/08ROM-FAL.htm>.

protestors?[3] Or is it reasonable to infer that religious freedom has to be a part of our evolving consensus? After all, though the numbers are declining, the 2016 Australian census confirms that 52% of the population still believe enough to affirm their Christianity and more than 60% have confirmed their continuing religiosity.[4]

In this article I outline the history of religious freedom as an inclusion strategy with a focus on its Western development. The core of that analysis holds that the discovery of the idea of religious toleration in the 17th century was not the product of Galileo or Newton. Rather it was the product of a peace conference at Augsburg in Westphalia when the parties gathered after thirty years of savage civil war and acknowledged that neither the Catholics nor the Protestants could conquer. Their primitive consensus, captured in the phrase *'cuius regio, eius religio'* (meaning that the religion of the ruler was to dictate the religion of those ruled), was developed by subsequent philosophers in England and in Europe, and in practical experiments in the United States before and after the War of Independence. That philosophy and those experiments form the core of this chapter, but in Part One I begin earlier and discuss the way religious diversity was managed in Assyria, Persia, Babylon, Greece and Rome before the advent of Christianity. The rulers of those civilisations wrestled with the same homogenisation, assimilation and tolerance problems that face Western civilisation today. Their nuanced solutions present empirical examples that should inform wise debate today.

---

3   'Xi warns China's adversaries of 'crushed bodies, shattered bones'', *Aljazeera* (online, 14 October 2019) <https://www.aljazeera.com/news/2019/10/xi-warns-china-adversaries-crushed-bodies-shattered-bones-191014015858714.html>.

4   Australian Bureau of Statistics, *2016 Census Data Summary: Religion in Australia* (Catalogue 2071.0, 28 June 2017) 1; see also Australian Bureau of Statistics, *Census of Population and Housing: Reflecting Australia: Stories from the Census, 2016: Same-Sex Couples in Australia, 2016* (Catalogue 2071.0, 18 January 2018). Note there were just under 47,000 gay couples in Australia in the 2016 census. See also Australian Bureau of Statistics, *Census of Population and Housing: Reflecting Australia: Stories from the Census, 2016: Sex and Gender Diversity in the 2016 Census*. Note that 1,260 people reported non-male-female sex/gender in Australia in the 2016 census.

I conduct a similar historical analysis in Part Two. The perennial problem of how a government best manages religious diversity was a core issue for the framers of the Peace at Westphalia and in the philosophical analysis that played out in the American state and federal experiments. All of the English colonies in America had established religions but those establishments were abandoned within the first 30 years of the formation of their republic.[5] I discuss the Westphalia treaties as part of the context for the American revolution; the philosophical discussion of the idea of religious freedom that followed in the writings of Locke and others, and the American experiments after Roger Williams and Anne Hutchinson were expelled from New England.

In Part Three I more fully canvass the American philosophical debates both before and during their constitutional conventions where Madison compromised in the final wording of the First Amendment which informed the Australian framers in 1897. In Part Four I discuss why we adopted those American words in Australia, and I focus on what I believe all those threads of history should teach us about the necessity of inclusion as we contemplate a renewed compromise in the interests of enduring consensus.

I conclude that our 2020 state and federal solutions must avoid an oppressive Versailles flavour since that peace bore such bitter fruit. That our solutions will be worked out in 2020 gives me hope since 2020 vision symbolically means we can factor all the history in.

---

5   'Separation of church and state in the United States', *Wikipedia* (Web Page, 23 July 2020) <https://en.wikipedia.org/wiki/Separation_of_church_and_state_in_the_United_States>. Wikipedia includes a nuanced table that recognises that dis-establishment came by degrees. For example, though the Congregational Church in Massachusetts was dis-established in 1780, state funding for any church was not discontinued until 1833.

Part One – Religious Freedom in Ancient History

I begin with a platitude for rhetorical affect. There were no *Universal Declaration of Human Rights*[6] (UDHR) or *International Covenant on Civil and Political Right*[7] (ICCPR) one thousand years before the common era (BCE). Religious freedom as we know it since the Westphalia treaties and the American democratic experiment, did not exist. There was occasional reluctant comity dictated by Dawkinian self-interest, but mostly might was right. Pre-Christian humans grouped together for protection. Type A personalities and selfish ambition, were largely tolerated because there was "no other way" to ensure safety for one's family. There were occasional stories (legends?) in pre-biblical scripture about the city states of Enoch and Melchizedek which achieved social justice led by righteous leaders who may have subliminally inspired the idea of the philosopher-king in Plato. But the legends said that the city states of Enoch and Melchizedek excluded others and were taken to heaven. Those who survived on earth coalesced around ambitious self-serving and often greedy strong men. The stories of David, Solomon, and the Assyrian, Persian, Median and Babylonian Kings followed by Alexander in Greece and the Romans, are manifestations of that story played out on a larger stage as human ambitions grew.

In another place I have explained how traditional Israelite Divine Council theology went underground and was eventually lost because the Persian One God policy did not accept any god greater than Ahura Mazda.[8] But that is a simplification. The gods of conquered nations were tolerated in the quest for civil obedience if Persian authority was accepted. Hence the Jews were able to rebuild Jerusalem because Cyrus decreed it. The Jews learned

---

6   *Universal Declaration of Human Rights*, GA RES 217A (III), UN GAOR, UN Doc A/810 (10 December 1948) ('*UDHR*').

7   *International Covenant on Civil and Political Rights*, G.A. Res 2200A (XXI), U.N. GAOR, 21st Sess., Supp.No.16 U.N. Doc.A/6316 (16 December 1966, entered into force on 23 March 1976) ('*ICCPR*').

8   A Keith Thompson, *Trinity and Monotheism: A historical and theological review of the origins and substance of the doctrine* (Modotti Press, 2019) 29, 33-4.

to accommodate themselves to the Persian worldview.

But the Greeks and Romans chose a different approach towards religious diversity and accommodation. They interpreted the mythology and religion of other cultures using their own religious concepts and practices as comparative analogues which assisted understanding and enabled homogenisation.[9]

The gods of people who became subject to Greek and Roman authority were assimilated and reinterpreted. Translation was a defensive strategy pursued in the interests of empire. But the result was different religious postures for external and domestic use. At times, Jews were willing to resist their overlords to the point of violence. But not always and not everyone.[10] The overall strategy of the ancient superpowers was assimilation and homogenisation with some accommodation manifest by the multiplicity of temples in ancient Greece and Rome.

Part Two – The Reformation and its wars

While it may be easier to interpret the Westphalia treaties and the American democratic experiment beginning in the 16th and 17th centuries as a continuation of the ancient story if we could withdraw a millennium or two, we have many more records to explain the detail of what happened. The Reformation eventually played out on European battlefields. But the commitment and the conversion of the people and the rulers was so great that neither side could win. Hence, after thirty particularly bloody years, a peace was negotiated at Augsburg in Westphalia, Germany in 1648. A summary of that settlement has been captured in the phrase '*cuius regio, eius religio*' – the religion of the ruler was thereafter to dictate the religion of those ruled, so that Europe was divided into Catholic and Protestant principalities.

---

9   Ibid 34 nn 123-4.
10   Ibid 35.

In England, the ruler had also changed his religion and there was insufficient power within the nation to force a Westphalian compromise, especially after the Spanish Armada was defeated by Sir Francis Drake in 1588. If the English wished to enjoy worship according to the dictates of their own consciences, they had to leave as Pauline Hansen might have suggested. And many did leave. There were four principal English settlements in America and all had a different religious flavour. The Puritan Pilgrims sought to establish a 'city on a hill' in New England. Virginian and other southern planters sought to transplant the ways of the English gentry and brought with them, an Anglican establishment. A Friends or Quaker migration established itself in the Delaware valley and the borderers found non-conformist peace in the borderlands and backcountry and had a lot to do with the establishment of American ranch culture.[11]

The American experiments

The New England Puritan settlement was most conspicuously established in pursuit of freedom of conscience, but famously found limits early on. The majority did not like the way that Roger Williams and Anne Hutchinson exercised their consciences. They both escaped to avoid the death penalty and Williams established the separate colony of Rhode Island premised on a more accommodating concept of freedom of conscience. Later Jefferson, Mason and Madison all bristled against the strictures of the established Anglicanism in Virginia and haggled a statute of religious liberty in 1786 which served as part of the template for what became the First Amendment to the *US Constitution* in the Bill of Rights in 1791.

Because the framers of the *US Constitution* were never going to be able to agree on a national religion, that was a necessary early compromise in

---

11   David Hackett Fischer, *Albion's Seed: Four British Folkways in America* (Oxford University Press, 1989) 7.

their conventions. What was not so clear was whether some generic or civil expression of religion could still play a part in their national settlement. While the constitutional words they chose suggest the answer was no, the superabundance of official prayers, paid chaplains and the existence of religious holidays which have endured for more than 200 years, prove that there was much more nuance in their settlement than one would guess from the words they used. And while the federal settlement did not require the abandonment of their existing state religious establishments, the fact of the abandonment of all of those establishments as they strove to unify their nation by including everyone suggests their experiments, and the arguments which enabled them, are pregnant with enduring wisdom.

Eighteenth century religious liberty philosophy

The question of how best to protect religious freedom in eighteenth century America may be illustrated by understanding the differing views of George Mason and James Madison when they debated what form that protection should take in the Virginia *Bill of Rights* in 1776. Mason insisted that it was enough that religious exercise should be fully tolerated unless it 'disturb[ed] the peace, happiness or safety of society'.[12] Madison insisted that was too narrow and advocated that full and free exercise of religion must be protected 'unless under color of religion the preservation of equal liberty and the existence of the State [we]re manifestly endangered'.[13] Mason's idea resonates with the limitation now found in art 18(3) of the *ICCPR* which holds that the '[f]reedom to manifest one's religion or beliefs may be subject only to such limitations as are prescribed by law and are necessary to

---

12   Michael W McConnell, 'The Origins and Historical Understanding of Free Exercise of Religion' in Thomas C Berg (eds), *The First Amendment: The Free Exercise of Religion Clause, Its Constitutional History and the Contemporary Debate* (Prometheus Books, 2008) 84, 87.

13   Rodney K Smith, *James Madison: The Father of Religious Liberty* (Plain Sight, 2019) 121.

protect public safety, order, health or morals or the fundamental rights and freedoms of others'.[14]

Madison's broader view of the appropriate bounds of religious liberty was the product of his concern about the Anglican establishment in Virginia. Though he was raised in that faith,[15] he was opposed to its establishment because he wanted to place religious exercise entirely beyond the reach of the state.[16] Establishment gave the state a measure of control of the mind which was inconsistent with a natural right which included every individual's duty to God.[17] Madison was thus opposed to government support for the payment of clergy salaries which suggested a privilege that was inconsistent with equality or equal treatment in matters of religion.[18] Establishment and privilege would enable majority religionists to tyrannize minorities. Madison also asserted 'that the regulation of religion was not within the province of civil power'.[19]

Jefferson inclined to Mason's view that the state was justified in preventing religious exercise which interfered with the rights of others and his distinction between protected beliefs and action also resonates with the modern distinction between the *forum externum* and the *forum internum* in the *ICCPR*. Madison's duty to God idea has clear antecedents in the thought of William Penn and John Locke who held that 'conscience, the duty owed one's God'[20] was 'a form of property'[21] which was 'beyond the rightful reach of government'[22] regulation.[23]

---

14   *ICCPR* (n 7) art 18(3).
15   Smith (n 13) 51.
16   Ibid 109, 119-21.
17   Ibid 120.
18   Ibid 121.
19   Ibid 127.
20   Ibid.
21   Ibid.
22   Ibid.
23   Ibid 95, 98.

The religious freedom wording finally adopted on 12 June 1776 in s 16 of the Virginia *Bill of Rights* was:

> That religion, or the duty which we owe to our Creator, and the manner of discharging it, can be directed only by reason and conviction, not by force or violence; and therefore all men are equally entitled to the free exercise of religion, according to the dictates of conscience; and that it is the mutual duty of all to practise Christian forbearance, love, and charity toward each other.[24]

It manifests compromise between Mason and Madison and significantly influenced the language of the *Declaration of Independence* drafted later that same month by the 'Committee of Five' with Thomas Jefferson principal among them. To the extent that the *Declaration of Independence* ratified by the Continental Congress three weeks later on 4 July 1776 had anything to say about religious freedom, it read:

> We hold these truths to be self-evident, that all men are created equal, that they are endowed by their Creator with certain unalienable Rights, that among these are Life, Liberty and the pursuit of Happiness. – That to secure these rights, Governments are instituted among Men, deriving their just powers from the consent of the governed, - That whenever any Form of Government becomes destructive of these ends, it is the Right of the People to alter or to abolish it, and to institute new Government, laying its foundation on such principles and organizing its powers in such form, as to them shall seem most likely to effect their Safety and Happiness.[25]

Nearly ten years later, when those Declarants had secured their freedom and were contemplating the form their new government should take, and the principles upon which it should be founded, Jefferson wrote the Virginia *Statute of Religious Liberty* and it was passed into law by the Virginia General Assembly on 16 January 1786. It disestablished the Anglican Church and

---

24   *Virginia Bill of Rights* s 16.

25   Independence Hall Association, 'The Declaration of Independence: The Want, Will and Hopes of the People', *US History* (Web Page, 4 July 1995) <http://www.ushistory.org/declaration/document/>.

dealt with religious freedom in more detail but included the following text:

> I. Whereas Almighty God hath created the mind free; that all attempts
> to influence it by temporal punishment or burthens, or by civil
> incapacitations, tend only to beget habits of hypocrisy and meanness,
> and are a departure from the plan of the Holy author of our religion,
> who being Lord both of body and mind, yet chose not to propagate
> it by coercions on either, as was his Almighty power to do . . .
>
> II. Be it enacted by the General Assembly, that no man shall be
> compelled to frequent or support any religious worship, place, or
> ministry whatsoever, nor shall be enforced, restrained, molested,
> or burthened in his body or goods, nor shall otherwise suffer on
> account of his religious opinions or belief; but that all men shall be
> free to profess, and by argument to maintain, their opinion in matters
> of religion, and that the same shall in no wise diminish, enlarge, or
> affect their civil capacities.[26]

Jefferson felt so strongly about the successful passage of this statute into law that he left clear instructions that it should be memorialised as one of his two greatest accomplishment on his tombstone.[27] He wrote:

> On the faces of the Obelisk the following inscription, & not a word
> more:
>> Here was buried
>> Thomas Jefferson
>> Author of the Declaration of American Independence
>> of the Statute of Virginia for religious freedom
>> & Father of the University of Virginia
> Because by these, as testimonials that I have lived, I wish to be
> remembered.[28]

---

26   'Thomas Jefferson and the Virginia Statute for Religious Freedom' *Virginia Museum of History and Culture* (Web Page) <https://www.virginiahistory.org/collections-and-resources/virginia-history-explorer/thomas-jefferson> ('Thomas Jefferson and the Virginia Statute').

27   'Thomas Jefferson's Tombstone' *Sam Davidson* (Blog Post, 19 September 2011) < http://samdavidson.net/blog/thomas-jeffersons-tombstone> ('Thomas Jefferson's Tombstone'); see also 'Jefferson's Gravestone', *Thomas Jefferson's Monticello* (Web Page) < https://www.monticello.org/site/research-and-collections/jeffersons-gravestone>.

28   Thomas Jefferson's Tombstone (n 27).

He asked no mention of his two terms as President, his ambassadorial service in France or any of the many other offices he discharged in the service of his country. The Virginia Statute was passed 'because dissenting sects there (particularly Baptists, Presbyterians and Methodists) had petitioned strongly during the preceding decade for religious liberty, including the separation of church and state'.[29] The implication that Madison was correct to believe that the protection of religious freedom in s 18 of the Virginia *Bill of Rights* was insufficient to secure religious freedom in that state without disestablishment of the Anglican Church, appears to have been vindicated. Until disestablishment, in 18th century America, minority religion did not feel included in her civil society.

In due course, the Virginia expressions of religious freedom were the watershed from which the US *First Amendment* (and first clause in the US *Bill of* Rights) flowed. Madison's 1776 'free exercise of religion' phrase in the original Virginia *Bill of Rights* was carried forward:[30]

> Congress shall make no law respecting an establishment of religion, or prohibiting the free exercise thereof; or abridging the freedom of speech, or of the press; or the right of the people peaceably to assemble, and to petition the Government for a redress of grievances.[31]

I shall now outline the debate about religious freedom at a national level in what became the United States before the First Amendment was adopted.

Part Three – The debate in the US Constitutional Conventions

Madison originally did not think a Bill of Rights was necessary because the states had their own constitutions and as a government of limited powers,

---

29   Thomas Jefferson and the Virginia Statute (n 26).
30   Paul Matzko, 'Virginia's Religious Disestablishment', *Association of Religion Data Archives* (Web Page) < http://www.thearda.com/timeline/events/event_13.asp>.
31   *United States Constitution* amend I.

the proposed US federal government would not be able to exercise powers that it had not been given.[32] Madison was not alone. George Mason wished that the constitutional plan had been prefaced by a Bill of Rights but when 'Elbridge Gerry moved for the appointment of a Committee to prepare such a bill',[33] the delegates defeated the motion without debate.[34] Those delegates all thought a Bill of Rights unnecessary since the proposed federal government was limited to its enumerated powers. The only reason Madison eventually added a draft Bill of Rights was because a pledge that such amendments would follow, was politically essential to achieve ratification of the whole unification project in New York and Virginia where it would otherwise be a close run thing.[35] As a matter of law, he did not place a great deal of confidence in what he called 'parchment barriers'.[36] However, Vincent Blasi has written that Madison came to understand the protective importance of the US *Bill of Rights* ten years later when:

> during the Washington administration,…he witnessed with dismay how [his *Federalist Papers'* co-writer and] Treasury Secretary Alexander Hamilton implemented a complex system of public finance that permitted him to consolidate power in the national government in such a way as to overwhelm Madison's carefully designed system of checks and balances.[37]

For David Little, Madison's early 'reservations about a bill of rights…had nothing to do with a lack of conviction'. He was more concerned that the

---

32   Thomas C Berg (ed), *The First Amendment: The Free Exercise of Religion Clause, Its Constitutional History and the Contemporary Debate* (Prometheus Books, 2008) Editor's Preface, 12.

33   History.com Editors, 'Bill of Rights', *History* (Web Page, 25 September 2019) < https://www.history.com/topics/united-states-constitution/bill-of-rights#section_2>.

34   Ibid.

35   Ibid.

36   Ibid.

37   'First Amendment Author James Madison "Belated" in Discovering its Importance' *University of Virginia School of Law* (Web Page, 5 March 2004) <https://content.law.virginia.edu/news/2004_spr/blasi.htm>.

inclusion of express freedoms 'as part of the national Constitution, might suggest…that these rights were delegated by the government, rather than possessed inalienably by the people'.[38] McConnell's analysis adds that the free exercise formulation upon which both James Madison and George Mason finally agreed in 1776 included the idea that "full and free exercise of religion" was exempt from general law except in cases of overriding importance.[39]

During the Constitutional Convention, John Adams had written from England to Thomas Jefferson in Paris and asked: 'What think you of a Declaration of Rights? Should not such a Thing have preceded the Model?'. Jefferson is said to have replied that while 'he found much to like about the new plan for a federal government…he objected to the "omission of a bill of rights"' and wrote to Madison that 'a bill of rights is what the people are entitled to against every government on earth, general or particular, & what no government should refuse, or rest on inference'.[40]

Then, as now in Australia, there was argument against a Bill of Rights from even committed civil libertarians that a bill of rights would restrict rather than guarantee freedoms.[41] Partly that was premised on Madison's idea that the statement of natural rights in a Bill would infer that the government could grant them rather than that they were self-evident or inherent as had been affirmed in the Declaration of Independence. But there was also

---

38   David Little, 'Theological Source of the Religion Clauses in Historical Perspective' in James E Woods (ed) *The First Freedom, Religion and the Bill of Rights* (J.M. Dawson Institute of Church-State Studies, 1990) 22-3.

39   Michael W McConnell, 'The Origins and Historical Understanding of Free Exercise of Religion' in Thomas C Berg (ed), *The First Amendment: The Free Exercise of Religion Clause, Its Constitutional History and the Contemporary Debate* (Prometheus Books, 2008) 84, 88.

40   Jack Lynch, 'Debating the Bill of Rights: What No Government Should Refuse, or Rest on Inference' [2009] (Winter) *Colonial Williamsburg Journal* <https://research.colonialwilliamsburg.org/Foundation/journal/Winter09/rights.cfm>.

41   Ibid.

concern that if a list of rights omitted anything, then that other assumed inherent right would then have been excluded. There was also an argument that leaving natural rights out of the federal constitution would affirm that such protections belonged in state constitutions since they retained all the legislative power that was not granted by the new federal constitution to the federal government.

We do not know for certain what tipped the balance for Madison, but his decision to support a bill of rights by immediate constitutional amendment seems to have convinced the naysayers on the basis that if it was good enough for Madison, it was good enough for them. Originally, the Bill he drafted contained seventeen rights, but they were 'whittled down to twelve' by the Congress. Two more were rejected by the states – one of those, concerning congressional salaries, was only passed 201 years later in 1992.[42]

Madison's first draft of an amendment to protect religious freedom, introduced on 8 June 1789, was immediately challenged. It read: '[t]he civil rights of none shall be abridged on account of religious belief or worship, nor shall any national religion be established, nor shall the full and equal rights of conscience be in any manner, or on any pretext infringed'.[43]

While Madison said his intention was to prevent congress establishing a national religion, Benjamin Huntingdon of Connecticut thought the clause could hurt religion and be misconstrued so as to disallow any governmental religious observation. Some representatives took issue with the word "national" and on 15 August 1789, Samuel Livermore of New Hampshire proposed a new version: 'Congress shall make no laws touching religion, or infringing the rights of conscience'.[44] On 20 August 1789, Fisher Ames from Massachusetts proposed: 'Congress shall make no law establishing religion, or to prevent the free exercise thereof, or to infringe the rights

42   Ibid.
43   Ibid.
44   Ibid.

of conscience,'[45] but when this proposed amendment left the House
of Representatives for the Senate it read: 'Congress shall make no law
establishing religion or prohibiting the free exercise thereof, nor shall the
rights of Conscience be infringed'.[46]

In the Senate, there were a number of further versions before a Conference
Committee was appointed to resolve the differences. That Committee,
which included Madison from the House of Representatives, settled the
current language which was ratified without further debate by the States on
15 December 1791 and read: 'Congress shall make no Law respecting an
establishment of Religion, or prohibiting the free exercise thereof'.[47] For
Madison, the Establishment and Free Exercise clauses were both necessary to
prevent government overreach into individual conscience. No government
and no majority should have the right to interfere with the property that was
individual conscience. Any interference with conscience stood to exclude
the affected minorities from full inclusion within the relevant society.[48]
Majoritarian tyranny must be stopped by governmental institutional
structure and by protecting conscience from any government interference.
The only time government interference with conscience could be justified
was if the existence of the state itself was imperilled by some full and free
exercise of religion. The idea shared by Jefferson and Mason,[49] and which is
reiterated in modern terms in art 18 of the *ICCPR* – that government could
justify interference with religious practice if the existence of the state was

---

45   Ibid.
46   Ibid.
47   Ibid; see also Douglas Laycock, '"Nonpreferential" Aid to Religion: A False
        Claim About Original Intent' (1986) 27 *William & Mary Law Review* 875. Note
        Douglas Laycock's discussion of the various First Amendment options that were
        discussed by the House of Representatives and the Senate before they settled
        on the final text. See also Smith (n 13) 292. Note too Smith's speculation that
        Madison likely drafted the final version since he was a member of the relevant
        Committee and the final clause used his "free exercise" phrase: at 292.
48   Smith (n 13) 122-3.
49   Ibid 118-20, 130-3.

not threatened but if public peace and tranquillity were threatened – would have allowed far too easy inroads to the full and free exercise of religion. When he advocated religious liberty and drafted legislative instruments to protect it, Madison chose not to differentiate between what we now call the *forum internum* and the *forum externum*.

The meaning of the 'free exercise' phrase has not received a lot of jurisprudential attention since. I have written about this previously and said:

> [In Australia, where this phase] is the core part of the third of four clauses identifying religious space where the Commonwealth is prohibited from legislating,[50] it appears to protect what has become known in the 20th century as the *forum externum*. That focus stands in contrast to the focus of the fourth clause which prohibits religious tests for public office and thus prevents the Commonwealth from some legislative interference with the *forum internum*.[51] The US Supreme Court has suggested that religious beliefs are completely protected by this *internum-externum* dichotomy, but that acts done for religious reasons are not protected when they would offend the requirements of generally applicable law,[52] though they did not apply that standard from the 1960s until 1991.[53]

I also observed Carolyn Evans' view that the *forum internum-externum* dichotomy is not helpful because a clear line between these fora cannot be

---

50   *Australian Constitution* s 116.

51   The fourth subclause of s 116 prohibits the Commonwealth from making religious tests 'a qualification for any office or public trust under the Commonwealth'.

52   See, eg, *Reynolds v US* 98 US 145 (1878); *Employment Division v Smith* 494 US 872 (1990).

53   A Keith Thompson, 'Religious Freedom under the Australian Constitution and recommendations that religious confession privilege be abolished' in Iain T Benson, Michael Quinlan and A Keith Thompson (eds), *Religious Freedom in Australia: A New Terra Nullius?* (Shepherd Street Press, 2019) 239, 244-7; see also *Sherbert v Werner* 374 US 398 (1963); *Wisconsin v Yoder* 406 US 205 (1972). In the former, the Supreme Court overturned a State law which denied unemployment benefits denied to a Seventh Day Adventist woman who would not work on Saturdays. In the latter, the Supreme Court held that the State's interest in educating Amish children was outweighed by their parents' religious wish to continue their education after the eighth grade outside the state school system.

identified in practice.[54] She said that action cannot be easily separated from thought when it follows thought and the *forum internum-externum* dichotomy then denies protection for the conscience aspect of the resulting action even though many religious acts (like personal prayer and church attendance) are completely harmless. When this problem of the frequent indivisibility of religious thought and action is tracked to ground, the dichotomy can be seen to trivialise the dignitarian nature of religious belief and practice. And it is that risk of trivialisation which presents as the reason for the original disagreement between George Mason and James Madison in 1776 when they were debating how religious liberty should best be protected under their original Virginia statute. Madison was adamant that Mason's distinction was too weak. That is why Madison chose the "free exercise" phrase. And though that phrase did not feature in his first draft of the US First Amendment, it resurfaced and was cast in bronze by the Conference Committee that settled the final version of that language – and that language was then adopted by the Australian framers 110 years later. I have previously summarised where that analysis leads:

> The consequence of these insights is that religious belief and action are probably best understood as part of a conscience spectrum that should be considered in the context of other human rights demands. The essentiality of conscience and belief to human identity and dignity are manifest in the fact that the *ECHR* and *ICCPR* framers said that the internal part of religious belief and action should be inviolable or non-derogable. Whether actions taken for religious reasons should be protected is a matter of balance. How they are balanced depends upon how much those religious actions intrude into, or even violate the human rights and dignity of others. But the balancing that is done, must take into account the dignity of the religious believers involved, however unpopular or politically incorrect their belief choices may have become.[55]

---

54   Carolyn M Evans, *Freedom of Religion or Belief under the European Convention on Human Rights* (Oxford University Press, 2012) ch 5 and particularly 72-9; see also Paul M Taylor, *Freedom of Religion: UN and European Human Rights Law and Practice* (Cambridge University Press, 2005) ch 3 and particularly 117-24.

55   Thompson (n 53) 246-7.

In practical terms, the debate between Madison and Mason about what wording best protects religious freedom in practice begun in Virginia is still relevant today. The only difference in the Australian context is that because we have never had a Madison in our Parliament setting our nuances, we have never fully engaged with the issues that concerned him.

Part Four – What does "free exercise of religion" mean in Australia in the 21st century?

The introduction of the "free exercise of religion" phrase into the *Australian Constitution* came in the Australian Constitutional Debates at the instance of barrister H.B. Higgins in February and March 1898.[56] He had been lobbied by Victorian voters concerned that Patrick Glynn's successful introduction of the words "Almighty God" in the Preamble to the *Constitution*, presaged a de facto establishment of religion in this country. Higgins' lobbyists had tabled petitions stating their concerns and opposition to the Preamble wording in April 1897.[57]

---

56 *Official Record of the Debates of the Australasian Federal Convention*, Melbourne, 7 February 1898, 655-7 (Henry Higgins); *Official Record of the Debates of the Australasian Federal Convention*, Melbourne, 8 February 1898, 658-63 (Henry Higgins); *Official Record of the Debates of the Australasian Federal Convention*, Melbourne, 2 March 1898, 1732-79 (Henry Higgins); *Official Record of the Debates of the Australasian Federal Convention*, Melbourne, 17 March 1898, 2474 (Edmund Barton).

57 *Official Report of the National Australasian Convention Debates*, Adelaide, 6 April 1897, 405 (Vabien Louis Solomon); *Official Report of the National Australasian Convention Debates*, Adelaide, 7 April 1897, 406 (Vabien Louis Solomon); *Official Report of the National Australasian Convention Debates*, Adelaide, 12 April 1897, 429 (Sir George Turner); *Official Report of the National Australasian Convention Debates*, Adelaide, 20 April 1897, 943-4 (George Huston Reid). On 6 April 1897, 1,201 electors from Victoria, South Australia, Tasmania and New South Wales, prayed 'that neither the Federal Government nor any State Parliament sh[ould] make any law respecting religion or prohibiting the free exercise thereof'. On 7 April 1897, 1,663 electors from Victoria, South Australia and New South Wales delivered a very similar petition. On 12 April 1897, 2,606 residents of New South Wales, Victoria, South Australia and Tasmania prayed similarly. And finally on 20 April 1897, 2,337 persons from New South Wales, Victoria, South Australia and Tasmania prayed that 'no state in the Commonwealth should be allowed to make any law respecting religion or prohibiting the free exercise thereof'.

Higgins' original draft proposed that the Australian states should be prohibited from passing religious establishment laws. After debate, his proposal was amended to prevent both states and Commonwealth from establishing a religion, but further amendment forbade religious establishment to the Commonwealth but not the states so that the states might continue to regulate religious practice.

It is evident from this history and an analysis of the debates in our constitutional conventions, that the American language was adopted to prevent a national establishment of religion in Australia rather than to protect the conscience or practice of British subjects in Australia even though the American "free exercise of religion" words were used in full. While there was discussion of whether and how religious conscience and practice should be governed, the national debate did not fully engage with that issue and left it to the states where it has arguably never been the subject of the vigorous analytical debate that occurred in Virginia and then nationally between 1776 and 1791. Even though our Human Rights and Equal Opportunity Commission (HREOC) identified the need for national engagement with this issue in 1998, it is only the same-sex marriage debate, and the demise of Prime Minister Turnbull, that have focused the underlying philosophical issues for more complete consideration in Australia.

As the so-called 'father of religious liberty' in the United States, even though he was born and raised an Anglican, James Madison's primary concern was to disestablish the Anglican Church as the state religion of Virginia.[58] Eleven years after Madison and Mason had first engaged with these issue in Virginia in 1775 and 1776, when the debate had moved to the national stage, Madison was similarly concerned to prevent the national establishment of any religion in the new United States. But since no one religion had the power to assert its supremacy on that stage, there was more nuanced consideration

58   Smith (n 13) 109-13.

of the nature and protection that should be afforded to individual religious practice in the Bill of Rights. Parchment protection of natural rights was widely seen as necessary to avoid the oppressive experiences all had suffered at English hands.

For Madison, religious establishment was the primary threat to free exercise of religion. But he was also aware of the oppression minority Baptists had suffered at the hands of majoritarian established Anglicans in Virginia. Baptists had been told they were not Christians because they did not fully subscribe to the established creeds, and teaching their doctrine had been defined as sedition.[59] Madison was thus unwilling to subject conscience to majority will.[60] His original phrase in Virginia in 1776 was "full and free exercise of religion" by which he meant that no government should interfere with an individual's expression and discharge of what he considered his duty to God. The "full and free exercise of religion" could only be legitimately controlled by government if that exercise would manifestly endanger the state itself or if it infringed upon the equal liberty of others.[61]

Madison did not accept that the generic protection of public peace, happiness or safety justified state regulation of religious practice.[62] He would have rejected the idea expressed in the *Victorian Charter of Human Rights and Responsibilities* in Australia most recently copied in Queensland, that the state was justified in prohibiting "full and free exercise of religion" if that prohibition was *reasonable* as a measure to protect the rights, safety and even the peace of others. He would have preferred the language of art 18 of the *ICCPR* that forbids state interference with the manifestation of religion unless that was *necessary* to protect public safety, health or morals. But Madison would have added, as he did in repeated debate with Mason

---

59   Ibid 111, 128.
60   Ibid 130.
61   Ibid 121.
62   Ibid 122.

from 1776 onwards, that the state should only be allowed to interfere with the free exercise of religion if that free exercise manifestly endangered the existence of the state itself. Madison would have decried fuzzy notions of public safety, health or morals as the unjustified dilution of the God-given natural rights of every human being. Such dilution was simply not necessary and called to his mind both the tyrannical oppressions of the English king, and the majoritarian Anglicans, against the minority Baptists in his native Virginia.

The question for modern Australia is whether Madison's insights have anything to teach us today. While there are suggestions that the 2019 debate about religious freedom is simply majority Anglicans and Catholics protesting the fact that they have been displaced by "no religion" as the majority in the 2016 Australian census,[63] that argument trivialises concern about the plight of unpopular religious minorities which was spelled out with challenging examples in HREOC's 1998 report to the federal government.[64] Should the new "no religion" majority be allowed to dictate its beliefs to old and new minorities, or do broader notions of equality and inclusion require that all voices be heard in the modern Australian public square? Should laws be passed that proscribe minority religious expression which does not manifestly endanger the existence of the state or, in the words of Thomas Jefferson, break the bones or pick the pockets of those who think otherwise?[65] Should state and national anti-discrimination norms be updated to prevent terminations of employment or the foreclosure of other opportunities and services to those who have any minority status? In short, how should we adjust our laws to ensure that we can continue to live

63   Australian Bureau of Statistics, *2016 Census Data Summary: Religion in Australia* (Catalogue 2071.0, 28 June 2017) 1.

64   Human Rights and Equal Opportunity Commission, *Article 18: Freedom of religion and belief* (Report, July 1998).

65   'Extract from Thomas Jefferson's *Notes on the State of Virginia*', *Thomas Jefferson's Monticello* (Web Page, 1 January - 31 December 1782) <http://tjrs.monticello.org/letter/2260> ('Extract from Thomas Jefferson').

together in disagreement?[66] What is the wise and appropriate consensus of Australian shared virtues after the recommendations of the Ruddock Review?

My suggestion is that everything James Madison argued about the nature of religion and conscience between 1776 and 1791 is transferable to modern Australia. The only reason we should consider making speech or religious manifestation illegal is if it 'manifestly endangers the existence of the state'[67] or physically encroaches on the *ICCPR* rights of another. While I have disagreed with John Rawls' revision of his *Theory of Justice* post the *Smith* case in 1991,[68] I agree with his idea that the continued peaceful existence of a liberal democratic society rests on the reimagination of our overlapping consensus every time that is necessary. We simply have different religious beliefs and non-beliefs to reconcile in the present. Our wise goal must be to ensure we include everyone. All must feel they have a voice in society. History makes it clear that the suppression of dissenting voices is an unwise strategy. It cannot provide long term societal peace.

Conclusion

The aphorism that those who ignore history are destined to repeat it, is variously attributed.[69] Nor is it possible to prove whether it is true or not.

---

66   Cf Iain T Benson, *Living Together with Disagreement, Pluralism, the Secular and the Fair Treatment of Beliefs in Law Today* (Connor Court, 2012).

67   Smith (n 13) 121

68   Anthony K Thompson, 'Should 'Public Reason' Developed Under US Establishment Clause Jurisprudence Apply to Australia?' (2015) 17 *The University of Notre Dame Australia Law Review* 107, 107-34.

69   See, eg, Matthew Caleb Flamm, 'George Santayana (1863-1952)', *Internet Encyclopaedia of Philosophy* (Web Page) <https://www.iep.utm.edu/santayan/>; see also Dallon Christensen, 'Those who fail to learn from history are doomed to repeat it', *Whiteboard Business Partners* (Web Page) < http://www.whiteboardbusiness.com/those-who-fail-to-learn-from-history-are-doomed-to-repeat-it-sir-winston-churchill/>. Note that Winston Churchill is said to have paraphrased George Santayana's quote to the House Commons in 1948.

But there is no doubting that there is a circular quality to individual and human societal behaviour. It is similarly unlikely that we will ever be able to prove that the similar solutions we learn come because we think in parallel lines or crystallise transcendent ideas from the atmosphere in response to identical social stimuli. And yet previous experience, including the idea of precedent in law, is a giant on whose shoulders many generations of humanity have wisely built.

In this chapter, I have suggested that Australia's current debate about religious freedom and the idea that we need to make our society more inclusive, has more context than has been credited in the public square in recent Australian debate. Every human society that aspires to peaceful co-existence has wrestled with the ideas we now label minority, dissent and diversity. The underlying problem has always been whether we best achieve peaceful co-existence by suppressing or even crushing the dissenting voices, whether we force those who oppressed us in the past to pay for those sins of oppression in the future,[70] or whether we find a contemporary solution more respectful of physically harmless human difference and conscience.

There are many respects in which this recurring question is sad. It is sad that we seem to have to relearn how to live together in peace in every single generation of our existence.[71] While the Westphalia *'cuius regio, eius religio'* summary conclusion in 1648 did not respect human conscience enough to resolve the underlying problem, it did recognise that there are some human differences that are so inherently contestable and enduring that they are never going to be solved forever by suppression. And so those treaty

---

70   Many historians have suggested that causes of the Second World War may be found in the reparations payments imposed on the German people by the Versailles Treaty which concluded World War I. See, eg, Sarah Pruitt, 'How the Treaty of Versailles and German Guilt Led to World War II', *History* (Web Page, 3 June 2019) <https://www.history.com/news/treaty-of-versailles-world-war-ii-german-guilt-effects>.

71   Cf Martha Nussbaum, *Liberty of Conscience: In Defense of America's Tradition of Religious Liberty* (Basic Books, 2008) 359-60.

makers called 'quits' to their most recent thirty years of war. Mere tolerance is not an enduring solution either because tolerance is always condescending and makes people outsiders as Sandra Day O'Connor might have warned.[72] Long term solutions require respectful understanding of differences that do not threaten the existence of the state.

After the revolutionary Americans had created their new republic in the eighteenth century, they experimented with practical solutions that responded to the philosophical insights of the enlightenment. For the most part, those philosophical insights endure though the utility of their practical experiments is not as obvious. For example, their solutions to the problem of how to stop central governments accumulating power which the essayists wrestled with in *The Federalist Papers*,[73] has not resolved the problem. Despite their hopes, neither structural constraints nor a Bill of Rights have stopped the US Executive, Legislature or Judiciary accumulating power. And Australia's Westminster preference that final Commonwealth decisions come from politicians rather than unelected judges, has yielded no greater protection of the principle of subsidiarity. But the Americans did light on something valuable when under Madison's leadership; they insisted on religious disestablishment. While continuing national experiments in other countries confirm that disestablishment is not essential to religious freedom and is no cure for governmental intolerance of dissent,[74] in a liberal democracy there is some truth to the idea that peaceful co-existence depends on the idea that no orthodoxy should be imposed on anyone.[75]

---

72   *Lynch v Donnelly* 465 US 668 (1984); see also *McCreary County v ACLU* 545 US 844 (2005).

73   Originally published in 1788 under the pseudonym, Publius, this collection of 85 articles and essays was originally prepared by Alexander Hamilton, James Madison and John Jay to encourage the States of New York and Virginia to ratify the *US Constitution*.

74   See, eg, W Cole Durham and Brett G Scharffs, *Law and Religion: National, International and Comparative Perspectives* (Aspen Publishers, 2010) 112-62.

75   *West Virginia State Board of Education v Barnette* (1943) 319 US 624, 642 (Jackson AJ).

However, we have not learned the additional lesson that this principle does not just apply to the imposition of ideological or religious orthodoxy. If all minorities are to enjoy peaceful lives in any society, none of them can be straitjacketed into an identity with which they are not comfortable. Madison argued that there was only one sensible exception to that principle when he went further than does our modern *ICCPR*. While Jefferson would have limited minority manifestation if it 'picked his pocket or broke his leg',[76] Madison was emphatic that the only thing that justified suppression of conscience was a manifestation that threatened the existence of the state itself.[77] While he conceded the *ICCPR* idea that minorities could be controlled if their manifestations would interfere with the natural rights and freedoms of others,[78] he was not conceding dignitary harm. Though we cannot cross-examine him on the point, his concession to the rights and freedoms of others was part and parcel of his notion that the protection of minorities could not go so far as to endanger the state itself. And while I think he took for granted that ideological difference could never justify breach of the generally applicable criminal law, I do not think he would have conceded that the generally applicable criminal law should include prohibitions on simple moral harm as art 18(3) of the *ICCPR* allows.

My conclusion is that the American consideration of conscience protection in the eighteenth century went much deeper than our debates. When our framers decided to use the American conscience settlement words between 1897 and 1900, they did not engage with freedom of conscience. They reached for, and adapted, a formula that denied establishment and that has been confirmed by the Australian High Court.[79] But the words Madison used captured more of the enlightenment wisdom than we have yet pondered. When must we impose on conscience or identity? Need we do so when our

---

76   Extract from Thomas Jefferson (n 65).
77   Smith (n 13) 121.
78   Ibid.
79   *Attorney-General (Vic); Ex Rel Black v Commonwealth* (1981) 146 CLR 599.

self-image is challenged, or only if our physical peace or the existence of our nation are endangered? Should legal ideas about non-specific general damage and dignitary harm be imported into this constitutional space? If they are, can we find a satisfying answer, or do we need to withdraw to the more tangible notions of harm that Jefferson and Madison settled upon? My suggestion is that we can only safely regulate what we can touch and see. While we can and should pastorally empathise with all of those who are the victims of abuse including those who have inherited dignitary harm, our discrimination laws should not direct punishment for intangible harm.

Bibliography

Attorney-General (Vic); Ex Rel Black v Commonwealth (1981) 146 CLR 599.

Australian Bureau of Statistics, *2016 Census Data Summary: Religion in Australia* (Catalogue 2071.0, 28 June 2017).

Australian Bureau of Statistics, *Census of Population and Housing: Reflecting Australia: Stories from the Census, 2016: Same-Sex Couples in Australia, 2016* (Catalogue 2071.0, 18 January 2018).

Australian Bureau of Statistics, *Census of Population and Housing: Reflecting Australia: Stories from the Census, 2016: Sex and Gender Diversity in the 2016 Census.*

Australian Constitution.

Benson, Iain T, *Living Together with Disagreement, Pluralism, the Secular and the Fair Treatment of Beliefs in Law Today* (Connor Court, 2012).

Berg, Thomas C (ed), *The First Amendment: The Free Exercise of Religion Clause, Its Constitutional History and the Contemporary Debate* (Prometheus Books, 2008).

Christensen, Dallon, 'Those who fail to learn from history are doomed to repeat it', *Whiteboard Business Partners* (Web Page) < http://www.whiteboardbusiness. com/those-who-fail-to-learn-from-history-are-doomed-to-repeat-it-sir-winston-churchill/>.

Durham, W Cole and Brett G Scharffs, *Law and Religion: National, International and Comparative Perspectives* (Aspen Publishers, 2010).

Employment Division v Smith 494 US 872 (1990).

Evans, Carolyn M, *Freedom of Religion or Belief under the European Convention on Human Rights* (Oxford University Press, 2012).

'Extract from Thomas Jefferson's Notes on the State of Virginia', *Thomas Jefferson's Monticello* (Web Page, 1 January - 31 December 1782) http://tjrs.monticello.org/letter/2260.

Fischer, David Hackett, *Albion's Seed: Four British Folkways in America* (Oxford University Press, 1989).

Flamm, Matthew Caleb, 'George Santayana (1863-1952)', *Internet Encyclopaedia of Philosophy* (Web Page) <https://www.iep.utm.edu/santayan/>.

History.com Editors, 'Bill of Rights', *History* (Web Page, 25 September 2019) <https://www.history.com/topics/united-states-constitution/bill-of-rights#section_2>.

Human Rights and Equal Opportunity Commission, *Article 18: Freedom of religion and belief* (Report, July 1998).

Independence Hall Association, 'The Declaration of Independence: The Want, Will and Hopes of the People', *US History* (Web Page, 4 July 1995) <http://www.ushistory.org/declaration/document/>.

International Covenant on Civil and Political Rights, G.A. Res 2200A (XXI), U.N. GAOR, 21st Sess., Supp.No.16 U.N. Doc.A/6316 (16 December 1966, entered into force on 23 March 1976).

'Jefferson's Gravestone', *Thomas Jefferson's Monticello* (Web Page) <https://www.monticello.org/site/research-and-collections/jeffersons-gravestone>.

Jefferson, Thomas, *Notes on the State of Virginia* (John Stockdale, 2nd ed, 1787).

Laycock, Douglas, '"Nonpreferential" Aid to Religion: A False Claim About Original Intent' (1986) 27 *William & Mary Law Review* 875.

Lynch, Jack, 'Debating the Bill of Rights: What No Government Should Refuse, or Rest on Inference' [2009] (Winter) *Colonial Williamsburg Journal* <https://research.colonialwilliamsburg.org/Foundation/journal/Winter09/rights.cfm>.

Lynch v Donnelly 465 US 668 (1984).

Matzko, Paul, 'Virginia's Religious Disestablishment', *Association of Religion Data Archives* (Web Page) < http://www.thearda.com/timeline/events/event_13.asp>.

McConnell, Michael W, 'The Origins and Historical Understanding of Free Exercise of Religion' in Thomas C Berg (ed), *The First Amendment: The Free Exercise of Religion Clause, Its Constitutional History and the Contemporary Debate* (Prometheus Books, 2008) 84.

McCreary County v ACLU 545 US 844 (2005).

Nussbaum, Martha, *Liberty of Conscience: In Defense of America's Tradition of Religious Liberty* (Basic Books, 2008).

Official Record of the Debates of the Australasian Federal Convention, Melbourne, 7 February 1898, 655-7 (Henry Higgins).

Official Record of the Debates of the Australasian Federal Convention, Melbourne, 8 February 1898, 658-63 (Henry Higgins).

Official Record of the Debates of the Australasian Federal Convention, Melbourne, 2 March 1898, 1732-79 (Henry Higgins).

Official Record of the Debates of the Australasian Federal Convention, Melbourne, 17 March 1898, 2474 (Edmund Barton).

Official Report of the National Australasian Convention Debates, Adelaide, 6 April 1897, 405 (Vabien Louis Solomon).

Official Report of the National Australasian Convention Debates, Adelaide, 7 April 1897, 406 (Vabien Louis Solomon).

Official Report of the National Australasian Convention Debates, Adelaide, 12 April 1897, 429 (Sir George Turner).

Official Report of the National Australasian Convention Debates, Adelaide, 20 April 1897, 943-4 (George Huston Reid).

Pruitt, Sarah, 'How the Treaty of Versailles and German Guilt Led to World War II', *History* (Web Page, 3 June 2019) <https://www.history.com/news/treaty-of-versailles-world-war-ii-german-guilt-effects>.

Reynolds v US 98 US 145 (1878).

'Section 8: The Fall of Rome: Facts and Fictions', *Utah State University* (Web Page, 2019) < https://www.usu.edu/markdamen/1320Hist&Civ/chapters/08ROMFAL.htm>.

'Separation of church and state in the United States', *Wikipedia* (Web Page, 23 July 2020) <https://en.wikipedia.org/wiki/Separation_of_church_and_state_in_the_United_States>.

Sherbert v Werner 374 US 398 (1963).

Smith, Rodney K, *James Madison: The Father of Religious Liberty* (Plain Sight, 2019).

Taylor, Paul M, *Freedom of Religion: UN and European Human Rights Law and Practice* (Cambridge University Press, 2005).

'Thomas Jefferson and the Virginia Statute for Religious Freedom' *Virginia Museum of History and Culture* (Web Page) <https://www.virginiahistory.org/collections-and-resources/virginia-history-explorer/thomas-jefferson>.

'Thomas Jefferson's Tombstone' *Sam Davidson* (Blog Post, 19 September 2011) < http://samdavidson.net/blog/thomas-jeffersons-tombstone>.

Thompson, A Keith, 'Religious Freedom under the Australian Constitution and recommendations that religious confession privilege be abolished' in Iain T Benson, Michael Quinlan and A Keith Thompson (eds), *Religious Freedom in Australia: A New Terra Nullius?* (Shepherd Street Press, 2019) 239.

Thompson, Anthony K, 'Should 'Public Reason' Developed Under US Establishment Clause Jurisprudence Apply to Australia?' (2015) 17 *The University of Notre Dame Australia Law Review* 107.

Thompson, A Keith, *Trinity and Monotheism: A historical and theological review of the origins and substance of the doctrine* (Modotti Press, 2019).

United States Constitution.

Universal Declaration of Human Rights, GA RES 217A (III), UN GAOR, UN Doc A/810 (10 December 1948).

Virginia Bill of Rights.

West Virginia State Board of Education v Barnette (1943) 319 US 624.

Wisconsin v Yoder 406 US 205 (1972).

'Xi warns China's adversaries of 'crushed bodies, shattered bones'', *Aljazeera* (online, 14 October 2019) <https://www.aljazeera.com/news/2019/10/xi-warns-china-adversaries-crushed-bodies-shattered-bones-191014015858714.html>.

8

RELIGIOUS FREEDOMS AND INCLUSIVITY

Charles Wilson

Abstract

'Inclusivity' and 'religious freedoms' today are disputed terms. Conservative and faith-based groups and secular liberals alike exclude some from their idea of 'inclusivity'. The result is a civic life conducted in increasingly divisive tones. In finding a way through the impasse, this paper suggests that too much can be expected of the law although it has a role to play. It explores the possibility that it is on individuals and informal networks on whom responsibility instead falls and that people of faith have before them an opportunity to allow others to see that public life can be conducted in a different way, by drawing on the qualities that enrich and sustain faith-based life with humility and respect.

Recent academic exploration of the constitutive theory of the foundations of s 116 of the *Constitution* posits the idea that the section is a safeguard against religious intolerance.[1] It may equally be understood that s 116 is a safeguard against religious exclusivity. 'Safeguard' is not an inapt term. Sir Henry Higgins used the word repeatedly in the course of advocating for s 116 at the 1897-8 Federal Convention.[2]

Conceived as a 'safeguard' against 'religious exclusivity' captures well the point of s 116, at least as well as the idea of a safeguard against 'religious intolerance'. Section 116, among other things, forbids laws imposing a religious test for public office. It is a safeguard against 'intolerance' by striking at laws that deny access to public office to those who do not adhere to favoured religious beliefs or adhere to disfavoured ones.[3]

The concept of 'exclusivity', as Luke Beck observes,[4] is not the binary opposite of 'inclusivity'. 'Exclusivity' and 'inclusivity', he notes, are ideas sitting at the opposite end of a continuum. If the ideas were binary opposites, then the idea of a 'safeguard against religious exclusivity' would be the juridical equivalent of a 'guarantee of religious inclusivity'. That assuredly is not the legal operation or effect of s 116. The direction of s 116, as Mr Beck observes, is better viewed as essentially negative in character; it is concerned with avoiding a state of affairs, not with advancing a particular end in a positive sense, such as the elimination of all forms of religious intolerance or the promotion of inclusivity of religious belief and practice. Accordingly, it is elsewhere that one must look to find the agents of a commitment to 'inclusivity' as a possibility.

---

1   Beck, *Religious Freedom and the Australian Constitution: Origins and Future* (Rout-ledge, 2018), 118.

2   *Official Report of the National Australasian Convention Debates*, Melbourne 2 March 1897, 1734, 1779, accessible at <https://parlinfo.aph.gov.au/parlInfo/download/consti-tution/conventions/1898-1120/upload_binary/1898_1120.pdf;fileType=applica-tion/pdf#search=%22third%20session%22>, cited in Beck, (n 1), 118.

3   Beck, (n 1) 163-64.

4   Ibid.

Possible directions of inquiry are suggested by s 116. The philosophical literature on tolerance suggests two distinctions that are relevant to the theme of 'religious freedoms' and 'inclusivity'.[5] Firstly, a distinction is to be drawn between the subject of inclusivity and the object of inclusivity. The same distinction applies to the subject of exclusivity and the object of exclusivity. In the context of s 116, the subject of exclusivity is the Commonwealth. The objects of exclusivity are individuals or groups who may be excluded by reference to their religious beliefs or practices. What is evident is that s 116 does not place demands on private individuals. Section 116 only limits the legislative power of the Commonwealth as the subject of exclusivity,[6] without placing demands on the objects of exclusivity (private individuals or groups who may be affected by the actions of the Commonwealth). Section 116 does not oblige private individuals to refrain from religiously intolerant actions. It is not a guarantee of religious rights.[7] We return to the significance of this below.

A second distinction that is relevant to the theme of 'religious freedoms' and 'inclusivity', also suggested by the philosophical literature on tolerance, is to be drawn between 'inclusion' and 'inclusivity'. 'Inclusion' is a transitive concept: it requires an object. 'Inclusion' in this transitive sense invites the question, inclusion of what? So conceived, 'inclusion' is an action or a practice. 'Inclusivity' on the other hand does not necessarily require an object.[8] 'Inclusivity' is a quality. It is an attitude of the heart in which

---

5   This discussion is largely drawn from or suggested by observations in Beck, (n 1), 119-20.

6   *Attorney-General (Vic) (Ex rel Black) v Commonwealth* (1981) 146 CLR 559, 579-81; *Minister for Immigration and Ethnic Affairs v Lebanese Moslem Association* (1987) 17 FCR 373, 378.

7   For example, in *Kruger v Commonwealth (Stolen Generations Case)* (1997) 190 CLR 1, Justice Gaudron denied that the protection of religious freedom set out in s 116 of the *Constitution* was a constitutional guarantee because it "does no more than effect a restriction or limitation on the legislative power of the Common-wealth" (ibid 124-125).

8   Beck, (n 1), 119-20.

differences are embraced as a source of enrichment of a greater whole to which we all belong, not as grounds for marginalising or excluding another.

The same distinctions hold true for 'exclusion' and 'exclusivity', with 'exclusivity' viewed as a vice or unevolved state, at least in liberal circles, while many faith groups would want to defend an idea of 'exclusivity' on the basis that it is founded in the conviction of faith, not intolerance.

'Inclusivity' viewed through the lens of 'religious freedoms' is today a disputed term. It is a term that takes its meaning according to the interest using it.

Secular and progressive liberals expound an idea of 'inclusivity' that is opposed by conservative religious groups. Liberals of this kind are viewed by conservative religious groups as committed to marginalising differences of all kinds under the banner of 'inclusivity', and ignoring and thus subordinating to secular values, the beliefs and practices of people of different faiths.[9] On the other hand, conservative religious groups expound an idea of 'religious freedoms' that is opposed by secular and progressive liberals. Conservative religious groups are viewed by secular and progressive liberals as committed to establishing 'privileges' for conservative Christians in areas where public life intersects with religious belief or practice, an example of which is the push by conservative religious groups for legislative recognition of religion-based exceptions to secular and liberal standards otherwise of general application in the context of anti-discrimination, same-sex and end of life laws.

Secular and progressive liberals and conservative religious groups thus both espouse opposing ideas of 'inclusivity' that, in effect, exclude the other. In

---

9   A fully developed articulation of this view is found in the writing of Catholic lawyer, James Kalb. See, eg., James Kalb, 'Inclusiveness: A Harmful Ideology', *Crisis Magazine*, 5 December 2013, accessible at <https://www.crisismagazine. com/2013/inclusiveness-a-harmful-ideology>. And *Against Inclusiveness: How the Diversity Regime is Flattening America and the West and What to Do About It*, 2013.

short, both defend an idea of 'exclusivity' under the banner of 'inclusivity' that is dedicated to the protection of some, but not of all; and both groups are little different.

In recent years, the tension between the opposing ideas of 'inclusivity' espoused by secular and progressive liberals and conservative religious groups has become more acute as a consequence of two agencies. The first is in part the outplay of the second. The first is that we live in an age of statutes. Legislation now governs and controls large areas of activity in Australia that in earlier ages was the domain of the common law or societal consensus. The second is the emerging ascendancy of secular liberal values in civic life. This has seen conservative religious groups today perceive an existential threat to their place in the public square, so that they view legislative activity as an instrument for the advancement of secular agendas.

Confronted by the twin developments mentioned above, conservative religious groups have engaged in highly-organised efforts to defend their idea of 'inclusivity' and resist secular agendas under the banner of freedom of religious belief and practice. The result has been a public square dominated by debate conducted in increasingly divisive and shrill tones. Most troublingly, it has in places seen religion deployed as a force of bigotry, and secular and liberal ideals deployed as instruments of intolerance.

In many respects, the tension is not a new one. At its root is the tension of negotiating difference. What is of recent development however, at least in Australian and western democratic civic life, is the degree of polarisation and heightened divisiveness. The direction of civic life is in this respect not unique to the debate about 'religious freedoms' and 'inclusivity'. It can be found and is repeated in varying degrees in many conversations where what is in question is 'inclusivity' and belonging.

Confronted by the polarisation and heightened divisiveness of the debate about 'religious freedoms' and 'inclusivity' what is called for is a different, broader understanding of 'inclusivity' and a renewed understanding of the public square as a common space shared by liberal and socially progressive religious groups, and socially conservative religious groups alike, as opposed to a space that includes certain beliefs and is committed to the exclusion of others.

Attempts at establishing a different, broader understanding of 'inclusivity' in the public sphere, as a shared idea that can embrace all rather than only some, will be largely unsuccessful until ownership of the idea of 'inclusivity' is taken back from secular liberals. At the same time however, faith groups need to learn not to mistrust or reject the idea of 'inclusivity' in the public square as if it were an existential challenge to their existence. Equally, 'religious freedoms' as an aspiration for all people of all faiths and walks of life cannot be allowed to remain the exclusive property of conservative religious groups. How we are to advance this project calls for a renewed commitment as now outlined, below.

The distinction between the public and private spheres is increasingly difficult to define, as sociologists have observed.[10] What is evident is that public life has at least two dimensions. The first dimension of public life comprises a formal public space - the arms of government, democratic processes, the education system, and formal institutions (marriage, etc). The second dimension comprises the informal public space, in which people meet and build relationships and borrow and exchange ideas, the pulse of community life and social networks. Both of these dimensions inform and enrich the other.

What is in front of us today is how to restore ownership of the idea of

---

10   See, eg., Sales, A, 'The Private, the Public and Civil Society: Social Realms and Power Structures', (1991) 12(4), *The Public and the Private*, 295-312, accessible at <https://www.jstor.org/stable/1601467?seq=1>. See also, Charlesworth, H, 'The Public/ Private Distinction and the Right to Development in International Law', 1988 *Australian Year Book of International Law*, 190-204, accessible at <http://www.austlii.edu.au/au/journals/AUYrBkIntLaw/1988/9.pdf>.

'inclusivity' to its proper place by building an expanded idea of what it means. At the same time, our society needs to identify and use opportunities in the informal public space to foster and nourish inclusivity as an attitude of open heartedness which informs how we interact with one another and talk about our differences. This idea of inclusivity would restore the private individual and community groups of all kinds to the very centre of civic life, supplanting the assumption underpinning s 116 which asks nothing of private individuals and groups in the safeguard against exclusivity. This is not to overlook that the intention of the framers of s 116 was not to protect religious freedoms but to 'preserve the States' exclusive power to regulate religious practices'.[11] However, it is to highlight that we are to look elsewhere if we are to build impetus for the protection of religious freedoms in a civic life that is modelled on collaboration and inclusivity, where differences of belief, faith-based and secular, are accommodated.

Views differ as to whether the common law is an agency for the advancement of religious freedoms and inclusivity. While too much should not be expected of the common law in this domain, declarations at a high level of abstraction nevertheless may be found in the caselaw that the common law exhibits a 'tolerant indulgence [for] cultural and religious diversity' and that the courts 'pay every respect to religious belief'.[12] Just the same, the common law has never guaranteed an inalienable right of religious freedom.[13] The shifting attitude of the common law to confessional privilege,[14] especially in a post-Royal Commission landscape, highlights the point, as does the unpredictable

---

11   Dr Beck, *Committee Hansard*, Sydney, 6 June 2017, pp. 26-27, accessible at <https://parlin-fo.aph.gov.au/parlInfo/search/display/display.w3p;query=Id:%22committees/com-mjnt/dffdc74c-afad-4a3b-8bc7-7625b8050249/0003%22>.

12   *R(E) v Governing Body of JFS and the Admissions Panel of JFS* [2008] EWHC 1535 (QB), [107].

13   *Grace Bible Church v Redman* (1984) 36 SASR 376, 388. See also, Evans, *Legal Protection of Religious Freedom in Australia* (2012), 88.

14   AK Thompson, *Religious Confession Privilege at Common Law* (Martinus Nijhoff, 2011).

protection that the common law affords religious freedoms at the point of intersection with the implied right of political communication and protections of freedom of speech. The common law's halting recognition of a principle of statutory interpretation that Parliament does not intend to legislate in a manner that discriminates with respect to religion[15] further confirms the limits of the common law's commitment to the protection of religious freedoms and the promotion of inclusivity.

Limits in the protection of religious freedoms and the promotion of inclusivity under the common law do not necessarily reflect a failure in the common law. Arguably, our patchwork of anti-discrimination legislation and the absence of comprehensive legislative protection of religious freedoms in Australia, despite our ratification of the *International Covenant on Civil and Political Rights* suggest that the lacuna in the common law is a reflection of enduring Australian custom. And perhaps the gathering momentum for the enactment human rights legislation at state level in an appropriate Australian solution. Meanwhile, an opportunity exists and always has for expansion in new directions.

Embracing the opportunity before us involves recognising the risk that in an age of statutes we may expect too much of laws and in doing so abrogate a deeper personal responsibility for building the kind of society that we would choose for ourselves and our children. In the increasingly polarised atmosphere of civic life today, what is missing is a deeply held attitude of the heart, that each one of us is responsible for the world in which we live. We need to find ways to live lives which include others as we move through our day, choose our interactions with others of different faiths and walks of life, and thus how we choose to make society not just for ourselves but

---

15   See J Spigelman, *Statutory Interpretation and Human Rights*, (University of Queensland Press, 2008) vol 3, 29. But see Meyerson, D, 'The Protection of Religious Rights under Australian Law' [2009] *Brigham Young University Law Rev* 529, 540.

also everyone else.

Observers can be forgiven for concluding that in current days secularist worldviews have gained ascendancy in public policy circles in Australia and that faith-based worldviews come off second best. An example is the outcome of the same-sex marriage debate. The question, as Charles Taylor has posed, is not, 'How do we stop this?' The question is, 'How are all people, but people of faith in particular, to be in the face of this development?'[16] For, it may not fall to us to stop it. Do what we are called to do; stand and be a voice for a different way. But, strident forms of politics dedicated to stopping the forces of intolerance and exclusivity only lead to deeper levels of polarisation in public life. The bible would urge, 'Let the Spirit do its work'.[17] Other traditions arrive at a similar conclusion.[18] It is in drawing on this common understanding and asking how we are to be with one another, that people of faith have the opportunity of showing a different way. If they can find this different way, and give expression to it in the way that they conduct civic life, they need not descend into and thus perpetuate in the next cycle, the politics of old and deepening divisions.

In any democratic society, decisions are inevitably an exercise in majoritarianism in which some feel unsatisfied. As a result, many, are left with the feeling that their interests have not been considered or taken into account. The result is a widespread 'loss of faith in democracy', if not a disappointment in its capacity to advance and fulfil the lives of all people, not just the lives of people of faith.[19]

---

16   Charles Taylor, 'Democracy and Its Crisis: Losing Faith in Democracy', Walter-Benjamin Lectures 2019, 17 June 2019, accessible at <https://www.youtube.com/watch?v=sUAmhREFJxs>.
17   Cf Galatians 3:1-5; Ephesians 3:16-19.
18   Cf Giovanni Cereti, 'Presence and Action of the Holy Spirit in the World and Other Religions', The Activity of Commissions, Commission for Interreligious Dialogue, accessible at <http://www.vatican.va/jubilee_2000/magazine/documents/ju_mag_01091997_p-56_en.html>.
19   See Taylor, (n 16).

To date, with notable exceptions, opposition to secularist agendas in civic life has taken the form of a socially conservative politics: the political activism of faith-based groups largely has been right-leaning. However, such efforts are mainly conducted from within an attitude to civic life that is a part of why we find ourselves where we are. What is missing from the political activism of faith-based groups is a sense of how deeply felt religious experience can guide us in how we conduct ourselves in the public space. The sense of existential threat is allowed to overwhelm our deeper instincts and so the world is deprived of the opportunity of seeing that there can be a different way of engaging with others in public life that is an expression of dearly held values of faith groups, and guided by the source from which our deepest faith arises.

As observed by George Marsden, Emeritus Professor of History at University of Notre Dame, Indiana,[20] civic life today is conducted as a 'zero-sum game' in which the winner takes all instead of from a place of inclusivity and open-heartedness. Elevation to office is viewed as an opportunity to implement policies favouring one section of society over another. The sense that elected office at all levels of public life carries a deep responsibility to understand the needs of all equally is missing.

How to restore the missing dimensions in public life is a project that calls for a change at the level of the private individual and groups, those of whom s 116 asks nothing, and calls for us to find a renewed appreciation of our innate capacity for inclusivity and collaboration as an attitude of heart. It is not a change that legislative action or judicial fiat can mandate, although legislation and the decisional law do establish norms of conduct that operate as sign-posts indicating the direction in which society is headed.

---

20   Marsden, 'A More Inclusive Pluralism: A Constructive Proposal for Religion in a Pluralistic Society', *First Things,* February 2015, accessible at <https://www.firstthings.com/article/2015/02/a-more-inclusive-pluralism>.

What we must search for is a shared understanding of who we are, in a world where the Christian religion no longer provides that unifying understanding.

Reinvigorating inclusivity as a founding principle that guides the conduct of civic life starts with a willingness to understand another born of a recognition that all live under the same God and that in our shared humanity all are walking towards the same destiny. It is around this shared value and understanding that the possibility of inclusivity can grow. And it is on the private individual and groups that responsibility to strengthen and build this value in civic life ultimately rests.

Each individual and group has the possibility of finding within themselves a respect and deep interest in others no matter their outlook. Intensely held, deeply personal spiritual experience, and a meaning in life found in beliefs and practices that are different from those we hold, may be challenging. However, experience tells us that those sitting next to us with beliefs that we find strange are also intelligent, high functioning people with families like ours and who, like us, are contributing to society in important ways. A start is to explore honestly the ways in which we have allowed the fervour of belief to become a cloak for intolerance.

Indian Prime Minister, Indira Ghandi famously said, 'You cannot shake hands with a clenched fist'.[21] We must build respect and friendship with those of different outlooks because of an attitude of inclusivity and open-heartedness, and connection to our shared humanity. Individuals and groups committed to real inclusivity will draw their inspiration from their faith traditions, shared openly. Their humble sharing, without any intent to justify or convert, will see all advance beyond where we find ourselves today.

---

21   Press conference, New Delhi (October 19, 1971), quoted in 'Indian and Pakistani Armies Confront Each Other Along Borders' by Sydney H. Schanberg, *The New York Times* (October 20, 1971), page 6C, accessible at <https://www.nytimes.com/1971/10/20/archives/indian-and-pakistani-armies-confront-each-other-along-borders.html>.

As we explore our differences and seek willingly to understand each other, we can move beyond the tension between 'inclusivity' and 'religious freedoms'. In place of that tension, we can arrive at love of the innate equality of all people and a deep sense of our shared humanity, which existed long before there were any differences in theology or history or disputes over the meaning of 'inclusivity' and 'religious freedoms'.

Bibliography

Attorney-General (Vic); Ex Rel Black v Commonwealth (1981) 146 CLR 599.

Australian Constitution.

Beck, Luke, *Religious Freedom and the Australian Constitution: Origins and Future* (Routledge, 2018).

Cereti, Giovanni, 'Presence and Action of the Holy Spirit in the World and Other Religions', The Activity of Commissions, Commission for Interreligious Dialogue (2000).

Charlesworth, Hilary, 'The Public / Private Distinction and the Right to Development in International Law', 1988 *Australian Year Book of International Law*, 190.

Evans, Carolyn, *Legal Protection of Religious Freedom in Australia* (Federation Press, 2012).

Grace Bible Church v Redman (1984) 36 SASR 376.

Kalb, James, *Against Inclusiveness: How the Diversity Regime is Flattening America and the West and What to Do About It*, (Angelico Press, 2013).

Kalb, James, 'Inclusiveness: A Harmful Ideology', *Crisis Magazine*, 5 December 2013.

Kruger v Commonwealth (1997) 190 CLR 1.

Marsden, George M, 'A More Inclusive Pluralism: A Constructive Proposal for Religion in a Pluralistic Society', *First Things*, February 2015.

Meyerson, Denise, 'The Protection of Religious Rights under Australian Law' [2009] *Brigham Young University Law Rev* 529.

Minister for Immigration and Ethnic Affairs v Lebanese Moslem Association (1987) 17 FCR

373.

R(E) v Governing Body of JFS and the Admissions Panel of JFS [2008] EWHC 1535.

Sales, Arnaud, 'The Private, the Public and Civil Society: Social Realms and Power Structures', (1991) 12(4), *The Public and the Private*, 295.

Schanberg, Sydney H, 'Indian and Pakistani Armies Confront Each Other Along Borders', *The New York Times* (October 20, 1971).

Spigelman, James, *Statutory Interpretation and Human Rights*, (University of Queensland Press, 2008).

Taylor, Charles, 'Democracy and Its Crisis: Losing Faith in Democracy', Walter-Benjamin Lectures 2019, 17 June 2019.

Thompson, A Keith, *Religious Confession Privilege at Common Law* (Martinus Nijhoff, 2011.

INDEX

www.ingramcontent.com/pod-product-compliance
Lightning Source LLC
Chambersburg PA
CBHW060252220326
41598CB00027B/4068